Families in Ancient Israel

SERIES EDITORS

DON S. BROWNING AND IAN S. EVISON

Families in Ancient Israel

Leo G. Perdue
Joseph Blenkinsopp
John J. Collins
Carol Meyers

Westminster John Knox Press
Louisville, Kentucky

Book and cover design by Jennifer K. Cox

First edition

Published by Westminster John Knox Press
Louisville, Kentucky

This book is printed on acid-free paper that meets the American National Standards Institute Z39.48 standard. ♾

PRINTED IN THE UNITED STATES OF AMERICA

99 00 01 02 03 04 05 06 — 10 9 8 7 6 5 4 3 2

Library of Congress Cataloging-in-Publication Data

Families in Ancient Israel / Leo G. Perdue . . . [et al.].
        p.   cm. — (The family, religion, and culture)
    Includes bibliographical references and indexes.
    ISBN 0-664-25567-1 (alk. paper)
    1. Family—Palestine—History.   2. Bible. O.T.—Social scientific
criticism.   3. Sociology, Biblical.   4. Palestine—Social life and customs—
To 70 A.D.   5. Family—Biblical teaching.   I. Perdue, Leo G.   II. Series.
BS1199.F32F36   1997
221.8'30685—dc20   96-41778

Contents

Series Foreword

There is an important debate going on today over the present health and future well-being of families in American society. Although some people on the political right and left use concern about the state of the family primarily to further their respective partisan causes, the debate is real, and it is over genuine issues. The discussion, however, is not well informed and is riddled with historical, theological, and social-scientific ignorance.

This is not unusual as political debates go. The American family debate, however, is especially uninformed and dogmatic. This is understandable, for all people have experienced a family in some way, feel themselves to be experts, and believe that they are entitled to their strong opinions.

The books in this series, The Family, Religion, and Culture, discuss these issues in ways that will place the American debate about the family on more solid ground. The series is the result of the Religion, Culture, and Family Project, which was funded by a generous grant from the Division of Religion of the Lilly Endowment, Inc., and took place in the Institute for Advanced Study in The University of Chicago Divinity School. Part of the project proceeded while Don Browning, the project director, was in residence at the Center of Theological Inquiry in Princeton, New Jersey.

The series advances no single point of view on the American family debate and gives no one solution to the problems concerning families today. The authors and editors contributing to the volumes represent both genders as well as a variety of religious and ethnic perspectives and denominational backgrounds—liberal and conservative; Protestant, Catholic, and Jewish; evangelical and mainline; and black, white, and Asian. A number of the authors and editors met annually for a seminar and discussed—often with considerable intensity—their outlines, papers, and chapters pertaining to the various books. The careful reader will notice that many of the seminar members did influence one another; but it is safe to say that each of them in the end took his or her own counsel and spoke out of his or her own convictions.

The series is comprehensive, with studies on the family in ancient

Israel and early Christianity; economics and the family; law, feminism, and reproductive technology and the family; the family and American faith traditions; and congregations and families; as well as two summary books—one a handbook and one a critical overview of the American family debate.

To our knowledge, there has been no recent comprehensive review in the English language concerning the family in ancient Israel. The absence of such a study indicates how the family is often neglected in religious and theological studies, a situation that this book, *Families in Ancient Israel,* and others in this series hope to redress.

This book profits from the many breakthroughs in the study of the Hebrew scriptures—what Christians call the Old Testament. Of course, the family in ancient Israel should be understood as a complicated, multigenerational "household" system even though the covenanted father and mother and blood-related children were generally at its core.

The family as an economic and social system, as well as a religious reality, is described here in vivid detail. Reading this book will help place Hebrew theological ideas about the family in their economic and social context. Religious ideas gave order and significance to the practical realities of life in ancient Israel. Theological ideas about the family were not disconnected from the contingencies of labor, land, wealth, poverty, procreation, inheritance, profit, loss, underpopulation, government, sickness, dependency, and death. Theological ideas about the family interacted with concrete material realities. Understanding how this worked in ancient Israel sharpens one's insight into how the same interactions function in our society.

Readers may catch more vividly the drama of this interaction if, early in their study, they move to the end of Chapter 5 and review Leo Perdue's analysis of the importance of "household" in a proper understanding of "covenant." He argues that covenant was a highly integrative idea relating God's love and promise to both land and household, king and parent, and God's rule in both society and the family. Reading *Families in Ancient Israel* will improve the American family debate by forcing all parties to ground their biblical references on the firm knowledge contained herein.

We give our deepest thanks to Carol Meyers, Joseph Blenkinsopp, John Collins, and their chairman, Leo Perdue, for their splendid contribution to our knowledge of the family in ancient Israel.

Don S. Browning
Ian S. Evison

Preface

In recent years, scholars of ancient Israel and early Judaism have devoted a great deal of attention to various features of the family. However, there is currently no comprehensive overview of the family that makes use of contemporary social-scientific methodology, archaeological data, and contemporary biblical scholarship. In addition, there is no study at present that considers in detail the relationship between the Israelite and Jewish family as a social institution and Old Testament theology and ethics. Also lacking is a serious, scholarly effort to determine what, if anything, the understanding of the family in ancient Israel and early Judaism may contribute to the modern debates about this important institution in contemporary North American society. This volume seeks to remedy these omissions by providing an in-depth social-critical analysis of the family in ancient Israel and early Judaism; an indication of the connection between the social reality of the family and Israelite and Jewish understandings of God, Israel, the world, and ethics; and a proposal of what the ancient understandings may or may not contribute to the nature and character of the family in modern North America.

In line with the Religion, Culture, and Family Project, this volume on the family in ancient Israel and early Judaism addresses the significant issues in the interpretation of this institution: the purposes of the family; the question of whether there is a normative family form; the meaning of gender and gender roles, especially in relationship to the issues of patriarchy and paternalism; the roles of children in families; the topics of intergenerational care and care that extends into the larger social network; and the question of an appropriate model for defining the relationship between family, religion, and the state. To this set of issues we have added a seventh, marriage and divorce, since this is an important topic not only in contemporary culture in North America but also in the Hebrew Bible and in early Jewish texts.

The first three chapters in this volume examine the origins and development of the Israelite and early Jewish family in its continuous and diverse expressions through three major social and historical periods: early Israel (1200 to 1000 B.C.E.); the monarchy, or first temple period (1000 B.C.E. to 586 B.C.E.); and the second temple period (586 B.C.E. to the beginning of the common era [C.E.]). What serves as a link between these chapters is the existence of a largely common and enduring form of the family, the household, that continues throughout these twelve centuries. In addition, these chapters examine the major features and purposes of the family in this ancient culture, including, in particular, economics (production and consumption), reproduction, nurture, and education. They also determine the important role that familial solidarity played in Israelite and early Jewish social ethics and indicate the relationship between the practice of household religion and the social character of the family.

The last two chapters provide a synchronic summary of the family in ancient Israel and early Judaism and propose that the family household became the social matrix for shaping much of the Hebrew Bible's understanding of God, Israel, and the world. The argument is made that the social reality of the household became the major crucible in which a great deal of Old Testament theology and ethics was formed; there the implications of faith and ethics for responsible living—both for the corporate community and for its individual members—were lived out. If this contention proves true, then the Israelite and early Jewish household may serve as a paradigm, suggesting how faith and the moral life may be integrated into and then actualized within the experiences and practices of contemporary Christian and Jewish families in North American society.

                                                        Leo G. Perdue

Abbreviations

AAR/SBL	American Academy of Religion/Society of Biblical Literature
AB	Anchor Bible
ABD	D. N. Freedman (ed.), *Anchor Bible Dictionary*
ABRL	Anchor Bible Reference Library
AnBib	Analecta biblica
ANET	J. B. Pritchard (ed.), *Ancient Near Eastern Texts*
AOAT	Alter Orient und Altes Testament
AOS	American Oriental Series
ArOr	*Archiv orientální*
ASOR	American Schools of Oriental Research
BA	*Biblical Archaeologist*
BAR	*Biblical Archaeology Review*
BASOR	*Bulletin of the American Schools of Oriental Research*
BETL	Bibliotheca ephemeridum theologicarum lovaniensium
Bib	*Biblica*
BJS	Brown Judaic Studies
BO	*Bibliotheca orientalis*
BT	*The Bible Translator*
BWANT	Beiträge zur Wissenschaft vom Alten und Neuen Testament
BZAW	Beihefte zur ZAW
CahRB	Cahiers de la Revue biblique
CBQ	*Catholic Biblical Quarterly*
Cn	Correction (NRSV); indicates most probable reconstruction
ConBOT	Coniectanea biblica, Old Testament
CRINT	Compendia rerum iudaicarum ad novum testamentum
DJD	Discoveries in the Judaean Desert

EncJud	*Encyclopaedia Judaica* (1971)
ET	English translation
EvTh	*Evangelische Theologie*
FS	Festschrift
HSM	Harvard Semitic Monographs
HTR	*Harvard Theological Review*
HUCA	*Hebrew Union College Annual*
ICC	International Critical Commentary
IDB	G. A. Buttrick (ed.), *Interpreter's Dictionary of the Bible*
IEJ	*Israel Exploration Journal*
JAAR	*Journal of the American Academy of Religion*
JANESCU	*Journal of the Ancient Near Eastern Society of Columbia University*
JAOS	*Journal of the American Oriental Society*
JBL	*Journal of Biblical Literature*
JCS	*Journal of Cuneiform Studies*
JJS	*Journal of Jewish Studies*
JNES	*Journal of Near Eastern Studies*
JQR	*Jewish Quarterly Review*
JSOT	*Journal for the Study of the Old Testament*
JSOTSup	Journal for the Study of the Old Testament— Supplement Series
JSS	*Journal of Semitic Studies*
JTS	*Journal of Theological Studies*
LD	Lectio divina
LXX	Septuagint
MT	Masoretic Text
NICOT	New International Commentary on the Old Testament
NRSV	New Revised Standard Version
NT	New Testament
NTS	*New Testament Studies*
OBO	Orbis biblicus et orientalis
OBT	Overtures to Biblical Theology
Or	*Orientalia* (Rome)
OT	Old Testament
OTL	Old Testament Library
OTS	*Oudtestamentische Studiën*
P	Priestly source
PEQ	*Palestine Exploration Quarterly*

RB	*Revue biblique*
RHPR	*Revue d'histoire et de philosophie religieuses*
SBL	Society of Biblical Literature
SBLDS	SBL Dissertation Series
SBLMS	SBL Monograph Series
SBLSP	SBL Seminar Papers
ScrHier	Scripta hierosolymitana
SNTSMS	Society for New Testament Studies Monograph Series
SWBA	Social World of Biblical Antiquity
TDOT	G. J. Botterweck and H. Ringgren (eds.), *Theological Dictionary of the Old Testament*
TLZ	*Theologische Literaturzeitung*
VT	*Vetus Testamentum*
VTSup	Vetus Testamentum, Supplements
WBC	Word Biblical Commentary
WMANT	Wissenschaftliche Monographien zum Alten und Neuen Testament
ZAW	*Zeitschrift für die alttestamentliche Wissenschaft*

Contributors

JOSEPH BLENKINSOPP, John A. O'Brien Professor of Old Testament, Department of Theology, University of Notre Dame, Notre Dame, Indiana

JOHN J. COLLINS, Professor of Hebrew Bible and Post-Biblical Judaism, The Divinity School, University of Chicago, Chicago, Illinois

CAROL MEYERS, Professor of Biblical Studies and Archaeology, Department of Religion, Duke University, Durham, North Carolina

LEO G. PERDUE, Professor of Hebrew Bible and Dean, Brite Divinity School, Texas Christian University, Fort Worth, Texas

1

The Family
in Early Israel

CAROL MEYERS

Virtually all considerations of human behavior operate under the
assumption that there is such a thing as a family in every society.
Indeed, the family is empirically ubiquitous. In every corner of the
globe and as far back in time as our lenses of historical and anthropological research can peer, a small, kinship-structured unit is visible on
the broad landscape of human existence. Yet the deceptively simple
English word *family* masks a unit of social connection and interaction
that is incredibly complex and varied. Not surprisingly, families exhibit wide variations across cultures. The shape, functions, and dynamics of a family group have distinctive features in each of the count-
less cultural forms that constitute the synchronic and diachronic
history of humankind.

Perhaps even more significant than the cross-cultural variations
among families is the fact that even within cultures there is considerable difference among family units. Families are constantly in flux—as
members are born, grow to maturity, and die. And the quality and character of family life are constantly changing—in dynamic relation to the
internal and external factors that affect the way the family encompasses
the interlocking life courses of its constituent members.

Yet, despite the great differences among families viewed cross-
culturally, the very ubiquity of this social unit and the fact that it is the
fundamental human collective mean that the study of the family should
be an important part of any attempt to understand a particular society.
This is especially true for ancient Israel, in which the levels and forms
of social organization were far less numerous and complex than in the
industrialized West, which traces its spiritual, if not social, origins to the
biblical world. A comprehensive understanding of ancient Israel must
include an examination of its constituent family units. Historical

research tends to be carried out from the top down, by first examining the largest sociopolitical structures and only later, if at all, attempting to recover the smallest units of society—perhaps because those units are usually least visible in the sources readily available to scholars, as is surely the case for biblical Israel. This historiographic bias often causes the profound impact of family structures on the course of national events to elude scholarship, with the result that national history is misunderstood or misrepresented.

When examining the period of Israelite beginnings, the study of early Israel is nearly equivalent to the study of the family. The term *early Israel* here designates premonarchical Israel. It refers to that period of time, about two hundred years long, before Israel existed as a national state. In terms of the periodization that is widely used to give chronological specificity to the ancient history of Palestine, early Israel is coterminous with the Iron I period, which begins around 1200 B.C.E. and, according to most (but not all) schemes, comes to an end with the transition to statehood. The emergence of a Benjaminite named Saul to the head of a supratribal polity that is perhaps best identified as a chieftaincy[1] marks a transitional period of some twenty years (ca. 1020–1000 B.C.E.). For most scholars, the true monarchical state, incorporating most of the territory attributed to the component tribal groups, begins with David's meteoric rise to national and supranational power around 1000 B.C.E.[2]

In short, the period of early Israel is barely of two centuries' duration, a small fraction of the thousand or so years of Israelite, Yehudite, and Jewish history during which the components of the Hebrew Bible gradually took shape. Yet those first two hundred years of Israelite existence were especially important because of their formative role. Many of the traditions, values, and forms of social organization that were to endure for most of the rest of the biblical period and that were to be foundational for Israelite society in the subsequent monarchical (first temple) and postmonarchical (second temple) periods can be traced back to the period of early Israel. Identifying the chronological and geographical location of the early Israelite family is thus important for the task of examining the features and dynamics of the Israelite family throughout history.

Before the rise of the national state, the levels of social organization were relatively simple. There can be no doubt that the family—which is the basic unit of human existence, no matter how complex the society in which it is embedded—was of paramount importance. The challenges of life in the Palestinian highlands, combined with whatever traditions the Israelites brought with them as their ancestral heritage, gave birth to distinctive and adaptive family units.

The economic role of the family figures prominently in this chapter. Recognizing that early Israel was an agrarian society from its very beginnings is therefore critical. Certain features of the ancestral stories in Genesis, as well as unexamined notions of what is meant by the "tribes" mentioned so often in biblical texts that purport to describe early Israel, underlie the popular notion of emergent Israelites as pastoralists. Yet that notion is fundamentally erroneous.[3] While there was an important pastoral component to the family economy, the Israelites were farmers. They were what we today might call smallholders: "rural cultivators practicing intensive, permanent, diversified agriculture on relatively small farms."[4] Consequently, their agrarian identity must play a central role in the consideration and reconstruction of the Israelite family.

In looking at Iron I family life, an understanding of the environmental constraints is also critical. At this point, suffice it to recognize that the early Israelites were, for the most part, pioneers. The earliest settlements in Palestine, dating back to the Epi-Paleolithic period (ca. 10,500–8500 B.C.E.), were among the oldest anywhere in the world. Yet the millennia of human occupation along the eastern Mediterranean coast did not involve settlements in all parts of the area. To be more specific, Palestinian sites from the Stone Age to the end of the Late Bronze Age (1550–1200 B.C.E.) tended to be along the coast or in the large valleys—notably the Jezreel Valley, cutting east-west from the rift valley to the Mediterranean at the southern edge of Galilee, and several other large, intermontane valleys. For the most part, the rocky, wooded central highlands were environmentally unfriendly and therefore remained largely uninhabited until the Israelite beginnings in the Iron I period.

The geographic environment of early Israel thus had critical implications for the nature of the family units that constituted the early settlements. And the lifeways and values of those families were foundational for subsequent Israelite family life, even after the transition to statehood. Indeed, it is safe to say that the characteristics of these "first families" of ancient Israel found their way into many of the features of later biblical laws and narratives dealing with family dynamics.

Resources

In dealing with this foundational period in the corporate existence of biblical Israel, it would seem that the *biblical text* would represent the

major source of information about the families that populated the Palestinian highlands in the Iron I period. That supposition is true in the
sense that the designation *Israelite* could hardly be given to those highland dwellers without the biblical assertion that Israelites were the ones
who occupied that territory in the premonarchical age. It is also true in
the sense that scattered details about family life are found in various
parts of Hebrew scripture. Yet the problems in using biblical materials
for understanding early Israelite family life are enormous.

For one thing, the Bible for the most part is a national document. It
focuses on the corporate identity of Israel at the larger sociopolitical levels in which the family is embedded: the tribe and the state. Although
the masses of individuals who comprised the national body—the people of Israel—were of great concern to the canon makers, the social units
in which they lived their daily lives are not clearly delineated. Also, most
of the biblical authors, as far as they can be identified, were urban-
dwelling elites. As such, they were several social and economic levels
removed from the lives of most Israelites. Their perspectives on the lives
of people inhabiting the Iron I settlements are likely to distort or ignore
the everyday reality of those lives. Furthermore, these authors were all,
or nearly all, adult males. Yet adult males were a minority in family
groups—outnumbered by females and children. All these authorial interests preclude the availability of a balanced set of scriptural data on
all members of a family unit.

Thus the official document that emerges from and records the Israelite national experience tends to obscure its core units. The lack of
information about families is accompanied by the inherent biases of a
normative document, for there is inevitably a disjunction between the
official, public character of the canonical text and the daily lives of the
community members represented in that text.[5]

These reservations about the utility and reliability of the Bible as a
source of information about the early Israelite family notwithstanding,
it is possible to highlight those texts that ostensibly chronicle the premonarchical era. The scriptural account of the growing presence of Israelite communities in Palestine is found largely in the books of Joshua
and Judges. These books relate how the Israelites took possession of a
sizable portion of the central hill country of Palestine, how they divided
up the newly acquired territory into inheritances for *mišpāḥāh* groups,[6]
and how a series of local military and civilian leaders experienced successes and failures in attempting to maintain the territorial integrity of
the Israelite settlements.

In their present form, the books of Joshua and Judges are part of a larger narrative, the so-called Deuteronomic History. That work provides an unmistakable editorial framework and perspective—one that reflects late monarchical events—to the conquest sagas, territorial inventories, and judge narratives of these books, which also contain many artfully constructed literary units, each with its own style and integrity.[7] However complex this configuration of traditional, historical, and literary materials may be, the books of Joshua and Judges are valuable repositories of material arising from the early Israelite experience.[8] Indeed, several passages, most notably the Song of Deborah in Judges 5, may date back in their present form to the very period they purport to represent.

Yet the value of these biblical books for understanding the early Israelite emergence in Palestine is not matched by a similar value for reconstructing family life at that time. After all, the narrative of Joshua and Judges is essentially a male conquest tale, obscuring the story of the families—of women and children as well as males—that were involved in securing their livelihood in a new territorial base. Even so, these two books, especially Judges, contain more female figures than most, attesting perhaps to a greater openness to women's leadership roles in noncentralized community life than in the subsequent long monarchical period.[9] Yet these women are of little use to the task of examining family life, for they are exceptional characters, not ordinary family members.

The limited usefulness of Joshua and Judges as resources for early Israelite family life does not, however, exhaust the possibility of finding relevant biblical materials. The Pentateuch deserves attention as an important resource. The so-called Covenant Code in Exodus 20:22–23:19, despite its long redactional history, has been shown to be rooted in the socioeconomic context of premonarchical Israel.[10] Consequently, some of its stipulations pertaining to kinship relations are relevant. The same can be said for some aspects of Levitical law: despite its priestly framework, which may be exilic or later, Leviticus contains demonstrably ancient materials. Indeed, some of the features that seem so idealistic that many scholars believe they could never have been applied may derive from the hoary past of the highland communities of early Israel. Legal passages dealing with land tenure are a case in point, as the discussion below suggests.

In addition to Joshua and Judges and some Pentateuchal passages, occasional texts elsewhere in the Hebrew Bible probably contain relevant information about Israelite families in the premonarchical period.

Given the relative paucity and unreliability of textual resources, other kinds of data become essential. First and foremost among extratextual resources are the results of *archaeological investigations* of the Palestinian highlands. A generation ago, such a statement would not have been possible. Archaeology in the land of the Bible had historically and persistently been the archaeology of urban sites. Driven by various motives—such as the desire to authenticate biblical tales, or to discover aesthetically valuable artifacts, or to uncover monumental architecture that could be readily appreciated by an endlessly curious audience of laypersons and Bible buffs—archaeologists for over a century have been drawn to the largest and deepest sites.

One might call those endeavors elitist archaeology, in that it focused on the structures (temples, palaces, fortifications) and objects (jewelry, statuary, weapons) that are the material remnants of the upper segments of urban hierarchies. As such, it completely ignored the communities in which most people—most families—lived. During the premonarchical period, virtually all the settlements that are tentatively identified as Israelite can be characterized as nonurban. Few such sites were explored in the heyday of biblical archaeology; and even for prominent cites such as Hazor in the north, in which a nonurban village interim can be identified for Iron I, the dominant urban character tended to obscure the rural nature of early Israelite communities. This distortion, it should be noted, is equally problematic for subsequent periods. According to numerous estimates 90 percent or more of the population of any preindustrial society was nonurban.[11] City dwellers and townsfolk were always a small minority, yet archaeologists disproportionately investigate their settings.

The social, economic, political, and cultural domination of urban centers—despite the fact that they contained a small percentage of the population—clearly affected the archaeological enterprise in the Near East for generations. In the 1960s, however, the general anti-institutional and anti-establishment atmosphere among many western academics, along with the impact of the so-called New Archaeology, with its emphasis on cultural process rather than political history, led archaeologists working in Palestine to turn with increasing frequency to some of the myriad sites that constituted the frontier settlements of early Israel. At about the same time, the Six-Day War (1967) opened the highlands of western Canaan to Israeli archaeologists. As on-the-scene investigators, they were able to carry out the kind of extensive and careful surveys that had never before been made of the highland areas of the

West Bank. These recent excavations, along with reliable survey evidence about the location and size of Iron I settlements, have provided a wealth of new information about the dwellings, artifacts, subsistence strategies, and other aspects of daily life of the agrarian communities in which virtually all the early Israelites lived. Similarly, concern with reconstructing ancient economies led to more careful collection of floral and faunal remains than had previously been the norm.

The availability of archaeological data pertaining to the early Israelite existence in Palestine, as welcome as it is, does not automatically translate into information about the family units that inhabited the buildings and used the artifacts of the early Iron Age. Material cultural remains are silent resources with respect to human behavior. They can speak to us only insofar as we can understand how and which human actors occupied the spaces and used the objects that archaeologists have unearthed. In other words, the mute remnants of the past are given voice only through interpretation. Much, if not all, interpretation rests on analogy, often done intuitively. More formally, analogic interpretation is carried out through that aspect of archaeology known as *ethnoarchaeology,* whereby ethnographic information is utilized for the interpretation of archaeologically retrieved data.[12] Knowledge of visible cultures, similar in critical ways to past ones, is used to reconstruct various aspects of an ancient culture. The use of analogical reasoning has some obvious risks, inasmuch as it assumes commonalities and continuities that cannot be independently verified; it nonetheless is of utmost value and can be used, albeit cautiously, with considerable reliability.[13] Indeed, one recent study of Israelite families—"The Archaeology of the Family in Ancient Israel"[14]—draws heavily on ethnographic observations. Similarly, a study of women in the context of Iron I families in early Israel[15] interprets biblical and archaeological data through the lens of ethnographic information.

The value of ethnoarchaeology for reconstructing the early Israelite family merges with the general use of *social science methodology.* Again, precisely because so little direct information is available, knowledge of visible agrarian cultures provides important clues about early Israel. This is especially true in considering families. To be sure, cross-cultural variations are manifold and divergences even within a society are the norm. Yet, despite such differences, the very ubiquity of the family as an institution—as a small, kinship-structured domestic unit—allows theorists to suggest certain commonalities for families living in similar environmental niches and with corresponding subsistence regimes.

The study of the family, along with kinship and marriage, has long been the special domain of social (or cultural) anthropology. Many theorists in that discipline now hold that, despite clear differences between modern and ancient farm families, the division between preindustrial and contemporary smallholders is not so great as some would suppose.[16] Indeed, there are systematic commonalities between them, with critical elements of farm families found virtually everywhere. For this reason, the results of contemporary social history as well as traditional ethnography and social anthropology are relevant to a consideration of the ancient agrarian family pioneering in the Palestinian highlands. Studies of families in colonial America and on the shifting American frontier[17] are full of insights into family dynamics and values that have parallels among pioneering farm families everywhere.

As an institution recognizable in all societies and subjected to generations of social-scientific analysis, the family is viewed in a variety of ways.[18] Three main perspectives have emerged.[19] One is a *functionalist* approach, which sees families performing certain functions directed toward universal goals (such as obtaining subsistence), with variations reflecting local adaptations. The second approach is *structuralist;* it examines kinship relations and the status and roles of family members in relation to one another. And the third approach, termed *interactionist,* focuses on the diversity of both function and structure, particularly as manifest among the multiplicity of social classes and ethnic groups in modern western society.

All three perspectives can contribute to the study of early Israelite family groups. Yet the interactionist emphasis on diversity makes it largely irrelevant to the relative homogeneity of Iron I Israel. And the structuralist concern with kinship relations and roles precludes a consideration of fundamental family activities and of the values and traditions that emerge to ensure that these activities can be performed. Consequently, the functionalist approach seems most appropriate to the aims of this chapter. Its concern with what a family does in order for its members to survive means it has a primary interest in the material aspects of existence. It is thus congenial to a cultural-materialist orientation, in which ecosystems are seen as standing in systemic relationship to the fundamental features of the cultures that inhabit them.[20]

The Highland Setting

The natural environment in which the early Israelite families established their farmsteads was far less friendly than the popular imagination supposes. Despite the biblical rhetoric of "a land flowing with milk and honey" (Deut. 26:15), the highland core of Palestine was hardly prime farmland; otherwise it undoubtedly would have been more extensively settled during one or more of the several demographic surges of the Bronze Age. Why the settlers, identified as Israelites by many scholars,[21] chose to occupy this inhospitable territory is part of a serious debate, which cannot be described here, about the beginnings of Israel.[22] However unclear the political and economic processes are that led to the opening of the highland frontier, the resources available to the pioneer families can quite readily be discerned. Generations of geologic, topographic, and climatological data collection have enabled recent scholarship to refine and provide nuance to the work of earlier generations of Holy Land geographers.[23]

It is now clear that the desire of the superpowers of the ancient Near East to control Palestine was a response to its strategic location on the military and commercial land route between Egypt and Mesopotamia and between Phoenicia or Anatolia and the Arabian peninsula, and not for access to any natural resources—no valuable minerals or stands of large trees—or to extensive grain-producing fields. The central hill country in particular was lacking in resources and arability.

From the perspective of an agrarian family, the dearth of level land in the highland core imposed restrictions on a family's ability to produce adequate cereal crops, the mainstay of the Palestinian agricultural regime.[24] The extensive and early development of agricultural terracing was a response to the terrain problem; terraces provided land that could be plowed and planted with wheat or barley and also helped reduce water runoff on the hillsides. At the same time, terracing placed considerable demands on the labor resources of farm families, for terraces require considerable effort to construct and then to maintain.

In terms of water retention, terraces were only minimally successful in offsetting major climatological patterns. Seasonal (winter) rainfall was the chief water supply in most of the highland territory. The amounts of rainfall were relatively low and unpredictable in the hill country as a whole. While the temperature ranges of the Mediterranean climate were quite conducive to agriculture, the borderline aridity, with serious droughts occurring three or four years in ten, meant that highland farmers were rarely free from the specter of crop failures, food shortages, and general economic distress. Indeed, the persistent pastoral component to the subsistence cropping pattern represented a kind of safety valve: Animal food supplies are less subject to decimation in drought years than are plant sources. Farmers dug cisterns in which to retain water from the rainy season for use in the dry season, but a meager rainy season mitigated the efficacy of such measures.

The varied soils of Palestine were also a resource of dubious value for farmers. None of the four main soil types has all the features needed for high crop yields, although some are more fertile or water retentive than others. Furthermore, good soils were often inaccessible; forestation and rocky outcroppings were obstacles—not entirely insurmountable—in many areas. As with the paucity of level land and the insufficient water, the scarcity of good soils required extra labor on the part of farm families, as well as technological adaptations, in order to achieve subsistence yields.

Perhaps the most important factor in ancient Israel's geographical setting is its diversity. Despite its relatively small size, the landforms and climatic zones are extraordinarily varied. In geologic terms, the basic limestone core and several overlays of softer limestones and chalk, along with basaltic-volcanic outcroppings and coastal sandstone, have been disrupted severely in many parts of Palestine, especially in Galilee, by strenuous tectonic activities. An unusually high degree of warping, folding, and faulting, in irregular directions, has affected the locations and depths of soils in profound ways. Great climatic diversity is also present. The averages of temperature and rainfall may look quite favorable in terms of agricultural potential, but they obscure a remarkable variation. Locales quite close to one another often receive dramatically different amounts of rainfall, depending on which side of the rain shadow—caused by mountainous interruption to prevailing winds—they may lie. Even the areas of higher rainfall would not necessarily have given early Israelite farmers an advantage, in that the concentrations of rain in the winter months rarely could have been conserved in sufficient quantities to provide water for cropping in the hot summer months.

The great diversity of landforms, climatic zones, elevations, and soil types, in various combinations, means that the land is incredibly fractured with respect to agricultural potential. Myriad small ecological niches dot the landscape. One would be hard pressed to find another part of the globe with such a remarkable confluence of geographical factors within so limited an area.[25] The significance for family patterns and dynamics of so many subtly different ecosystems in close proximity is discussed below.

The divergences among landforms and climatic factors did not produce widely different subsistence strategies. The agricultural potential of virtually all Israelite regions and subregions lay within what is called the "Mediterranean agricultural pattern," particularly as adapted to irregular landforms. The Israelite farmers, working without the possibility of irrigation, developed a basic tripartite strategy in which they grew (1) wheat or barley, the major cereal crop; (2) olive trees, which survive without irrigation in the dry summer months; and (3) grapevines, which have particularly deep roots and do well on hilly terrains. These major crops are probably reflected in biblical references to "grain, wine, and oil"; yet they hardly constituted the full extent of agricultural production. Other field crops included legumes of various sorts, such as lentils and chickpeas. Besides olive orchards and vineyards, tree crops included figs, dates, olives, the carob, and some nuts. Vegetable gardens produced various herbs and spices, as well as onions and greens; and other vegetables, herbs, and berries were gathered in the wild.

The overall variety of food products is notable. Yet it must be emphasized that individual farmers grew only a partial selection of these Mediterranean products. In each ecological niche the quality of the soil, the elevation, the rainfall amount, and the temperature variation affected the farmer's choices. Ethnographic evidence has recently been combined with archaeologically retrieved plant remains and with survey data to provide a good understanding of the divergent land use of various subregions of Palestine, especially in the hill country of Ephraim.[26]

One feature in this picture of diversity in cropping patterns must be noted. Whatever mixture of plowed fields, gardens, orchards, and vineyards constituted a particular family farm, the organization of farming for most of the crop selection involved items that were produced in sequential, small batches, seasonally staggered for the most part, rather than crops tended in continuous process for much of an annual cycle. Like the diversity of landforms and its impact on land management, the diversity of foodstuffs grown on an Israelite farm had implications for the dynamics of family life.

Village Setting

Some examples of isolated farmsteads of the early Iron Age have been recovered, particularly in the marginal areas of the highlands of the northern Negev, where soil and water conditions in most areas limited the productivity of the land to what could sustain a single family group. Elsewhere in the highland core, as surveys have conclusively shown, most settlements of the early Israelite period were small, rural sites. Certainly for that period, and probably for much of the ensuing era of the monarchy and concomitant reestablishment of urban sites in Palestine, the primary locus of family life was the village. Because several of these settlements have been extensively excavated, and because surveys have identified so many of them, the size and configuration of these highland sites are fairly well known.

What is most striking about these villages to the western observer is their small size. A fair number of them, hamlets really, were barely more than half an acre in size—less than the area of a football field. Others were somewhat larger, as much as two-and-a-half acres, but still tiny by western expectations. Only a few approached ten acres or more in size. Clearly, the population of any of these villages was proportionately small.

How many people inhabited such sites? Estimating ancient populations is one of the most challenging problems of ethnoarchaeology. Early studies computed population density for various periods of antiquity rather generously, so that well into the 1980s, scholars were suggesting that as many as 200 people lived on an acre of village land.[27] At present, as the result of more sophisticated measures of population density, a population-to-area coefficient of 100 persons per acre seems more accurate. Consequently, the smallest early Israelite villages were probably home to about 50 persons, with about 150 people living in the somewhat larger ones. Settlements of more than several hundred persons were exceptional; about 80 percent of the Iron I population inhabited villages of fewer than a hundred.

These villages were generally laid out rather haphazardly. Some sites suggest a modicum of planning, with dwellings forming an elliptical ring around a central space free of structures, a space perhaps used for village livestock pens.[28] Other sites, probably the majority, are more agglomerative in character, consisting of an irregular collection of home clusters arranged roughly in an oval. Both kinds of villages are marked by the absence of any perimeter walls that could be labeled defensive systems. They are similarly notable for the absence of public structures of any sort—no administrative buildings, sacred precincts, granaries, arsenals, or the like. This architectural profile strongly suggests that the villages were autonomous communities composed of self-sufficient family groups. There were no regularized village functions that required permanent space and that would have called on scarce family resources to build and maintain the needed public structures.

Careful sociological studies of the early Israelite period have linked these villages to biblical terminology for population groups. Although somewhat fluid in what it can denote, the term *mišpāḥāh* is generally understood to be coterminous with the inhabitants of a village. It can also, however, represent—perhaps in later time periods—a somewhat larger regional group or a subdivision of a larger settlement.[29] Nonetheless, the idea that Israelites held land in clusters of kin groups, called *mišpāḥôt,* and not actually by tribes, is contained in the allotment texts of the second half of the book of Joshua. (Cf. Num. 33:54—"You shall apportion the land by lot according to your *mišpāḥôt.*")

Offering an English translation for *mišpāḥāh* is difficult. Most English versions render the term "family" or sometimes "clan." Neither is quite appropriate, for it is more than a family, although it may well be a grouping of related family units. And *mišpāḥāh* does not quite fit the general anthropological understanding of a clan, which does not usually involve residential commonality. The suggestion "protective association of families"[30] is unwieldy, although it does convey the dimension of local cooperation involved in the *mišpāḥāh* and in the *'elep,* a related term that preserves the idea of military cooperation.[31] "Residential kinship group," or "kinship group" in shortened form, perhaps best conveys the nature of the village community: related farm families sharing common settled space and earning their livelihoods in the fields, orchards, and vineyards surrounding the village site. The farmlands themselves were held not by the kinship group as a whole but rather, it seems, by the constituent family groups.

Family Households

The units comprising the village *mišpāḥāh,* or kinship group, were the families of early Israel. Because these families were agriculturalists, their identity and survival were integrally connected with their material world—more specifically, with their arable land, their implements for working the land and processing its products, and their domiciles—as well as with the human and also animal components of the domestic group. In many ways, the term *family household* is more useful in dealing with early Israelite families (although that would not be the case for the monarchical period and later, when domestic units were more varied in their spatial aspects and economic functions). Combining *family,* with its kinship meanings, and *household,* a more flexible term including both coresident and economic functions, has descriptive merit.

The family household thus included a set of related people as well as the residential buildings, outbuildings, tools, equipment, fields, livestock, and orchards; it sometimes also included household members who were not kin, such as "sojourners," war captives, and servants.[32]

Conceptualizing the early Israelite family in terms of its material components means that archaeologically retrieved materials can be used to reconstruct the morphology of the family—the number and nature of its kinship components—as well as some aspects of its function. Excavated examples of Iron I domestic structures provide important clues about the size and makeup of the family group. A number of field projects have yielded relevant data. Not only have they explored the layout of Iron I villages; they also have mapped out the domestic spaces that comprise the villages. The agglomerative villages in particular have produced a clear picture of the residential units and their relation to one another.

Most of the domestic buildings that constitute the entirety of the architectural remnants of the Iron I highland villages are what are known as four-room houses.[33] That designation, however, is misleading in several respects. First, it represents only the ground floor, whereas it is quite likely that these dwellings had upper levels with additional living space. Also, the ground level has fewer than four rooms in many cases; such buildings are actually three-room or even two-room houses. Because "four-room" does not fit all examples, and because of a ubiquitous feature of all these dwellings, they are better labeled "pillared houses."

These pillared houses are small, rectilinear structures. Access was through a door leading into the largest room. On one or sometimes both sides of the entryway was a row of crude pillars (or piers); hence the designation *pillared house*. Sometimes there was a low partition wall connecting the pillars. The central area of the large room usually had a beaten earth floor, with the area between pillars and side walls having a cobbled surface. At the end of the main room, or along one side in some cases, were one or more doorways leading to one to three smaller rooms, usually with beaten earth floors. Several kinds of installations present in these structures contribute to an understanding of how space was organized and used. Stairways, usually attached to exterior walls, indicate upper stories. Troughs in the partition walls were apparently mangers, based on ethnographic analogy as well as similarity to troughs in large communal stables found at later Israelite cities.[34] The central room sometimes had ovens, cooking pits, or hearths; but such installations were generally in sheltered outdoor space, more congenial to the smoke, odors, and waste materials associated with many food preparation activities.

Recent careful examination of the nature, size, and layouts of the rooms in the pillared house, along with its other associated features, has allowed scholars to reach a new understanding of its function. That understanding differs from the supposition of earlier researchers[35] that a good part, if not all, of the two to four rooms was for family activity, by both day and night. It now seems clear that the ground-level space in the pillared dwellings represents a specialized layout that met the needs of agriculturalists with important agricultural and pastoral components to their subsistence strategy. The configuration and features of the space accommodated animal and storage needs; they provided space for all the goods, tools, and chattel essential for self-sufficient agricultural survival in a challenging environment.[36] These largely economic functions were met by the segmented spaces on the ground floor. The areas of the pillared house reserved for human occupation were largely on the unrecoverable second story. Ethnoarchaeological data contribute heavily toward the postulation that living quarters and auxiliary storage comprised an upper level.[37]

The kind of artifacts recovered within or near these pillared buildings contributes further to the reconstruction of the Iron I household. In fact, the range of objects and pottery types is relatively small. The objects, including simple farming implements, grinding stones and querns, spindle whorls and loom weights, attest to the domestic production and processing of food products and textiles. Ceramic remains are also instructive for this period in three respects. First, the repertoire is small and simple—mostly everyday, utilitarian vessels, and unlike the situation in nearly every other period of Palestinian history, the pottery is undecorated. Second, there are virtually no imported wares, which characteristically mark the presence of trade or barter in a rudimentary market economy. Third, the storage jars, or pithoi, are smaller than those of previous or subsequent periods; they were used for retaining household products and not for intersite transferal of products, in contrast with the larger jars of the Late Bronze and Iron II periods. These three features point to the self-sufficiency of the early Israelite family farm. The presence of storage pits sunk into the floors of the pillared buildings, far more common than in earlier or later eras, likewise attests to household economic autonomy.

This analysis of domestic equipment and space is important for identifying the nuances of the economic base of the Iron I families: mixed farming and also some livestock, mainly sheep and goats. The necessity for winter folding of the animals and storage of a harvest's yield for subsequent usage combined with space needs for tools and implements to create the internal spatial arrangement of the pillared house. The subsistence regime that determined these space allocations and types also governed labor needs, technological features, and patterns of land tenure. The recoverable material elements allow us to see the human actors on the ancient landscape and to re-create their activities, concerns, and relationships.

One further piece of archaeological information about the pillared buildings—courtyard space—leads directly to a consideration of the early Israelite family. Some scholars believe that the central room of the pillared houses was at least partially open, creating an internal courtyard area.[38] However, most cooking ovens and hearths were found in spaces exterior to the buildings. Moreover, space requirements for daily or seasonal food-processing activities and textile production could not be met in the relatively cramped, dirt-floored area of the main room. The main courtyard areas of the Iron I dwellings therefore were probably outside the living-stabling-storage components of the house itself. In looking at the location of these external courtyard areas in relation to the domestic units, certain configurations of indoor and outdoor space become apparent: that is, the houses appear in clusters of two or three, with one or more walls in common, apparently sharing common courtyard space and, presumably, the activities carried out in that space.[39] Each group is separated from other ones, sometimes by enclosure walls, in other instances by pathways or passageways winding through the Iron I hillside hamlets.

These dwelling clusters constitute evidence for a family unit in early Israel larger than that of the nuclear family (or conjugal couple with unmarried offspring). Each pillared house in a cluster may represent the living space of a nuclear family or parts thereof, but the shared courtyard space and common house walls of the linked buildings indicate a larger family grouping. Early Israelite dwelling units were thus complex arrangements of several buildings and housed what we might call extended families. Furthermore, these compound dwelling units were not isolated buildings within a settlement of single-family homes.

What might the human composition of these dwelling clusters have been?[40] Precise determination of the extended family or compound family patterns of these household compounds is hardly possible. All such complex families are, by definition, in a state of flux; they are typically multigenerational, and therefore the ratio of older members to younger ones, or vice versa, shifts as new generations are born and older ones die, as one spouse predeceases another, as one or more offspring (usually female) leave, as affinal spouses join. Nonetheless, the clear biblical data on patrilineality suggest that the core of the compound family was an elementary unit of a senior family (spousal pair) extended downward (children and grandchildren), with the middle generation extended laterally (siblings and their spouses). In other words, this pattern consisted of all living persons, with the exception of married females, who were descended from a person (and his spouse) still living.[41]

This basic set of kin was no doubt augmented at one or more levels by more distant kin, whose own family groups may have met disaster through disease or economic failure. Military captives, transients (sojourners), and supplementary workers, indentured from other families, may also have been included in the compound family.

In addition to the genealogical materials indicating patrilineality, several texts in the book of Judges reflect a family arrangement that would inhabit the kind of dwelling cluster known from the archaeological record. The story of Micah in Judges 17—18 provides a picture of a man living with his widowed mother, his sons (and probably their wives), and a young priest, hired to serve household cultic needs. In Judges 18:22, the text describes several members of Micah's household who go off in pursuit of Danite raiders as the "men who were in the houses comprising the household of Micah."[42] This passage fits the material evidence remarkably well and also provides clues about family household functions (cultic, economic, social, military). Similarly, in Judges 6—8, Gideon is presented as a married man—a parent of at least two children (Judg. 8:20)—working the land of the household identified as that of his father Joash (Judg. 6:11). This is a multigenerational compound family. Another indication of an extended family household is the multigenerational accountability of the Decalogue (Ex. 20:5), which is relevant only in a context of families extending across three or even four generations.

The incest regulations of Leviticus 18 and 20 likewise reflect a compound family household as the basic domestic unit of society. These regulations are embedded in a late (exilic?) Priestly context. Yet, when examined from an anthropological perspective, they apparently preserve a set of proscribed relationships indicative of a family group meeting the labor requirements and social roles of the Iron I period, rather than of any subsequent time.[43] The relatively large number of prohibited liaisons among consanguinal and affinal kin arises from the necessity to create taboos among the residents of an extended family household.[44] In other words, the family is described negatively in the incest laws by listing the family members with whom marriage is prohibited; marital unions could not be made with certain kinfolk, whose proximity and kinship bonds presupposed a complex, not a nuclear, family.[45] Incest taboos, in such a context, serve as coping mechanisms for dealing with the tensions and temptations present when closely related persons live in close quarters. At the same time, they maintain the possibility for endogamy within the larger hamlet or village population, the mišpāḥāh.

The confluence of archaeological and biblical materials provides evidence that many early Israelite families consisted of more than a single nuclear pair with unmarried offspring. The environmental constraints of the highland settlements add further support to this picture. Despite somewhat romantic notions that an extended family is somehow more harmonious and provides more emotional stability for its members, such configurations in reality were fraught with potential difficulty and strife,[46] about which more is said below. For that reason, compound or extended families are actually not all that common. They tend to form in situations in which labor requirements are so demanding that a residential group cannot survive at subsistence level without the productive labor of more than a conjugal pair and their children, who would have married off at a relatively early age, given the limited average life span (about thirty years for females, about forty for males) and the need for reproductive processes to begin soon after puberty.

Those labor requirements in early Israel were especially intense for several reasons: cropping patterns, with their seasonal demands for many hands to do certain sowing or harvesting tasks within a relatively short window of environmental opportunity; sporadic needs for terrace maintenance and land clearing; a constant set of time-consuming daily procedures for tending to livestock, securing water, and transforming food products to comestibles. The number of persons needed for the family, as the primary, self-sufficient economic unit, to perform the myriad tasks in a regime with critical labor-intensive periods was greater than a nuclear family could supply. Extended or compound families were essential for survival.

The probable size of those families can be calculated using the techniques of population density estimation mentioned above. For the nuclear families (brothers with their spouses and offspring) that were present in family compounds, a maximum of seven persons can be estimated, although that supposes a reproductive rate higher than what might in fact have existed, given the high number of infant mortalities (as many as one in two children did not survive to the age of five)[47] and the risk of maternal death at childbirth. But if we suppose that a compound held two nuclear two-generation family subunits of five or six persons, as well as a senior pair and perhaps a random cousin, aunt or uncle, or sojourner, we reach a family size that would rarely exceed fifteen.[48]

Just as the small villages or tiny hamlets of early Israel can be linked with the lineage or kinship group (mišpāḥôt) terminology found in the Bible, so too can the compound family household be connected with biblical language: bêt 'āb. Although usually translated "father's house" or "house of the father," this term is perhaps better rendered "family household," which more successfully reflects the integral relationship between kinship-linked persons and the material basis for their survival. In terms of persons, bêt 'āb denotes the extended or compound family that inhabited a residential unit of several linked dwellings. The biblical usages of the term are somewhat fluid and can sometimes refer to groups other than a complex residential family group or even to a schematized social-genealogical fiction. In many texts, however, especially those stemming from or reflecting the premonarchical period,[49] the term probably denotes a multigenerational living group. The structure of these groups, as has been noted, was in flux as families expanded or contracted as the result of births, marriages, deaths, or other circumstances that augmented or depleted family size. Still, whatever the configuration of the bêt 'āb at a given moment, the governing kinship relationship was father-son descent, or patrilineality; and the governing territorial determinant was patrilocality—males inheriting family land from their parents and females moving out to the bêt 'āb of their husbands.

Land, like labor, was a major feature of an Israelite family household. That the family's immovable or real property (land as well as whatever is more or less permanently built on it) is the sine qua non for the livelihood and survival of an agrarian family need hardly be mentioned. Yet the specific identification of each family household with its inherited domain (naḥălāh, "patrimony" or "inheritance") was exceptionally strong; family land was to be held in perpetuity.

The idea of the inalienability of family property was, for agriculturalists, no less a function of the environmental constraints of the Palestinian highlands than was the need for extended family groups. The extraordinary diversity of the ecosystems of the hill country meant that virtually every family household experienced a different set of challenges in establishing a productive subsistence strategy. Under such conditions, it makes most adaptive sense for the property to be transferred to those most familiar with appropriate technologies, cropping patterns, planting times, and so forth.[50] The passing of property to those who had grown up on it and knew it best was the most efficient way to exploit successfully the marginal habitats of the hill country settlements.

The functional advantage of keeping real property within the small kinship group that farmed it is manifest in parent-child dynamics, to be considered below, and in traditional ways of preventing extrafamily land transfers. The latter—land-tenure regulations—were eventually encoded in biblical legal stipulations often considered among the most puzzling in scripture. Land was held in patrimonial units, not to pass out of the control of the family group. Institutions such as levirate marriage (Deut. 25:5–6; Ruth 4:10), jubilee provisions (Lev. 25:10, 28), and redemptive procedures (Lev. 25:24ff.) can best be understood as customs arising to prevent group/land fission, which would render holdings too small for viability or otherwise compromise the delicate balance between individual habitat and its successful exploitation. These customs would have emerged early in Israelite history as ways to continue or restore the socioeconomic basis of the family household.[51] That the protection of the inalienability of the land became fixed in legal materials undoubtedly testifies to the difficulty in maintaining patrimonial integrity. Indeed, the concept of divine ownership of land— all Israel viewed as inhabiting Yahweh's inheritance (e.g., Lev. 25:23), which was parceled out to designated kinship groups—provides powerful sanction for customs and laws not readily adhered to in the realities of human behavior.

In this regard, the absence of epigraphical evidence from Palestine for the sale or purchase of real property is striking, even though it is negative evidence, in comparison to the ample presence of such documents dealing with land transactions from Canaanite and other neighboring peoples.[52] Similarly, in contrast with the detailed Pentateuchal legal materials dealing with restitution of property, there are no laws that regulate land transfer except through inheritance.[53] One can also point to narrative materials in the Bible that have family land retention as a motif: the daughters of Zelophehad incident, the book of Ruth, and the story of Naboth's vineyard.

Inalienability of family property is a recurring concept in biblical law and lore. Its very unmanageability in socioeconomic reality probably should be viewed as a sign of its authentic origins in the exigencies of highland farm life. Policies and folklore encouraging the integrity of family lands thus are not depictions of idealized behavior, never carried out, although that may have been the case for the urban context in which the Bible reached its final canonical form. But in the period of Israelite beginnings, in a socioeconomic landscape composed of tiny hamlets and villages, inalienability was a powerful way to link land resources with labor resources and to integrate property with family. The identity of any family unit was thus inseparable from its land, which was the material basis of its survival.

Family Identity

Just as the family was inextricably connected with its landholdings, so too were individual family members economically and psychologically embedded in the domestic group. As is widely recognized by anyone looking at premodern societies, the concept of the individual and of individual identity as we know it today did not yet exist in the biblical world. This was especially true on family farms—and is even to this day, under certain circumstances. Whatever sense of individual agency a person may have had derived from his or her contribution to household survival rather than from individual accomplishment. The profound interdependence of family members in self-sufficient agrarian families thus created an atmosphere of corporate family identity, in which one could conceive not of personal goals and ventures but only of familial ones. People located themselves on the superimposed domains of land and kin group and did not view themselves as independent actors in domains of their own choice or making. In the merging of the self with family, one can observe a collective, group-oriented mind-set, with the welfare of the individual inseparable from that of the living group.[54]

To put it another way, family life was not distinct from whatever roles, prescribed according to age and gender, that individual family members may have played. Work and family were not independent spheres, just as property and family were not independent entities. The family as a residential, landed group was a collectivity, with its corporate goals and fortunes valued above the welfare of any of its constituent members. The power of the agrarian mode to establish corporate identity as more important than individual freedom should not be underestimated. In fact, even in contemporary America, with its strong pull toward individualism and its flood of media messages urging people to indulge themselves and make self-referent choices, small, independent farm families sustain an ethos that values the whole—the family farm—more than the constituent family members. In such agrarian households, the more marginal the family's economic status, the greater the sense of collectivity.[55]

This collective aspect of the farm family, in which working the land is inextricably tied up with family roles and values, is sometimes called the "property" model of the family.[56] It contrasts rather strongly with the kind of family that evolved along with the structural differentiation of society in the Industrial Revolution. Modern families in industrialized societies are separated from their economic basis, which lies in external domains—the workplace—and involves interaction of individual family members with a wide range of unrelated others. This person-centered arrangement fosters the notion of individual choice, interests, freedoms, gratification, and fulfillment and is the fundamental structure of most American families. Yet it is not determinative for many smallholding households. In agrarian settings in the United States and in many parts of Asia and Africa, household collectivity persists: People *belong* to a family rather than, if they so choose, *have* a family.[57]

In premodern agrarian settings such as early Israel, therefore, individualistic elements of human existence, including a person's range of psychological processes and feeling states, were characteristically subordinate to the person's role in the family unit.[58] Accepted and adaptive role behavior determined the character of the component family members. A person was not an autonomous entity but someone's *father, mother, daughter, son, grandparent,* and so forth. These terms designated behavior as much as biology; they represented life-sustaining as well as life-creating activities. Despite the strands of continuity that link the modern Judeo-Christian world with its biblical origins, there are significant areas of difference. Perhaps none is so radical as the corporate identity and family solidarity of the early Israelite farm family as opposed to the achievement-oriented individualism of the industrialized West.

Family Functions/Family Members

It is against the backdrop of collective family identity, in which individual roles and behaviors are embedded, that the functions of the early Israelite family as a unit as well as the particular responsibilities of its component members can be viewed. Even though the morphology of those families was in flux, so that no two households were exactly alike in their human configuration, the basic functions of a household were common to all such units compromising agrarian communities.[59] As has long been recognized by functionalist anthropologists, those functions consist of all activities imperative for the continuity of the coresidential group: economic (production and consumption of goods), sexual-reproductive, educational, and perhaps judicial.[60] All these activities contribute to family household continuity, that is, the transmission across generations of the skills, values, and resources necessary for survival. Although listed as discrete categories, Israelite household functions were dynamically interlocked and interdependent.

Family life for agrarian householders in the unremittingly marginal habitat of the Palestinian highlands was task-oriented. Certain daily, seasonal, and annual activities, in addition to unpredictable, sporadically occurring ones, formed the core of the everyday life of smallholders. As a unit for the mobilization and pooling of enough human labor resources for survival, the household was both workforce and workplace. The *economic* role of the family was all-pervasive.

For the early Israelites, the ecological constraints mentioned above—limited water, periodic drought, paucity of bottomlands, erodible soils, circumscribed planting seasons—required exceptionally intense labor output. The physical work required for subsistence agriculture would have taken up all available daylight hours virtually year-round.[61] In addition to the great demands of animal and vegetable food production, families had to process food products into forms to be stored for the seasons when few foods could be grown, and they had to prepare those products for consumption. These core tasks were accompanied by other survival chores: producing and maintaining most tools and implements, garments and other textiles, and built structures (dwellings, pens, terraces, and sheds). The arduous and time-consuming regime of subsistence tasks required, as noted above, a labor force greater than that of a nuclear family. Men, women, and children of several generations collectively carried out the multifarious household activities.

The density and intensity of shared family labor, in ancient Israel as in all agrarian societies, involved role specializations according to gender and age. At this point, it becomes possible to look at the specific kinds of family responsibilities borne by the component members of a highland household. Farm work was a family enterprise, but it was most efficiently carried out by individual family members learning the technologies and nuances of a relatively fixed set of operations.

A combination of archaeological, biblical, and ethnographic data provide evidence for the roles of those individuals. Archaeological materials help us reconstruct the nature of the requisite tasks but do not identify those who performed them. Occasional hints in the biblical record help identify some of the labors done by men, by women, and, to a lesser extent, by unmarried offspring; but the Bible hardly provides complete job descriptions. Because family farms, especially under frontier conditions, have remarkably congruent labor patterns across cultures, ethnographic information is invaluable for reconstructing the roles of Israelites in their households.[62]

The differential allocation of productive tasks along gender and age lines meant that adult males, for the most part, engaged in the plow agriculture necessary for growing field crops. In relation to that activity, men were also normally the ones to clear new fields of undergrowth or trees (see Josh. 17:18), to hew out cisterns, to build homes, and to construct terraces—that is, to carry out "start-up" operations.[63] The gender differentiation that placed men in fields and in constructive tasks perhaps hinged on their greater ability, relative to females involved in parenting infants and small children, to work at uninterrupted tasks at a distance from the residential compound,[64] and also, perhaps, on their somewhat greater strength. Whatever the reasons, and despite the inevitable exceptions to this pattern,[65] it is reasonably safe to assume that the males on Israelite farms performed these tasks and also that they made and repaired most of the requisite tools. The initial planters of the perennial horticultural stocks cannot be identified; perhaps, as performers of a start-up activity, those too were predominantly men.

Other kinds of agricultural tasks were probably performed by both men and women. Seasonal tasks such as harvesting required all available hands at key periods. The ongoing, sporadic tending of orchards and vineyards and the regular need to milk animals may also have been activities distributed across gender as well as age lines.

In assessing the participation of adult woman in family labor, it is important to avoid the trap of looking at female household work as somehow less important than male tasks.[66] That perception, emerging from the industrial splitting of workplace (and paid labor) from home (and unpaid labor), is hardly relevant to a premodern agrarian family, where both males and females worked in the household, broadly construed to include all the material and human components of a family. That is, the boundaries of a woman's world were virtually the same as those of a man's in the highland hamlets and villages of early Israel.

Having said that, the fact that women's productive tasks were more closely aligned to the domestic structure itself—"indoor work"—is recognizable as an aspect of the labor of agrarian females (an aspect that links them, erroneously, with the indoor and relatively menial work of women in industrialized contexts). Common female tasks in frontier farm settings involved keeping the home in order, caring for small children (with the help of the mother-in-law, older children, or unmarried sisters-in-law), tending gardens and small animals, producing textiles, and taking responsibility for food preparation and preservation.

These last two activities deserve special comment. First, they were not housebound chores. Many of the complex processes of turning the raw materials of farm fields, vineyards, and orchards into edible form were carried out in the courtyards or on the roofs of dwelling units or even at some distance from the family compound.

Second, both activities were time consuming. For example, cereal crops, which were the dietary core of the Israelite agricultural regime, require a complex series of operations to make them edible. The grains must be processed by soaking, milling, grinding; the flour is then mixed into a dough, set to rise, and baked in order to produce bread. Grain processing alone could easily consume two hours or more per day of a woman's time,[67] not including the procurement of fuel and tending of the oven fires that were the prelude to baking. Similar estimates of extensive periods of time exist for the procedures involved in transforming other foodstuffs—olives, herbs, fruit, and milk—to forms that could last beyond harvesttime. Women also participated in field work at harvesttime and performed myriad other operations. With some seasonal variation, upward of ten hours per day were spent in indoor, outdoor, and courtyard chores. Clearly, women carried an extraordinarily large workload.

Finally, the technology involved in such tasks was highly specialized. A wide range of learned skills was necessary to deal with the array of foodstuffs involved in the mixed agricultural regime. Similarly, the steps involved in taking wool or flax and producing garments involved many complex operations. Some of those tasks, such as sheepshearing or the related making of leather, may have been done by males. But the carding, spinning, weaving, and sewing were part of a woman's repertoire of household labors. The same can be said for other craft specializations, such as basketry and ceramic production, that were probably female jobs in the gendered division of labor in Israelite farm families. Considerable expertise—planning, skill, experience, and technological knowledge—was necessary for the performance of a woman's tasks, many of which involved precise chemical and physical processes.

The qualitative difference between the specialized tasks of adult men and of women deserves comment. For one thing, women's productive work was significantly more varied than that of men. Although men who worked farms are often conceptualized as jacks-of-all-trades, there is little doubt that women's farm work involved a greater variety of discrete tasks. If such was the case on the American frontier, for example, where families had some access to market commodities,[68] it would obtain to an even greater degree in fully self-sufficient agrarian households, such as in early Israel. Another distinction between male and female labor is that, taken as a whole, female tasks required a higher degree of expertise, judgment, and skill than did male tasks. Not that judgment and skill were lacking as requirements for men's work; but as a whole, technological knowledge was less characteristic of men's labor than of women's, although other aspects of men's work, such as sensitive awareness of ecological variables, involved the acquisition of experience over extensive time periods, a pattern not present for female tasks.

Another distinction involves the interlocking and sequential nature of many female tasks. A woman's labor involved an organic progression of operations—a "self-perpetuating chain."[69] Fire building and tending, bread making, the weaving of cloth—all required an integrated sequence of activities. The kinds of work performed almost exclusively by males, in contrast, tended to involve more discrete tasks, with one operation performed in relative isolation from another. Indeed, the extension of a field operation into the next phase usually meant that women took over the sequence of activities—as in cereal production, for example, when harvested grains were transformed to flour and then bread.

Finally, the success of men's work tended to be measured in quantitative terms. The number of ephahs of wheat or measures of wine or jars of oil (cf. Hag. 2:16) represented the ability of a male farmer to assess environmental conditions in relation to productive resources and thereby to achieve a significant yield. Such a yield would mean enough to satisfy current needs, with enough surplus to be preserved for later use and with sufficient seeds to be retained to plant for the next season. Such measures of agrarian male success in early Israelite farms meant periodic failures. Shortfalls were inevitable, even with risk-spreading techniques, because of recurring natural disasters: periodic droughts, hailstorms, plagues of locusts or grasshoppers, and blights. Women's productive tasks differed in that many of their expenditures of energy provided items of food and clothing that were immediately useful. And women had more direct control over the results of their labor in that their activities were related more to managed technology than to unmanageable nature. If men produced amounts, women produced things. Clearly, these two kinds of work were interdependent parts of the whole of the household economy. Yet one can imagine that specialized female tasks produced a different and more immediate feeling of accomplishment than did male labors.[70]

Whatever their qualitative differences, men's and women's labors together were marked by their sheer quantity and also by their interdependence. With respect to the first of these features, the need for extended or compound families to make up the basic economic unit has already been mentioned. The labor of several male and female adults was thus pooled. In addition, the labor of juveniles was essential to the household economy; many light but time-consuming tasks were undoubtedly assigned to children.

As early as age five or six, both boys and girls might be assigned tasks of fuel gathering, caring for younger children, picking and watering garden vegetables, and assisting in food preparation. For the most part, children of that age eased the burden of female labor, which probably consumed more total hours per day than did the male-specific tasks. By the age of thirteen, children typically reached nearly full adult labor input in farm households, with workloads easily exceeding nine hours per day.[71] These older children normally worked with same-sex adults, insofar as their adult tasks by then had become gender specific. Children under thirteen worked proportionately less; by age seven or eight, they may have labored up to four hours a day. Clearly, the labor value of children soon exceeded whatever cost in caloric intake they represented.

The essential role of child labor in agrarian households meant, of course, that childbearing was an additional component of a woman's life. Reproduction in such a context was not simply a biological process; and it certainly was not a process subject to the choice of an individual woman as she reached childbearing age. Rather, it was integral to the fundamental issue of family survival. It is no wonder that biblical texts contain injunctions for human fertility—"be fruitful and multiply" is addressed to males and females—and narratives about females overcoming infertility. Economic conditions mandated large families.

Despite the reproductive imperatives, childbearing may have been a less dominant aspect of women's lives than might be imagined. Today we tend to single out childbearing as a discrete and major aspect of women's lives because of the way in which the bearing and rearing of children constitute a distinct component of family life, with returns that are rarely immediate. For the agrarian parents of early Israel, with children very early folded into the economic activities of the household, children in some ways were, paradoxically, less central to individual women's lives than we might assume.[72] For a large percentage—as much as a third—of their life spans, women were inextricably involved in the physical processes of motherhood, such as pregnancy, breast-feeding, and taking care of infants. Few women survived to menopause, and childbearing began soon after puberty. The contrast between that situation and contemporary American experience is striking; women today devote barely a seventh of a seventy-five-year-plus life span to maternal processes.[73] Yet, despite the significant proportion of the early Israelite female life span taken up with motherhood—or perhaps because of it—women's productive work was largely unaffected by maternal activities. Production and reproduction in agrarian Israel were not experienced as such distinct or competing categories of female existence as they are in the industrialized world.

The compatibility of subsistence tasks and maternity in an agrarian regime and the importance of children for supplying labor should not mask the kind of difficulty that childbearing did pose for women. It surely diminished their life expectancies. As already indicated, infant mortality rates were high; it is likely that early Israelite farm families rarely reached the typical size, for example, of nineteenth-century American farm families, which had five or six surviving children (out of seven or eight births). Therefore a woman in Iron I Israel would have had nearly two pregnancies for every child who survived to the age of five. The risk of death through multiple pregnancies meant a life span for women nearly ten years shorter than the average of forty years estimated for men.

The life-and-death difficulties of pregnancy were thus of roughly the same magnitude as the life-and-death economic conditions for the members of the family households of early Israel. Unremittingly hard labor for both males and females and a nearly continuous sequence of pregnancies for the females were the salient features of existence in the highland settlements. One wonders how eager the inhabitants of these sites were to shoulder their unending and not always successful burdens.

Encouragement to endure the arduous nature of early Israelite farm life is embedded in a foundational biblical text. As is often the case, sacred or authoritative literature has a functional role in sanctioning behaviors that are difficult or demanding. What people are reluctant to do or apt to not do is presented as a divine mandate if such actions are for the overall stability or survival of the group.[74] Religious ideology in archaic societies both reflects and undergirds mundane as well as lofty aspects of human behavior.[75]

Such is surely the case for the Eden narrative. As a wisdom tale, it responds to the human anguish over the crushing responsibilities of daily life.[76] Embedded in the Yahwistic narrative of the early monarchy is a poetic fragment, probably somewhat older, that describes and prescribes the realities of highland farming. God proclaims that males shall, with much hard work and unending "toil" (Gen. 3:17), struggle to produce bread (sustenance) from reluctant soils (ground that has been cursed). At the same time, the lot of females is laid out in a verse that is virtually always mistranslated and typically read through the interpretive lenses of Augustine, Milton, and many other postbiblical commentators. Genesis 3:16 in fact sets forth the notion that God will increase both the female's "toil" (same word as in 3:17; not the Hebrew word for pain) and the number of her "pregnancies" (not "childbirth," as in many translations); women will have to work hard and bear many children.[77] The text reads:

> I will greatly increase your toil and pregnancies;
> [along] with travail shall you beget children.
> (author's translation)

Population increase is thus a contingent desideratum. It was mandated for a pioneer agrarian population with labor shortages, just as other ancient mythic expressions sanctioned diminished human fertility when the opposite demographic condition—overpopulation—was present.[78] Increasing family size, despite possible female reluctance to endure repeated pregnancies, and laboring long hours at subsistence tasks are the adaptive imperatives of the Genesis tale.

The labors of all the males and females of a family group were thus heavily directed toward the household economy and toward assuring the survival of the family group on its landholdings. Even procreation was part of a context of supplying labor and maintaining land tenure. All other family functions were similarly integral to the economic ones.

This can be readily seen in the *educative/socialization* dimension of the farm family. The interconnection of production and reproduction for family survival is reflected in all family interactions that have the effect of transmitting to younger family members the skills and procedures necessary for maintaining a household's agricultural regime.

The experience of senior males with respect to the nuances of soil types, terrain, climate, tool types, crop choices, and livestock management was gradually passed to the next generation as older male children were apprenticed to the fathers, uncles, and grandfathers of the compound family. Because the environment in the highland setting was so fractured and diverse, virtually every family's holdings had a unique configuration of ecological factors to which an assortment of technologies and strategies were applied. Older males were thus repositories of family-specific ecological knowledge. Their familiarity with the specific microenvironments of the patrimonial lands enabled the family to maximize its limited potential. This is probably a major reason for the strong emphasis on land inalienability.[79] The optimal ways for using the resources of one ecological niche could not always be successfully transferred to another one. Because the chances for adequate yields were dependent on extremely localized conditions, retaining both family lands and the specific knowledge base to exploit them was crucial to family survival.

A similar pattern of transmitting knowledge across generations affected female lives. In their daily activities, older females instructed younger ones in all the technical aspects of gardening, food processing, meal preparation, textile production, and other tasks within their specialized economic domains. In general, as noted above, women's tasks required somewhat greater technological expertise than did men's. However, their subsistence activities were somewhat less dependent on sensitive awareness of local ecological conditions. That is, women's skills were somewhat more transferable to other locales. In the patrilineal system of Israelite farmers, it was more pragmatic for daughters to marry out—their skills required little honing as they moved to farmsteads occupying slightly different habitats—than for sons. Nonetheless, as is noted below, there were limits to the range of female outmarrying in terms of the most advantageous use of the learned skills in the female repertoire of household labor.

Closely connected with the roles of both parents in transmitting the knowledge needed by their offspring to contribute to their natal households and eventually, in the case of daughters, to their affinal ones are the nature and degree of parental authority. The diverse and technical nature of the various subsistence activities required the exercise of considerable parental guidance; and responding to parental directives meant that children had to "honor" their parents, as in the Fifth Commandment of the Decalogue. Parental interaction with children, insofar as it was organized around bringing the children into the orbit of household productivity, required a considerable level of authority.

Indeed, parental educative roles merged with managerial ones, as senior family members orchestrated the complex set of subsistence operations carried out in their farming households. The varied tasks of the mixed agricultural regime required a high degree of integration of family labors. There would be little leeway for juvenile dalliance or resistance; offspring of all ages—young children as well as adult ones—had to provide labor and develop know-how. Because multigenerational or laterally extended families are characteristically more difficult to manage than are nuclear ones, senior family members wielded a significant degree of authority. The extreme penalties attached to legal strictures that aimed at ensuring parental authority (Ex. 21:15, 17) are most likely a function of the critical importance of establishing the household authority of mother and father, especially over adult children. When subsistence resources are scarce, as in early Israel, the exercise of parental authority is even more marked.[80]

The authority of senior parents over a multigenerational unit of more than twelve persons gave a jural cast to their roles. Decision-making processes involving marriage contracts, allocation of resources, and assignment of tasks were carried out in a household framework of quasi-legal parental authority. Any difficulties in these processes were largely resolved internally, through the adjudication of the family elders. Only when internal family redress failed to control tensions among members of the household might there be recourse to a suprafamily judicial body—perhaps a group of elders drawn from each household in a mišpāḥāh or village community (cf. Deut. 21:18–21 and Zech. 13:3).[81]

The educative and authoritative role of parents was thus determined and dominated by the economic functions of the household. But it involved other, less tangible features. It included, no doubt, passing on to children accounts of the family's patrimony, of its historical understanding of its claim to the land it held in relation to the holdings of the other family households in the settlement. The relation of households to one another, to be examined below, was important in many ways to the survival of any individual family group. The interrelatedness of the component units of a settlement, as a *mišpāḥāh,* helped link the land and its inhabitants beyond the level of individual family households. In that sense, the cultural heritage of a farm family served to mediate and solidify the relationship among families that lived in close proximity and that understood themselves as kin.

Although virtually invisible in the biblical record, ethnographic evidence suggests that household religious or ritual activities, along with family storytelling traditions, served to preserve and pass on unifying elements of connected family households. Standards of interpersonal and interfamily behavior, encoded as traditional sapiential morality on the one hand and incipient legal regulations on the other hand, were likewise part of the family heritage transmitted didactically across generations and probably reinforced by a framework of religious rites and beliefs.

Family and Community Solidarity

The multiple ways in which all members of an early Israelite family contributed to the household economy meant that families experienced a marked degree of solidarity. The corporate as opposed to individual identity of the farm family emerged from interdependence across gender and age boundaries. Beginning as early as age five or six, all residents of the family household were bound together by their mutual goals, needs, and tasks. This family solidarity is what made it possible for the household unit to achieve its self-sufficiency and to withstand recurrent economic crises. Shortfalls arising from the various adverse environmental conditions to which the highland communities were subjected were characteristically met by some combination of increased efforts—intensifying the workloads of an already arduous life for some period—and reduced consumption. Willingness to participate in such taxing measures would not have been possible without a work ethic produced by the corporate solidarity of the family household.[82]

The cross-generational interdependence, in which adults relied on a significant number of labor hours per day from their offspring, had the effect of making parents dependent on children in ways that western families virtually never experience. In industrialized nations, the words *children* and *dependents* are virtually synonymous. Not so in premodern agrarian households. Children were, of course, dependent on their parents; but the opposite was also true. This interdependence included the often overlooked fact that at the end of the life cycle, aging parents were cared for by those children (sons) and their spouses who were to inherit the family holdings. Property transfer within farm families mediated intergenerational bonds and ensured that the landholding ascendants would be cared for by succeeding generations for as long as they lived.[83] This fact may also have contributed to the reproductive imperative: higher fertility means greater old-age security.

The interdependence of husband and wife is another, often unrecognized feature of early Israelite family households. Androcentric aspects of biblical materials, including the designation of the family household by the masculine term *bêt 'ab* (father's house), have given the impression of male dominance in the economics and dynamics of family life. That impression should be challenged in view of the undisputed interdependence of men and women in carrying out the myriad household tasks. Men and women under such conditions are "farm partners."[84] It is difficult to maintain that there was a hierarchical relationship between the members of the conjugal pairs that comprised the household unit. Men were hardly the "breadwinners," with the rights and status that accrue to such a role in the industrialized West. Men and women were clearly interdependent, because of the essential contributions of both to subsistence labor. Women probably performed more jobs requiring technological skills than did men. In that regard, the division of labor by gender created a female workforce in each household in which women controlled sets of knowledge without which the family group could not have survived.

The amount of work women do in mixed agrarian regimes that support self-sufficient families seems to be remarkably congruent across cultures. For example, it has been estimated that women on pioneer American farms were responsible for one-third to one-half of all food production, aside from their other activities of household labor and management. For early Israel, a figure of about 40 percent can be suggested, based on a reading of the labor equivalencies in the table of commutation of vows in Leviticus 27.[85] That passage, typically read as indicative that males were valued above females, actually is a very different kind of text. Certain features of its language and content are rooted in archaic practices, so that despite its position at the end of probably later, Priestly materials, this appendix to Leviticus is discrete and much older. It contains valuations that allow for the redemption of property or persons from a shrine. The vowing of persons to a cultic establishment was meaningful in terms of the labor such persons would contribute; redeeming persons thus meant supplying other resources that could purchase an equivalent amount of labor. At a given age—there are four age categories in this passage—labor potential of females is calculated at 38 to 40 percent of the combined efforts of a male and female for three of the four age groups.

This figure fits well with what is known ethnographically and historically. And it also indicates a level of female contributions to subsistence that more or less means parity between male and female contributions to family survival, if some percentage (10 percent or so?) is reserved to reflect female time and energy bound up in reproductive contributions. It is perhaps no accident, then, that this kind of economic gender parity, with females contributing about 40 percent of productive labor, marks societies with the highest status for women.[86]

The high level of gender interdependence in early Israelite farm families, along with the important managerial role of senior females in the life activities of the household, may mean that the biblical term for the complex family unit—*bêt 'āb* (father's house)—refers to the descent reckoning along male lines but not necessarily to male dominance in household functioning. That is, from the male perspective on property transmission, the terminology reflects patrilineality. There is evidence, however, that when viewed from within, the family household had another designation: *bêt 'ēm*, or "mother's house." Although used rarely in comparison with "father's house," this term does appear in several biblical texts, all apparently generated by female experience: Genesis 24:28, Ruth 1:8, and Song of Solomon 3:4 and 8:2 (cf. Prov. 9:1ff.; 14:1; 31:10–31). In these few passages, the androcentrism of the biblical corpus has not completely obliterated the social reality of daily life, where women were powerful actors in daily affairs and family decisions.[87]

Recognizing that biblical androcentrism typically, though not completely, masks female agency and power calls into question the validity of labeling early Israel "patriarchal." That designation is virtually ubiquitous in assessments of the nature of Israelite society, by feminists as well as by others. Yet, arising as it does from nineteenth-century macrosociology, the idea of patriarchy may not be appropriate for an analysis of early Israelite farm families.[88] Patrilineal descent (a system that traces descent and group membership through males) and patrilocal residence (a norm that requires newly wed couples to live with or near the husband's parents) both involve the privileging of the male with respect to property; but adding patriarchy to that list places cultural baggage on the family households of the Iron I period that they may not legitimately need to bear. The term *androcentrism*, representing both Israelite society and biblical literature, may provide a more useful concept than patriarchy (or sexism) for examining how male power is produced in cultures.[89]

Calling early Israel "patriarchal" may also mask other kinds of power differentials and problems among family members. The fact of the overall interdependence of men and women, of adults and children, and of young and old in extended Israelite farm families might give the impression of a large harmonious unity—"one big, happy family." That was not necessarily the case, as our comments about the need for strong parental authority, for example, indicate. If parents survived into old age, their grown offspring took on an increased share of the physical labor and became increasingly eager to take on the concomitant decision-making roles. The subordination of adult children to older adults is nearly always problematic; norms of respect for elders and even customary legal strictures favoring the parents are not always able to contain intergenerational tensions or even outright hostility.[90] Families, after all, are dynamic groups with changing configurations of members and idiosyncratic developmental processes.[91] Internal conflict was thus inevitable; and there is no dearth of biblical materials—notably in the family narratives of Genesis, virtually the only texts allowing a glimpse of domestic life—to suggest otherwise.

When village populations expanded and land resources proportionally diminished, conflict among heirs was hardly unusual. Israelite legislation favoring firstborn sons with a double portion (Deut. 21:17) is not quite compatible with the structure of the compound families of early Israel and may date from a later period. Yet the similar principle that one adult brother—presumably the eldest—must exercise seniority over his siblings in the household on the death of the father would be a conflict-producing situation. Indeed, the departure of younger sons from the family household to join the militia units of early Israel (and later, the national army) was probably one mechanism for defusing conflict among male members of the same generation in a complex household.[92]

Intergenerational conflict and violence were less likely to affect female members of early Israelite farm families. Daughters left the family unit at marriageable age and thus were not present to contest the authority of their mothers. And daughters-in-law entering the family household, as newcomers, were unlikely to question managerial decisions of the senior female—unless, of course, the older female lived well beyond the usual life span and impinged on the growing competence and experience, to say nothing of the greater energy, of a mature younger woman. Even if daughters-in-law maintained respect for their husbands' mothers—a value strongly present in the book of Ruth— their position as outsiders, at least in the early years of marriage, may have made life difficult at times.

Sons' spouses probably fared best if they came from within the larger kinship group, the *mišpāḥāh*. In terms of family dynamics, they would thus have shared some part of the cultural and territorial heritage that linked kin groups. Biblical materials, while recording examples of ex- ogamy, clearly favor endogamy, whereby wives are taken from within the male's group. Perhaps the ideal form of endogamy, despite its con- sanguinity, was cross-cousin marriage, in which a man married the daughter of his mother's brother—someone outside the household unit but closely connected to it (as in Jacob's marriage to his cousins Rachel and Leah, Gen. 29:12).[93] Such daughters-in-law, usually from nearby households in the same village or from a village close by, would have been socialized into labor patterns and skills that most closely approx- imated those of their affinal families. This functional aspect of endogamy, given the diverse microenvironments in the Israelite high- lands, is surely a pragmatic justification for the frequent biblical stric- tures against exogamy (e.g., Ex. 34:16; cf. Gen. 24:3; 27:46). Those strictures are couched in theological terms—foreign daughters will bring foreign gods to the Israelites. Such language encodes the notion that foreign culture, technical as well as ideological, would not fit the household habitats of early Israelite communities. In contrast, marry- ing a woman from one's larger kin group meant obtaining someone with expertise more suitable to one's subsistence tasks.

The larger kinship group was important to early Israelite families in more ways than providing spouses for male offspring. The family household, though largely self-sufficient, was hardly a self-contained or fully circumscribed unit. The pathways and byways within a village or hamlet and those leading to nearby water sources, fields, and pastures were community spaces, frequently traversed by all family members. In spatial terms alone, Israelite families occupied the larger world of the settlement in which their households were situated. The small scale of the Israelite villages meant that people knew each other well, probably in kinship terms—as someone's mother or husband or grandparent, and so on.[94]

The archaeological recovery of village plans can provide some notion of the proximity of family households and thus of the inevitability of interhousehold contacts. What is lacking in such data is a sense of the dynamics of those contacts. What experiences and tasks were shared? What kind of community solidarity was established? Was there any interdependence among the household units that constituted the tiny hamlets and villages of early Israel?

As for many aspects of this foundational period of Israelite existence, the answers to such questions must be interpretive suggestions based on ethnographic analogy. And although the nuances of the connections among the various extended families of a settlement are difficult to discern, the likelihood is very great that such connections existed and were highly significant. Even in cultures in which households have a tradition of being fiercely independent, a wide variety of interactions among households, in a number of interlocking ways, is the norm. This is especially true for cultures inhabiting difficult environments, where the very survival of household units is an ever present concern. In such situations, cooperation between neighboring households is often the key to their ability to inhabit territories with marginal resources.[95] Intertwined economic and family responsibilities are inextricably embedded in the larger world of the village.[96]

Traditional agrarian families are thus inevitably bound to the fabric of a wider social structure, for economic, psychological, social, and often military reasons. For ancient Israel, the suprahousehold social unit was the *mišpāḥāh,* for which the descriptive rendering "protective association of families"[97] is appropriate. The *mišpāḥāh*—with its sense of being bound by a common heritage, by kinship ties, and by shared subsistence concerns—represented a solidarity of nearby family units that interacted with and sustained one another.

The suggestion that the family units were bound to one another in a kinship network gives us some idea of how the village or *mišpāḥāh* functioned. In the prestate period, with few, if any, institutions beyond the local level to guarantee behavior and mediate conflict, the concept of "shared blood" was a critical way for securing trust and assuring willingness to engage in mutual aid.[98] It is no wonder that biblical genealogies weave a comprehensive fabric of kin relationships for all the family households. The existence of an actual biological basis to that structure is irrelevant. People everywhere tend to think of themselves as kin, or use kinship language to characterize their commonality, if they have some historical experience, standards, and life patterns in common. Whether literary, sociological, biological, or, more likely, some combination of all three, the firm placing of each *bêt 'āb* (or *bêt 'ēm*)—father's (or mother's) house—in a wider, kinship-based structure was essential for the supportive and protective roles of the *mišpāḥāh*.

These roles can be reconstructed using historical, ethnographic, and biblical data. At the village level, there was surely some pooling or exchanging of both resources and labor. Family units at a stage of growth where they had relatively few capable laborers would be aided by units at the peak of their complement of able-bodied workers, as when there were adolescent daughters still at home or if there were a number of prepubescent grandchildren. One might even imagine interhousehold work groups that perhaps mended terraces or harvested adjacent fields together. In terms of the need for military protection, males from nearby villages within certain territories (tribes?) came together to form temporary, militia-type forces. Some shared activities, such as those involving heavy field work or military actions, were largely gender specific—that is, men's cooperative work—although extreme needs could allow crossover of gender roles. In Judges 9:51–54, for example, a woman of Thebez kills the erstwhile king Abimelech by throwing a millstone down on his head.

Other cooperative activities involved just women, who were hardly a segregated or isolated subset of the family household. Indeed, recent attention to the specifically female worlds of traditional farming communities reveals a rich assortment of shared activities across household boundaries. Ubiquitous among these activities were birthing procedures, attended by one or more women skilled in midwifery (cf. Ex. 1:15ff.). The gathering of females to assist a pregnant woman in childbirth created an atmosphere of physical and emotional intimacy among women. Similarly, daughters were in the company of mothers for all their premarital years (whereas sons were partly with mothers and partly with fathers). As a result, intimacy among females was perhaps even greater than that among males (cf. Ruth 4:17).

Along these lines, one can also point to female associations for learning and performing certain ritual activities. For example, funeral rites—mourning and lamenting (cf. Jer. 9:17–22)—involved calling on women with expertise in keening. And a set of celebratory events (e.g., Ex. 15:20; 1 Sam. 18:6) was predicated on women's musical talents and techniques. Both kinds of activities involved women learning musical skills, including the composition of dirges or songs, and practicing them together, so that they would be prepared to perform, individually or in ensembles.[99]

The ritual-religious nature of women's performance skills, whether for mourning or celebrating, draws attention to another aspect of community life and solidarity. Surely there were household sacred customs and rites, many of which have become visible as increasing attention is paid to women's roles in domestic religion.[100] At the same time there were local festivals and celebrations that transcended the family household, as there were in premodern farming communities everywhere. Such festivals were typically keyed to the agricultural calendar and marked the completion, usually a harvest, of some vital aspect of the cropping regime. The annual festival at Shiloh, mentioned in Judges 21:19–21, was undoubtedly related to the grape harvest. Similarly, the consumption of a lamb to mark the birthing season of a household's flocks apparently involved suprahousehold cooperation and community celebration; the text of Exodus 12:3–6, which describes that ritual, despite later accretions, surely stems from ancient agricultural festivities.

The biblical emphasis on one God, Yahweh, as the deity of the entire people of Israel obscures the way family religion was at the core of the religious culture of early Israelite settlements. At the same time, our contemporary sense of religion as a matter of individual choice and commitment makes it difficult to see that there probably was no such thing as personal religion in early Israel, or in the ancient Near East as a whole.[101] Just as individualism, as we experience it today in the West, was not present in the highland villages of Palestine, so too were individual belief systems nonexistent. Rather, a person's relationship to the deity was a function of that deity's connection to his or her family. Note the language of one of the oldest poems in the Pentateuch, the Song of Miriam/Moses: "This is my God, and I will praise him, / my father's God, and I will exalt him" (Ex. 15:2). Similarly, the ancestral narratives of Genesis repeatedly use the language of family in reference to God. Jacob in particular invokes the God of his lineage: the God of Abraham and of Isaac (e.g., Gen. 31:5, 42, 53; 32:9; 46:1–2).

In the early Israelite villages, family religion extended beyond the nuclear and compound families and included the local community—the kin group, or mišpāḥāh. Family groups inhabiting the same settlement shared an attachment to a deity or deities linked to their common ancestor, who was understood to be the founder of their lineage. Surely there were rituals and ceremonies that took place within individual or compound dwelling units; these may have had some connection with the "household gods" of Genesis 31:19, 34 and the images and cultic

objects in Micah's household (Judg. 17:4–5). Households probably had
their own cult corners.[102] Villages, too, had shrines or locales for ritual
events—natural rather than constructed spots. Such rocks or trees,
rather than discrete buildings or hewn altars, may have been the "high
places" of the Israelite villages.

Our holidays and holy days in the modern West are so historicized
and so few in number in comparison with those of traditional societies that it is often difficult to appreciate the level of community solidarity fostered by socioreligious gatherings at the village or
mišpāḥāh level. Such occasions contributed to and preserved the
sense of common heritage and destiny and helped cement the feelings of interconnectedness among households and thus of social responsibility across household boundaries. Indeed, shared values of
cooperation and mutual assistance are typically inculcated and perpetuated through cultural forms that highlight corporate experience,
past and present.[103] What we would designate *religion* was present in
the cultural practices, predicated on shared meanings of land and
kinship, that shaped the social occasions of early Israelite settlements. Such cultural practices served to produce and reproduce
larger social relationships and assure the willingness of family units
to contribute to one another's welfare.

An awareness of the interlocking network of social experiences and
connections that characterized the village or mišpāḥāh level of Israelite
family life makes it clear that the private-public dichotomy often used
as a paradigm for analyzing and understanding family life is inadequate
in considering early Israelite family households. Enmeshed as they were
in the larger kinship community, the activities of the household members were hardly contained by the family household. Or to put it another way, the spheres of activity of a family household transcended its
own persons and property.

The affairs of a household thus took on a public character, with the
integration of private and public domains mediated by the socioreligious life of the village community.[104] In both formal and informal
ways, in modes dealing with economic needs as well as emotional ones,
in activities geared to the life course or to the seasons, the social sphere
served to weave the family household units into the fabric of the larger
village community on which they depended. The socioreligious sphere
of life, often overlooked in studies of premodern families, stands out
as a critical feature in the overall culture of the constituent units. Corporate family identity through subscription to a larger social identity

provided meaning and security that the household unit alone could not achieve.

Just as we cautioned against idealizing the family household as a harmonious unit, so too we note the problems or limitations of the larger unit. Ultimately, it could not always or completely provide the protective roles, economically and militarily, that were its raison d'être. In some parts of Israelite territorial holdings, environmental constraints were too severe to be overcome by even the most concerted efforts of individual families and their larger kinship groups. The periodic droughts were sometimes too sustained or harsh for any families or groups of families to endure. Outbreaks of disease at times decimated too large a part of the tiny population of a settlement, or the raids of marauding groups on the unwalled villages jeopardized the sufficiency of precious supplies of foodstuffs and of seeds for the next plantings.

In addition, ironically, the very success of family households in some instances could cause corporate community distress. Too many sons surviving into adulthood could lead to interhousehold struggles over property rights, especially as households sought to expand their holdings.

The precariousness of the highland environment of early Israelite villages ultimately made it impossible, no matter how successful the solidarity of the family household and of the village kinship group, for all such units to survive. Many of the new settlements that dotted the highlands in the Iron I period did not continue into the age of the monarchies, the Iron II period. Although agrarian household families would continue to be a mainstay of Israelite life in succeeding centuries, they became increasingly part of the orbit of larger settlements—towns and cities. Many features of family dynamics, of marriage patterns and kinship values, were no doubt altered during the momentous changes brought about by state formation and national institutional systems. Yet it is also true that many of the patterns and values associated with early Israelite family structures were incorporated into the legal systems and community values of subsequent Israelite life. In many cases that continuity was advantageous. But that might not always have been the case, and further adaptations were necessary in the more densely populated settlements of monarchical Israel. In looking at the Israelite family in any period, but especially in the formative era, it is important to refrain from privileging either its form or its functions. Its adaptability to even the harshest circumstances, rather than the specific features generated by that adaptability, seems to be its most salient quality.

NOTES

1. James W. Flanagan, "Chiefs in Israel," *JSOT* 20 (1981):47–73.
2. Carol Meyers, "Kinship and Kingship: The Early Monarchy," in *The Oxford History of the Biblical World,* ed. Michael D. Coogan (New York: Oxford University Press, forthcoming).
3. See George E. Mendenhall, "The Hebrew Conquest of Palestine," *BA* 25 (1962):66–87.
4. Robert McC. Netting, *Smallholders, Householders: Farm Families and the Ecology of Intensive, Sustainable Agriculture* (Stanford, Calif.: Stanford University Press, 1993), 2.
5. Cf. E. R. Leach, *Social Anthropology* (Glasgow: Fontana, 1982).
6. This terminology is explained below, p. 13. See also pp. 36–40.
7. Norman Gottwald, *The Hebrew Bible: A Socio-Literary Introduction* (Philadelphia: Fortress Press, 1985), 252–60.
8. Norman Gottwald, *Tribes of Yahweh* (Maryknoll, N.Y.: Orbis Books, 1979), 150–87.
9. Jo Ann Hackett, "In the Days of Jael: Reclaiming the History of Women in Ancient Israel," in *Immaculate and Powerful: The Female in Sacred Image and Social Reality,* ed. Clarissa W. Atkinson, Constance H. Buchanan, and Margaret R. Miles (Boston: Beacon Press, 1985), 15–38.
10. Jay W. Marshall, *Israel and the Book of the Covenant: An Anthropological Approach to Biblical Law* (SBLDS 140; Atlanta: Scholars Press, 1993).
11. Gerhard E. Lenski, *Power and Privilege: A Theory of Social Stratification* (Chapel Hill, N.C.: University of North Carolina Press, 1984), 199–200.
12. Charles E. Carter, "Ethnoarchaeology," in *The Oxford Encyclopedia of Near Eastern Archaeology* (New York: Oxford University Press/American Schools of Oriental Research, 1997).
13. Richard A. Gould and Patty Jo Watson, "A Dialogue on the Meaning and Use of Analogy in Ethnoarchaeological Reasoning," *Journal of Anthropological Archaeology* 1 (1982):355–81.
14. Lawrence E. Stager, "The Archaeology of the Family in Ancient Israel," *BASOR* 260 (1985):1–36.
15. Carol Meyers, *Discovering Eve: Ancient Israelite Women in Context* (New York: Oxford University Press, 1988).
16. Ray Abrahams, *A Place of Their Own: Family Farming in Eastern Finland* (Cambridge: Cambridge University Press, 1991), 70.
17. Such as Linda K. Kerber and Jane Sherron De Hart, eds., *Women's America: Refocusing the Past,* 4th ed. (New York: Oxford University Press, 1995); and Clyde A. Milner, Carol A. O'Connor, and Martha A. Sandweiss, eds., *The Oxford History of the American West* (New York: Oxford University Press, 1994).
18. See Meyers, *Discovering Eve,* 128–32.
19. Bernhard Farber, ed., *Kinship and Family Organization* (New York: John Wiley & Sons, 1960), 1–9.

20. Emilio Moran, ed., *The Ecosystem Approach in Anthropology: From Concept to Practice* (Ann Arbor: University of Michigan Press, 1990); Marvin Harris, *Cultural Materialism: The Struggle for a Science of Culture* (New York: Vintage Books, 1980).

21. See Amihai Mazar, "The Iron I Age," in *The Archaeology of Ancient Israel*, ed. Amnon Ben-Tor (New Haven, Conn.: Yale University Press, 1992), 295–96; William G. Dever, "Cultural Continuity, Ethnicity in the Archaeological Record and the Question of Israelite Origins," *Eretz Israel* 24 (1993):22*–33* (Please note that this journal uses asterisks for pages within its English language section; journal also contains a Hebrew section); and William G. Dever, "Ceramics, Ethnicity, and the Question of Israel's Origins," *BA* 58(1995):200–213.

22. For a convenient and accessible discussion of this issue, see Hershel Shanks, William G. Dever, Baruch Halpern, and P. Kyle McCarter, *The Rise of Ancient Israel* (Washington, D.C.: Biblical Archaeology Society, 1992); cf. Gottwald, *Tribes of Yahweh*.

23. See, e.g., David Hopkins, *The Highlands of Canaan* (SWBA 3; Sheffield: Almond Press, 1985).

24. Oded Borowski, *Agriculture in Iron Age Israel* (Winona Lake, Ind.: Eisenbrauns, 1982), 87.

25. Carol Meyers, "Of Seasons and Soldiers: A Topological Appraisal of the Pre-Monarchic Tribes of Galilee," *BASOR* 252 (1983):47–60.

26. Israel Finkelstein, *The Archaeology of the Israelite Settlement* (Jerusalem: Israel Exploration Society, 1988), 121–39.

27. For example, Yigael Shiloh, "The Population of Iron Age Palestine in the Light of a Sample Analysis of Urban Plans, Areas, and Population Density," *BASOR* 239 (1980):25–35.

28. Finkelstein, *Archaeology of the Israelite Settlement*, 238–50.

29. Gottwald, *Tribes of Yahweh*, 257–94; Stager, "Archaeology of the Family," 22.

30. Gottwald, *Tribes of Yahweh*, 257.

31. George Mendenhall, "The Census Lists of Numbers 1 and 26," *JBL* 77 (1958):52–66.

32. Meyers, *Discovering Eve*, 128–32.

33. Yigael Shiloh, "The Four-Room House: Its Situation and Function in the Israelite City," *IEJ* 20(1970):180–90; John S. Holladay, Jr., "House, Israelite," *ABD* 3(1992):308–18.

34. John S. Holladay, Jr., "Stable, Stables," *ABD* 4(1992):178–83.

35. For example, Ze'ev Herzog, *Beersheba II* (Tel Aviv: Institute of Archaeology, 1984); and Frank Braemer, *L'Architecture domestique du Levant à l'âge du fer* (Paris: Editiones Recherche sur les Civilisations, 1982).

36. Holladay, "House, Israelite," 315–17.

37. Patty Jo Watson, *Archaeological Ethnography in Western Iran* (Viking Fund Publications in Archaeology 57; Tucson: University of Arizona Press, 1979).

38. Amihai Mazar, *Archaeology of the Land of the Bible—10,000–586 B.C.E.*

(ABRL; New York: Doubleday, 1990), 485–89; idem, "Iron I Age," 288–89.

39. Stager, "Archaeology of the Family," 18–19.

40. See Meyers, *Discovering Eve*, 132–38.

41. Francis I. Andersen, "Israelite Kinship Terminology and Social Structure," *BT* 20(1970):29.

42. Translation of Gottwald, *Tribes of Yahweh*, 291.

43. Madeline McClenney Sadler, "The Incest Taboos of Leviticus 18" (paper presented at the Southeast Regional AAR/SBL Meeting, Gainesville, Florida, March 1995).

44. See Nancy Wilmsen Thornhill, "An Evolutionary Analysis of Rules Regulating Human Inbreeding and Marriage," *Behavioral and Brain Sciences* 14 (1991), 247–93.

45. Meyers, *Discovering Eve*, 135; Andrew D. H. Mayes, *Judges* (Sheffield: JSOT Press, 1985), 49; cf. Joshua R. Porter, *The Extended Family in the Old Testament* (London: Edutext Publications, 1967).

46. Burton Pasternak, Carol R. Ember, and M. Ember, "On Conditions Favoring Extended Family Households," *Journal of Anthropological Research* 32 (1976): 121.

47. J. Lawrence Angel, "Ecology and Population in the East Mediterranean," *World Archaeology* 4 (1972):94–97.

48. Stager, "Archaeology of the Family," 21, Table 4; Hopkins, *Highlands of Canaan*, 253; cf. Thomas K. Burch, "Some Demographic Determinants of Average Household Size: An Analytical Approach," in *Household and Family in Past Times*, ed. Peter Laslett and Richard Wall (Cambridge: Cambridge University Press, 1972), 91–102.

49. Gottwald, *Tribes of Yahweh*, 285–92.

50. Mark R. Rosenzweig and Kenneth Wolpin, "Specific Experience, Household Structure and Intergenerational Transfers: Farm Family Arrangements in Developing Countries," *Quarterly Journal of Economics* 100 (1985):961–87.

51. Christopher J. H. Wright, *God's People in God's Land: Family, Land, and Property in the Old Testament* (Grand Rapids, Mich.: Wm. B. Eerdmans Publishing Co., 1990), 119–28.

52. Ibid., 56–57.

53. S. Herbert Bess, "Systems of Land Tenure in Ancient Israel" (Ph.D. diss., University of Michigan, 1963), 91.

54. Nancy Grey Osterud, "Land, Identity, and Agency in the Oral Autobiographies of Farm Women," in *Women and Farming: Changing Roles, Changing Structures*, ed. Wava G. Haney and Jane B. Knowles (Rural Studies Series; Boulder, Colo.: Westview Press, 1988), 77–79.

55. Ida Harper Simpson and John Wilson, "Proprietary Family Orientations of Black and White Farm Couples" (paper presented at the Conference of Rural/Farm Women in Agriculture, University of California at Davis, June 26–28, 1992).

56. Cf. Bernhard Farber, *Family and Kinship in Modern Society* (Introduction to Modern Society Series; Glenview, Ill.: Scott, Foresman & Co., 1973), 2–8.

57. Michael Elliott and Christopher Dickey, "Body Politics," *Newsweek*, September 12, 1994, 24–25.

58. Teodor Shonin, "Peasantry as a Political Factor," *Peasants and Peasant Society*, ed. Teodor Shonin (Harmondsworth, Middlesex: Penguin Books, 1971), 240–43.

59. Netting, *Smallholders, Householders*, 58–59.

60. This listing is not necessarily the only way household functions can be construed. Various researchers, going back to George P. Murdock, *Social Structures* (New York: Macmillan Co., 1949), provide listings with different nuances or subdivisions (e.g., Farber, ed., *Kinship and Family Organization*, 3; Shonin, "Peasantry as a Political Factor," 240; Marion J. Levy and Lloyd A. Fallers, "The Family: Some Comparative Considerations," in Farber, ed., *Kinship and Family Organization*, 10–13; Netting, *Smallholders, Householders*, 2; Kathleen Neils Conzen, "A Saga of Families," in Milner, O'Connor, and Sandweiss, eds., *Oxford History of the American West*, 319).

61. David Hopkins, "Life in Ancient Palestine," in *New Interpreter's Bible* (Nashville: Abingdon Press, 1994), 1:213–224; Øystein S. LaBianca, "Everyday Life at Hesban through the Centuries," in *Hesban: After 25 Years*, ed. David Merling and Lawrence T. Geraty (Berrien Springs, Mich.: Institute of Archaeology/Siegfried H. Horn Archaeological Museum, 1994), 197–210; Carol Meyers, "Everyday Life of Women in the Period of the Hebrew Bible," in *The Women's Bible Commentary*, ed. Carol A. Newsom and Sharon H. Ringe (Louisville, Ky.: Westminster/John Knox Press, 1992), 244–51.

62. See George P. Murdock and Caterina Provost, "Factors in the Division of Labor by Sex: A Cross-Cultural Analysis," *Ethnology* 12 (1973):203–25.

63. Ernestine Friedl, *Women and Men: An Anthropologist's View* (New York: Holt, Rinehart & Winston, 1975), 53.

64. Judith Brown, "A Note on the Division of Labor," *American Anthropologist* 72 (1970):1073–78.

65. See James Peoples and Garrick Bailey, *Humanity: An Introduction to Cultural Anthropology* (St. Paul: West Publishing Co., 1988), 250–61.

66. Laurel Thatcher Ulrich, "The Ways of Her Household," in Kerber and DeHart, eds., *Women's America*, 37–46.

67. Laurel Bossen, "Women and Economic Institutions," in *Economic Anthropology*, ed. Stuart Plottner (Stanford, Calif.: Stanford University Press, 1989), 318–50.

68. John Mack Faragher, "The Midwestern Farm Family, 1850," in Kerber and DeHart, eds., *Women's America*, 122.

69. Ulrich, "Ways of Her Household," 39.

70. Faragher, "Midwestern Farm Family," 127.

71. Netting, *Smallholders, Householders*, 70.

72. Louise A. Tilly and Joan W. Scott, *Women, Work, and Family* (New York: Holt, Rinehart, & Winston, 1978), 167.

73. Rayna Rapp, Ellen Ross, and Renate Bridenthal, "Examining Family History: Household and Family," *Feminist Studies* 5 (1977):182.
74. Clifford Geertz, *The Interpretation of Cultures* (New York: Basic Books, 1978), 167–72.
75. Meyers, *Discovering Eve*, 22.
76. George E. Mendenhall, "The Shady Side of Wisdom: The Date and Purpose of Genesis 3," *Light unto My Path*, ed. Howard N. Bream, Ralph D. Heim, and Carey A. Moore (Philadelphia: Temple University Press, 1974), 319–34.
77. Carol Meyers, "Gender Roles and Genesis 3:16 Revisited," in *The Word of the Lord Shall Go Forth*, ed. Carol L. Meyers and M. O'Connor (Philadelphia: ASOR, 1983), 337–54; and idem, *Discovering Eve*, 95–109.
78. Anne D. Kilmer, "The Mesopotamian Concept of Overpopulation and Its Solution as Represented in the Mythology," *Or* 41 (1972):160–77.
79. Mark R. Rosenzweig and Kenneth Wolpin, "Specific Experience, Household Structure and Intergenerational Transfers: Farm Family Arrangements in Developing Countries," *Quarterly Journal of Economics* 100 (1985):961–87.
80. Abrahams, *A Place of Their Own*, 73.
81. Christopher J. H. Wright, "Family," *ABD* 2 (1992):764.
82. Shonin, "Peasantry as a Political Factor," 64.
83. Netting, *Smallholders, Householders*, 75.
84. Osterud, "Land, Identity, and Agency," 77.
85. Carol Meyers, "Procreation, Production, and Protection: Male-Female Balance in Early Israel," *JAAR* 51 (1983):569–93.
86. Peggy R. Sanday, "Female Status in the Public Domain," in *Women, Culture, and Society*, ed. Michelle Z. Rosaldo and Louise Lamphere (Stanford, Calif.: Stanford University Press, 1974), 189–206.
87. Carol Meyers, "To Her Mother's House: Considering a Counterpart to the Israelite *Bêt 'āb*," in *The Bible and the Politics of Exegesis: Essays in Honor of Norman K. Gottwald on His Sixty-Fifth Birthday*, ed. David Jobling, Peggy L. Day, and Gerald T. Sheppard (Cleveland: Pilgrim Press, 1991), 39–51, 304–7.
88. Meyers, *Discovering Eve*, 24–26.
89. Cf. Sandra Bem, *The Lenses of Gender: Transforming the Debate on Sexual Equality* (New Haven, Conn.: Yale University Press, 1993).
90. Netting, *Smallholders, Householders*, 81.
91. Abrahams, *A Place of Their Own*, 7.
92. Stager, "Archaeology of the Family," 25–28.
93. See Robert Oden, "Jacob as Father, Husband, and Nephew: Kinship Studies and the Patriarchal Narratives," *JBL* 102(1983):189–205.
94. Sara Evans, "The First American Women," in Kerber and DeHart, eds., *Women's America*, 30.
95. Abrahams, *A Place of Their Own*, 163, 191.
96. Cf. Ulrich, "Ways of Her Household," 44.

97. See above; and Gottwald, *Tribes of Yahweh*, 257ff.

98. Cf. Conzen, "A Saga of Families," 327.

99. Carol Meyers, "The Drum-Dance-Song Ensemble: Women's Perfor- mance in Biblical Israel," in *Rediscovering the Muses: Women's Musical Tra- ditions,* ed. Kimberly Marshall (Boston: Northeastern University Press, 1993), 49–67, 234–38.

100. Phyllis Bird, "The Place of the Woman in the Israelite Cultus," in *Ancient Israelite Religion: Essays in Honor of Frank Moore Cross,* ed. Patrick Miller, Jr., Paul D. Hanson, and S. Dean McBride (Philadelphia: Fortress Press, 1987), 349–419; cf. Susan Starr Sered, *Women as Ritual Experts* (New York: Oxford University Press, 1992).

101. Karel Van der Toorn, "Family Gods in Israel, Syria, and Mesopotamia" (paper presented at the AAR/SBL annual meeting, San Francisco, No- vember 21, 1992).

102. Cf. the Iron II materials; see Yigael Shiloh, "Iron Age Sanctuaries and Cult Elements in Palestine," in *Symposia Celebrating the Seventy-fifth Anniver- sary of the Founding of the American Schools of Oriental Research (1900– 1975),* ed. Frank Moore Cross (Cambridge, Mass.: ASOR, 1979).

103. Conzen, "A Saga of Families," 320.

104. See Karen V. Hansen, *A Very Social Time: Crafting Community in Antebel- lum New England* (Berkeley: University of California Press, 1994), 1–9.

2

The Family in
First Temple Israel

JOSEPH BLENKINSOPP

In reading the biblical account of the history of Israel under the monarchy, we are reminded constantly that, in spite of the encroachment of the state system with its bureaucratic apparatus, the family remained the primary context in which the individual's location, functions, and roles in society were understood and transacted. So, for example, a good part of the legal material promulgated during the four centuries of the existence of the kingdoms was designed to regulate social relations within and among families, including such matters as marriage, land tenure, and inheritance on which the survival of the family unit depended. Much of the narrative of the Hebrew Bible is basically family history, obviously so in the story of the ancestors (Genesis 12—50) but no less with that of the monarchy itself—for example, the history of struggle and intrigue within David's family (2 Samuel 11—1 Kings 2). The idea of Israel as a cluster of families held together in a precarious unity was never far below the surface. Eventually this kinship substratum was eroded by the encroaching state system, though it never disappeared altogether and even reemerged in a somewhat different pattern in the period of the second temple. Archaeological evidence currently available also seems to suggest that the idea of a state took a long time to take hold, and that the basic prerequisites, including a minimum level of literacy, were not fully in place until the eighth century B.C.E., not much more than a century before the end of the kingdom of Judah.[1]

For information on the family we depend primarily on the biblical texts. Relevant archaeological data are not abundant, partly because—until recently, at any rate—the main interest of Palestinian and Near Eastern archaeologists has been to uncover monumental architecture; and in so doing, much potential source material for the living conditions of the mass of the population has been neglected or destroyed. With respect to Samaria, capital of the Northern Kingdom, for example, only the royal enclave was excavated, with the result that we know nothing about how the 27,290 inhabitants, whom the Assyrians claim to have deported in 722 B.C.E., lived.[2] Since space is an important dimension of social life, something can be learned from the layout of settlements and compounds and from house plans, where these have been recorded.[3] Not much written material relevant to the family or other aspects of social life has come down to us, largely because papyrus, the preferred writing surface for texts of any length, has a hard time surviving the Palestinian winter; in fact, only one papyrus has survived from the time of the kingdoms.[4] Some relevant information can be gleaned from such extant sources as the ostraca from Samaria, Lachish, and one or two other sites, but it does not amount to very much.

Using the biblical texts as source material for the family, or for anything else, calls for an acute sense of their special character as *canonical* texts. This means that the selection, arrangement, and point of view were dictated by the agenda and ideology of those who put the collection together and the circumstances and constraints under which they did the collecting and redacting. On all of this we are very poorly informed. We shall nevertheless examine selectively the laws, narrative, aphoristic and didactic material, and prophetic and cultic texts with a view to what they tell us about the family during Israel of Iron Age II, the time of the kingdoms. Where available, data from comparable societies is also taken into account.

The Israelite Household

The Broader Kinship Network

If we begin by asking what the Israelite family was like, it is very important to avoid taking for granted assumptions based on any particular contemporary understanding of *family*. It is by now well known that ideas about the family have changed rather drastically over the last few decades and that, historically, the term can refer to widely different structures and concepts of social interaction. The standard term in Hebrew, classical and modern, is *mišpāḥāh*. In the Hebrew Bible it is often used in quite unspecific ways, with reference to large social groups or nations (e.g., Gen. 10:5, 32; 12:3; Amos 3:2) and even species of animals (Gen. 8:19). It can also be used of Israel as a whole (Amos 3:1), the Northern and Southern Kingdoms (Jer. 33:24), and—on one occasion—of an individual tribe (Judg. 13:2). In a more precise and technical sense, however, the *mišpāḥāh* is the kinship unit intermediate between the tribe (*šēbeṭ*, *maṭṭeh*) and the ancestral household (*bayit*, *bêt 'āb*). This is clearly the sense of the term where it occurs routinely in genealogies, including lists of clergy to whom the fiction of biological descent could also be applied (e.g., Ex. 6:14, 25; Num. 1:2). The closest English equivalent, therefore, would be the originally Gaelic term *clan*, meaning a group of individual families or households forming a major unit of the tribe and claiming common, unilineal descent from a real or fictitious ancestor.[5]

It may be helpful to think of the individual as existing at the center of at least three concentric circles of kinship—namely, the nuclear unit based on filiation and siblingship, with its various extensions and ramifications; then the clan, or phratry; and finally, the tribe—or, to use a different spatial model, at the point of intersection of a horizontal line, representing siblings and more distant collateral kin, and a vertical line, representing past and future members of the kinship network, the dead and those not yet born. Deceased members were commemorated and venerated as an essential component of this organic whole, and we shall have occasion to note a close connection between patrimonial domain, burial site, and the postmortem existence of ancestors; hence the frequent expression "to be gathered to one's kin" (e.g., Gen. 25:8, 17; 35:29; 49:29, 33), or "to be gathered to one's ancestors" (Judg. 2:10), which might be paraphrased as aggregation, at death, to the totality of the tribe or clan.[6] We may be sure that the sense of identity and self-awareness of the individual living in this kind of network of social relations were significantly different from those of the typical privatized individual of postindustrial, urban society.

Whatever their historical value, several biblical narratives about the early phase of the history illustrate this basic structure of tribe, clan, and household. The parade example is the account of the violation of the ban during the conquest of Canaan:

> Joshua . . . brought the Israelites forward according to their tribes, and the tribe of Judah was singled out. He brought the clans of Judah forward and singled out the Zarhi clan. He brought the Zarhi clan forward according to its adult males and Zabdi was singled out. He then brought the male members of his household forward and there was singled out Achan ben Carmi ben Zabdi ben Zerah of the tribe of Judah. (Josh. 7:16–18; author's translation)

The violator of the ban was therefore discovered by casting lots, which identified first the tribe (Judah), then the clan (Zerah), then the household (Zabdi), and finally the guilty individual, the hapless Achan ben Carmi (Josh. 7:16–18). We may note, incidentally, how the individual's identity is conferred and recognized with reference to patrilineal or agnatic descent. In a later incident, Gideon (alias Jerubbaal) explained to a supernatural visitant that he could not be expected to save Israel since his claim or phratry (*'elep*) was the poorest in (the tribe of) Manasseh and he was the youngest member of his household (*bêt 'āb*) (Judg. 6:15). Later still, the usurper Abimelech won the allegiance of the *mišpāḥāh* to which his mother's *bêt 'āb* belonged and then proceeded to annihilate seventy male members of his father's household as potential rivals (Judg. 9:1–6). Saul son of Kish was picked out by lot, beginning with the tribe (Benjamin), then the *mišpāḥāh* (Matri), then finally Saul himself, skipping mention of his household (1 Sam. 10:21). In these and similar cases, the social existence and visibility of the individual are determined by his (less commonly, her) place within the kinship network.

The Ancestral Household

For obvious reasons, the micro-unit of the household bore most directly on the social consciousness, identity, and daily agenda of the individual Israelite. The ancestral household (*bêt 'āb*) was the basic building block of the tribal structure and continued as such throughout the entire period under consideration. Ethnoarchaeological studies based on excavated dwelling complexes in Israel and elsewhere in the Near East suggest that, at that time, a nuclear family unit of two parents and between two and four children would not be atypical.[7] Accurate demographic data on ancient societies are notoriously difficult to come by, so even these modest estimates can serve only as a rough guide. For what, in this respect, it is worth, the biblical record corroborates this rough estimate. We must, of course, leave aside royalty and those of sufficient wealth to maintain several wives or harem women and a correspondingly large number of children, thus enhancing their status and honor. David and Solomon are obvious examples, and we hear that several of the "judges" had anywhere between seventy and thirty sons (Judg. 8:30; 10:4; 12:9, 14). The undoubtedly high rate of infant mortality must also be factored in and would help to explain, for example, why we hear so often of a couple having only two or three (surviving?)

sons. Moses, Eli the priest of Shiloh, the wise woman of Tekoa, and the widow Naomi each had two sons. Judah had three, as had, apparently, Isaiah and Hosea, whether in reality or figuratively.[8]

Depending on its economic assets, and especially the state and extent of its inherited landholding, the typical household would also have included some or all of the following: grandparents, the families of grown children (since postmarital patrilocal [based on husband's family] residence must have been very common), an adopted child or adopted children, a divorced adult daughter who had returned to the paternal homestead, male and female servants or slaves, and other dependents. It is interesting to observe that dependents, including resident aliens (gērîm) and slaves, were—ideally and in theory, at any rate—considered members of the household, taking part in festivals, profiting by the Sabbath rest, and so on, not unlike servants in a pious household in colonial New England who were expected to attend church, take part in family prayers, and the like.[9] With respect to the larger and better-off households, therefore, we are really dealing with an extended family group and its dependents, occupying a compound with several houses in close proximity. The Ephraimite Micah lived with his widowed mother, his sons, perhaps also their families, and a Levite who was hired to tend the family shrine (Judges 17—18), rather like a chaplain resident in one of the great houses in nineteenth-century England. This Levite, it seems, had his own house (18:15), and there were other dependents living in outbuildings in the same compound (18:14–22). The entire unit, composed of several dwellings and apparently defended by a wall (we hear of people standing near the gate, 18:16), constituted a distinct ancestral household (bêt 'āb, 18:29, 25), one presumably much more populated and wealthier than most.

Though the Passover ritual as formulated in Exodus 12 is almost certainly quite late, no earlier than the neo-Babylonian period, the stipulation that adjacent small households join forces for the purchase and consumption of the Passover sacrifice may be taken to reflect the same situation.

For our purpose, it is not necessary to dwell at length on domestic architecture—fortunately so, since little is known for the period in question. Ground plans have survived from several sites (Tell el-Farah North, Beth Shemesh, Tell en-Nasbeh, Tell Qasile), the most salient feature being a courtyard in which food was prepared and cooked and other domestic activities took place. Even less information is available on house furnishings. The poorest would have eaten off the floor, used smooth stones to sit on, and slept in their clothes directly on the floor or on a pallet. The widow who hosted Elisha had an upper room furnished for him with a bed or couch (*miṭṭāh*), a table (*šulḥān*), a chair *kissē'*), and a lamp (*měnōrāh*) (2 Kings 4:10). This was considered adequate even for a fairly wealthy household, as hers was (4:8). Most of the seventy or so biblical allusions to tables locate them in either temple or royal palace, though we hear occasionally, in Psalms and elsewhere, of setting the table for a meal and of children gathered around the table with their proud parents (Ps. 23:5; 128:3; Job 36:16).

The ancestral household was therefore the basic unit of social interaction. It did not constitute an exclusively biological unity (filiation, siblingship, affinity) but functioned as an economically interdependent unit occupying its own space, generally in a plurality of individual dwellings or at least rooms. Its place within the larger entity of the clan to which it belonged was expressed by descent from a common forebear (e.g., Matri for Saul's household) and reinforced by occasional religious festivals and commemorations. David's *mišpāḥāh*, for example, held an annual sacrifice in the ancestral village of Bethlehem (1 Sam. 20:6, 29), an important piece of information to which we shall return. However, social interaction with other households in immediate proximity could have been even more important than kinship ties, especially at times of crisis or for such large-scale enterprises requiring cooperative effort as deforesting, irrigation, terracing, or defense against marauding neighbors.

In stressing the idea of fictive kinship, contemporary sociologists have helped us see how the primary function of a kinship system such as existed in ancient Israel transcends the obvious biological aspects by providing a network or grid for the social location of the individual and the determination of expectations and roles, with their attendant rights and duties. By the same token, it provided a measure of emotional security and stability for all members of the household, including those not biologically affiliated, the only condition being a willingness to live by the consensual ethic and ethos of the larger kinship group.

The Household
as an Economic Unit

As an economically interdependent unit, the typical household depended for its survival on possession of a plot of land for growing crops and access to grazing land for raising livestock, mostly sheep and goats.

In identifying the typical household as an agrarian unit, we should add that we know practically nothing about the urban family during the Israelite monarchy. The land-redemptive law distinguishes between dwellings in a walled town and those in the open country, namely, in unwalled settlements or villages (ḥǎsērîm, Lev. 25:23–28), and there was a close symbiosis between these settlements and the towns. The relationship may be illustrated by the Samaria ostraca discovered during the Harvard expedition of 1910. These sixty-three potsherds inscribed in black ink, dating from the eighth century B.C.E., record shipments of oil and wine from settlements in a neighboring region to the royal household and its dependents in the city.[10] On town dwellers in general, however, who constituted probably no more than about 5 percent of the population during the early monarchy, we are not at all well informed. In addition to the elite element, including royal dependents, clergy, and well-to-do urban families living off rents and the usufruct of country estates, there were those who supported themselves by engaging in a trade, often as members of a guild. At the bottom of the heap, finally, there would be the landless and dispossessed who had drifted to the towns from the countryside.

But if we are to speak of the *typical* household, another qualification is in order. The biblical narrative and the laws for the most part have in mind fairly prosperous households. The Decalogue, for example, is addressed to landowners and slave owners, and several of its stipulations are aimed directly at the economic well-being of this class and the protection of its property. What percentage of the population belonged at any given time to the landless underclass we do not know, but they are much in evidence at all times. We meet them at a later point in this chapter.

Ownership of a plot of land was, at any rate, essential for the survival of the typical *agrarian* family. In keeping with the common theology of the ancient Near East, the land of Israel belonged to Yahweh, the national deity who, as landlord and head of the household, leased it out in fief to the twelve tribes.[11] It was this theological idea that was used to justify and explain the inalienability of patrimonial domain (Lev. 25:23). Transfer of the family plot of land (naḥǎlāh, 'ǎḥuzzāh) could therefore be effected legally only through inheritance; hence Naboth's perhaps ill advised and, in the event, fatal refusal of Ahab's offer to buy his vineyard—"Lord forbid that I should give you my ancestral naḥǎlāh!" (1 Kings 21:3).[12]

On the death of the head of the household, title to the property would normally but not invariably pass to the eldest son, who became the new paterfamilias. Other male heirs inherited some of the estate, depending on the wealth and prosperity of the family unit (cf. the parable of the prodigal, a younger son who demanded and received his share, Luke 15:11–32). A daughter could inherit if there were no surviving sons, though with the proviso that she marry within the tribe, a practice inscribed in the narrative about the daughters of Zelophehad (Num. 27:1–11; 36:1–12; Josh. 17:3–6).[13] We might note too that Rachel and Leah were disgusted at being deprived of a share of their father's property (Gen. 31:14–16), and that the daughters in Job's second family received an inheritance alongside their brothers (Job 42:15). Widows also occasionally entered into possession of their husbands' estates—for example, the woman from Shunam (2 Kings 8:1–6), Naomi (Ruth 4:3, 9), and Judith (Judith 8:7)—though the law did not apparently guarantee their right to do so.[14]

The account of Esau selling his birthright to Jacob, though fictional, suggests that, at the time of writing and perhaps earlier, immovable property could be transferred by sale within the immediate family (Gen. 25:27–34). If the paterfamilias died childless, the property passed to the nearest of kin within the clan, beginning with a surviving uncle, if there was one (Num. 27:5–11). Other arrangements not mentioned in our sources may also have been in vogue.

It seems, then, that the head of the household held title to the patrimonial plot in the name of the entire kinship group and was responsible for passing it on intact to the next generation. This would not always have been easy. Drought is not uncommon in Palestine, and it might only take back-to-back crop failures to drive a household to mortgage future usufruct of its property against the purchase of seed and other necessities at a confiscatory rate of interest. The economic situation of many households was rendered even more marginal as a result of royal impositions and requisitions of the kind detailed in Samuel's response to the popular demand for a ruler (1 Sam. 8:10–18). Insolvency could very easily lead to indentured service and the resulting breakup of the household unit (Ex. 21:2–11; Lev. 25:39–43; 2 Kings 4:1), a situation that continued essentially unchanged into the second temple period (Neh. 5:1–5).

Only in the most desperate straits would one have to turn over the nahălāh itself in payment of outstanding debt, and even in this extreme case there were safeguards against permanent alienation. The basic purpose of the jubilee law with respect to land tenure was to exclude the sale of agricultural land as freehold and forbid the grant-ing of leasehold in excess of fifty years (Lev. 25:8–55). The idea was to give the individual household a new lease on life at half-century in-tervals by restoring its real estate and the liberty of members who had been forced into indentured service. The law in question is part of the Priestly material in the Pentateuch and therefore could have been promulgated at a rather late date, if indeed it was promulgated at all. And even if it was in force during the time of the monarchy, it must have been as easy to circumvent as it was difficult to enforce.[15] The only instance actually described is the proclamation of manumission (*dĕrôr*) of slaves or those in indentured service issued during the siege of Jerusalem in 586 B.C.E. (Jer. 34:8–17), and that was clearly a desper-ate ad hoc measure, one rescinded as soon as the immediate danger was thought to be over.

We are on somewhat firmer ground with the custom of land re-demption, which carried the legal right to repurchase after a forced sale or expropriation for insolvency when the opportunity presented itself. It also stipulated that the obligation to repurchase the plot fell to the next of kin (the *go'ēl*, redeemer) when the original owner was unable to do so. The legal situation governing land redemption (Lev. 25:23–28) is illustrated by Jeremiah's purchase of a field belonging to his cousin Hanamel (Jeremiah 32) and the refusal of Ruth's next of kin to purchase a parcel of land belonging to Elimelech, deceased husband of Naomi (Ruth 4).[16] Such measures, designed to maintain the eco-nomic independence of the small agrarian household, are reminiscent of the reforms of Solon during his archonship of Athens in the first decade of the sixth century B.C.E. He related that he took the radical step of canceling debts and prohibiting loans *epi tois sōmasin,* that is, with the debtor's own person, or that of one of his kin, as collateral. He also claimed to have freed the land by removing the *horoi,* or boundary stones, which suggests that these may have recorded the in-solvency of the owner and consequent foreclosure under mortgage of the property.[17]

The running of the agrarian household did not call for much in the way of role specialization. As almost everywhere in the Mediterranean rim, the basic activities were encapsulated in the annual round of plow-ing, planting, harvesting, threshing, and winnowing—raising cereal crops (wheat, barley, millet) and legumes, tending and harvesting fruit-bearing trees (especially grapevines and olives), and looking after live-stock, which shared living quarters with the household members in inclement weather, incidentally providing an inexpensive if malodorous central heating system.[18] Where circumstances permitted, diet would have been supplemented by hunting or fishing. In detailing the evils of monarchical rule, Samuel mentions several traditional gender-related roles—military activities, plowing, reaping, and making various implements for the men and baking and making perfume for the women press-ganged into the service of the court (1 Sam. 8:10–18)—that probably reflect the real situation throughout most of the history. Since the household was largely a self-sufficient unit, all members were expected to be productive, and therefore children were socialized into gender-specific roles at the earliest possible opportunity. Once the male child had passed from the care of women and came under the harsher authority of the father, childhood was, in effect, over.

There must have been many settlements capable of producing a surplus, especially in the staples of Mediterranean economies, olive oil and wine, resulting in a higher-than-average standard of living. Archaeological evidence for local industries, in the form of beam olive presses, looms, and storerooms full of pottery, is fairly abundant, but whether it points to an extensive cottage industry is doubtful.[19] The production of a significant marketable surplus would, one imagines, in most cases have called for a cooperative effort involving several households or an entire village.

Little time would have been available for leisure activities for any members of the rural household. It is worth noting that Amos (6:4–7) condemns leisure activities not in themselves reprehensible, such as singing and playing musical instruments, as characteristic of *urban* living. At the end of the six-day week, the Sabbath provided—in principle, at least—respite for all, including male and female slaves. Apart from that, the life of the average member was punctuated by the celebrations connected with the high points of the agricultural calendar—the harvesting of the barley in the spring, the wheat in the early summer, and the grapes and olives in the early autumn. Then there were events involving several households, such as threshing and sheep shearing, which provided occasion for male bonding, feasting, and imbibing (1 Sam. 25:2–38; 2 Sam. 13:23–29). Most important of all was the annual clan sacrifice, to which we shall return. Day-to-day interaction, reinforced by gossip, which has always played an important social role in village life, was focused primarily on the open plaza by the gate complex (where this existed) and the local well, frequented mainly by the women.[20]

Marriage and Divorce

Marriage Then and Now

Historically, economic interests and property rights have always been an important aspect of the institution of marriage. Traditional definitions of marriage presuppose a stable arrangement, legally and often religiously sanctioned, by which two persons of different sex agree to cohabit for the purpose of procreation, sexual communion, mutual support, and economic cooperation. Having said this, however, it is hardly necessary to add that no part of the definition could at the present time hope to pass unchallenged. But it is also worth pointing out that throughout history, marriage has assumed many forms that would not be covered by this definition.

The practice of appealing to the Bible in support of the traditional Jewish or Christian view of marriage is understandable, but it calls for some qualifications. First, theoretical or theological statements about marriage (e.g., Gen. 2:24, about man and woman becoming one flesh) must not be mistaken for or confused with the relevant social realities. Second, the physical, psychological, and emotional environment of the household at that time was quite different from that of the privatized nuclear family of today. Third, more than one form of marriage is attested, and polygamous unions occurred throughout most of the biblical period. And finally, the economic aspects of marriage are always clearly in evidence, for example, in laws concerning rape, adultery, and injury to a woman that leads to a miscarriage.

Legal Theory and Practice

It may come as a surprise to learn that there are no biblical laws dealing directly with marriage and none with marital dissolution—who may initiate it, under what circumstances, for what reasons, and with what consequences. This will remind us that the compilations of biblical laws (Ex. 20:23–23:19; Deuteronomy 12—26; much of Leviticus and Numbers, including the so-called Holiness Code in Leviticus 17—26) are not really law codes, since they made no pretense at comprehensiveness. Moreover, those formulations generally classified as apodictic law—especially the prohibitives of the "you shall not" kind, as in the Decalogue—are *moral* norms rather than laws in the usual meaning of the term, while the case laws define the *legal* consequences of specific actions or behaviors without defining their moral status. There has been much discussion as to the origin of the biblical case laws based on precedent—whether they are in continuity with the cuneiform legal tradition or represent an abstract of actual trial records, collections of special cases for the guidance of magistrates, or paradigmatic school exercises used in training law scribes. For our purpose, it is not necessary to decide this question.[21] The standard form states the circumstances of the case in the protasis ("if a man does X") and the legal consequences in the apodosis ("then Y follows"). The casuistic formulation, the Israelite equivalent of the common law, is therefore quite distinct from the explicitly moral apodictic statements, though such legal definitions could and generally would have moral implications.

We are also poorly informed on ancient Israelite legal praxis in general; for example, as to which of these laws were actually promulgated and which enforced, or which of them may have been redacted as part of an ideal order or polity as envisaged by the authors—Priestly, Levitical, scribal, or whatever. Scholars have, for example, argued that the family laws in Deuteronomy constitute a form of moral instruction rather than legislation in the strict sense.[22]

We can say at once that marriage in Israel of the biblical period was not, for the vast majority, a matter of individual decision and choice, least of all for the woman. The choice of a partner for an unmarried woman was a matter of concern for the entire household to which she belonged, and for the one to which she was destined to be transferred. The exchange of women was the most important of the transactions between households, too important to be left to the vagaries of individual choice. Marriage practices in specific societies are generally characterized as either *exogamous* or *endogamous,* but these terms take on definite meaning only in relation to specific social groups between which marriage alliances may be transacted. Since the woman introduced into her husband's household always remained, in a certain sense, an outsider, there was some pressure to seek an alliance with a household as close in terms of consanguinity as possible. This would also be conducive to retaining control of economic assets, especially patrimonial domain. But there was also pressure in the opposite direction, driven by the need to make alliances, renew the household's labor pool, and in general promote its economic interests. The laws governing forbidden degrees of consanguinity in Leviticus 18:1–18 are motivated by these concerns and by the need to preserve order within the household, not by eugenics.

To what extent the economic interests of the household are involved in the marriage of its women can be gauged in the laws concerning seduction and rape, the earliest of which is the following from the so-called Covenant Code:

> If a man seduces a young woman who is not engaged to be married and sleeps with her, he must hand over the marriage fee in order to make her his wife. But if the father refuses absolutely to give her to him, he must pay an amount equal to the marriage fee for young women. (Ex. 22:15–16 [ET 22:16–17; author's translation])

In this instance, the final decision is made by the paterfamilias as the proprietor, and it is to him that the marriage fee (*mohar*), perhaps fifty shekels (Deut. 22:29), is payable. The final clause suggests that this was the set price, but there was probably room for negotiation. Shechem, for example, offered to pay any amount to marry Dinah—a rare case of sexual violence followed by genuine affection, but one that ended badly nevertheless (Gen. 34:12). The fee could also be paid in kind; witness the grotesque story of the Philistine foreskins paid by David to Saul for his daughter (1 Sam. 18:25) and the marriage price of fifteen shekels of silver, together with barley and wine, paid by Hosea for Gomer (Hos. 3:2). The young woman's status is carefully specified (engagement was legally the equivalent of marriage), since an unmarried daughter was a valuable part of the household's economic assets. She herself receives no compensation for the violence visited on her and has no voice in the arrangements for her future.

We may note in passing that our sources have curiously little to say about the bridal dowry. The Hebrew terms *zebed* (Gen. 30:20) and *šillûḥîm* (1 Kings 9:16; Micah 1:14) refer to property ceded to the woman at marriage and therefore to the household of destination (Gen. 30:20; 31:14–16). The bridal gift could include land (Josh. 15:18–19; 1 Kings 9:6), and the value of the dowry was an index of the wealth, status, and honor of the bride's household. This feature is, however, much better attested elsewhere in the ancient Near East than in Israel.[23]

The law in Deuteronomy 22:28–29, corresponding to and presumably updating the one in the Covenant Code (Ex. 22:15–16 [ET 22:16–17]), envisages the same situation but no longer gives the woman's father the option of rejecting the seducer or rapist as a future son-in-law—one of several examples of the encroachment of state law and curtailment of the discretionary power of the paterfamilias (cf. also the treatment of the ungovernable son, Deut. 21:18–21). The sexual aggressor must now pay a fee of fifty shekels and may never divorce his victim. The intent of the law was the laudable one of guaranteeing the woman's economic security, but the modern reader would tend to think of it as resulting in a thoroughly bad situation for everyone involved except the father, and especially bad for the victim of sexual aggression—one of many examples of the social and psychological gap between text and reader.

This revised and updated version of the law in the Covenant Code is one in a series dealing with sexual relations, in or out of marriage (Deut. 22:13–23:1 [ET 22:13–30]). In contrast to the earlier collection in Exodus, the urban character of these laws is much in evidence. The first (22:13–21) envisages a consummated marriage in which a husband, looking for a pretext to divorce his spouse and recover the marriage fee, brings an accusation of premarital sexual irregularity against a newly married wife, an accusation that also indirectly accuses the woman's parents of giving their daughter in marriage while knowing she was not a virgin.[24] The parents, and presumably the woman herself, could refute the charge by producing evidence that she entered into marriage a virgin. The evidence is generally taken to have been a garment or cloth with stains from either the last premarital menstruation or the first marital cohabitation. Once the case was settled in her favor, the slanderer was subjected to corporal punishment and considerable damages, again payable to the father, and the couple had to stay together without the option of divorce. If the evidence was not forthcoming, the woman was stoned to death in front of the paternal domicile to make amends for the damaged reputation of the household of origin (Deut. 22:20–21). It is obvious, however, that there are so many loopholes in this law and so many ways of faking the evidence as to leave us wondering whether it was ever, or could ever have been, implemented.[25]

In view of the utopian and programmatic character of the Deuteronomic law in general, it would make sense to ask, again, whether such laws were ever actually promulgated and enforced. Similar questions have been raised about the ritual prescribed in the case of suspicion of the wife's infidelity, vaguely described as "the spirit of jealousy" on the part of the husband, involving ordeal by the woman drinking holy water mixed with dust from the sanctuary floor and the pronouncing of a self-imposed curse (Num. 5:11–31).[26] The least we can say is that allusions to marital infidelity in prophetic and narrative contexts (e.g., David and Bathsheba) confirm the general impression that adultery was considered an act striking at the roots of the established social order and therefore meriting death.[27]

Stringent protection of the marital bond is, in fact, what we find as we continue our survey of the relevant laws in Deuteronomy. The next formulation in this short series (Deut. 22:22) imposes the death penalty on both parties for adultery—perhaps by stoning, as in the well-known Gospel account of the woman taken in adultery (John 8:5), but the manner of execution is not specified. The basic intent of the prohibition is apparent in that it is addressed to the man having relations with the wife of another man, rather than the reverse. The wife is *bĕ'ulat ba'al,* literally "owned by a master," and the act therefore violates the proprietary rights of the husband in the woman. Adultery is also proscribed in the Decalogue (Ex. 20:14; Deut. 5:18). The prohibition of coveting—that is, having designs on—the neighbor's wife provides another indication that the Decalogue is addressed to the property-owning head of household. In one version (Ex. 20:17) the wife is, in effect, listed with the itemized assets of the household that are not to be coveted; that she is taken out of the itemization in the other version (Deut. 5:21) may therefore indicate a slight raising of consciousness. Something similar with respect to the legal status of women may be identified in the Deuteronomic version of the law on slavery (Deut. 15:12–17; cf. Ex. 21:2–11), though we should be wary of claims on behalf of the alleged humanitarianism of Deuteronomy. Adultery is also listed as a capital offense in another decalogue, in the so-called Holiness Code (Lev. 20:10).

The economic and proprietary aspects of adultery are nowhere more clearly stated than in Proverbs 6:29–35, in which adultery is compared to theft:

> So it is with the one who sleeps with his neighbor's wife,
>   Whoever touches her will not go unpunished;
> People don't despise a thief if he steals
>   To satisfy his appetite when hungry,
> But if he is caught he must pay sevenfold,
>   He must deliver up all the wealth of his household.
> So the one who commits adultery is senseless,
>   He who does it destroys himself. . . .
> For jealousy makes the husband furious,
>   He will have no pity when he takes revenge;
> No amount of compensation will appease him,
>   And no bribe however great will he accept.
>   (author's translation)

The approach here is somewhat prudential, not to say cynical: If you must gratify your sexual urges, do so with a prostitute (v. 26) but not with another man's wife. You might get caught, in which case the outcome could be economic destitution and even loss of life—almost as if the young man is being advised that it just isn't worth the risk.

The last section of the Deuteronomic series (Deut. 22:23–29) provides a detailed treatment of the sexual offense of seduction and rape, dealt with more summarily in Exodus 22:15–16 (ET 22:16–17). A distinction is made with respect to location in the case of a woman engaged to be married. If the seduction happened in an urban location, the legal presumption is that she consented since she could have called for help, and both are subject to the death penalty; if in the country, only the man is executed.[28] The distinction is inapplicable if the young woman is not engaged, in which case the offender pays fifty shekels of silver to the woman's father, the equivalent of the marriage fee of which the father is deprived now that his daughter has been seduced. The sexual aggressor must also marry the young woman without the option of divorce. While this last stipulation was intended to provide security for the wronged woman—a point made earlier—the law's indifference to her interests in general is too clearly in evidence to require comment.

Looking back over these legal provisions governing adultery and other sexual irregularities in and outside of marriage, what is most striking is the extent to which they were designed to protect the economic interests of either the woman's father or her husband, depending on whether she was single or married. But there was more to it than that. What was fundamentally important was paternity and inheritance, the extension of the man's "house" into the future, the preservation of his name and that of his ancestral house, and perhaps also an atavistic need for permanent, postmortem security within the same kinship network.[29] Into all of this the premarital and marital infidelity of the woman was seen to introduce an element of confusion and disorder of a more direct and threatening kind than that of the male.

Levirate Marriage
and Other Variations

A particularly striking example of this cultural view of the family is the custom of levirate marriage, the subject of a legal enactment in Deuteronomy 25:5–10. According to this custom, by no means confined to ancient Israel,[30] the widow of a husband who died childless would cohabit with the brother of the deceased with a view to raising up an heir who would carry on the name of the deceased. In other words, the first son born of this proxy marriage would be the legal heir and legatee of the deceased. The intent of this (to our modern view) extremely odd arrangement was to prevent the widow's marrying outside the household or clan ("to a stranger," Deut. 25:5); to ensure legal descendants of the deceased, as well as his decent burial and peaceful postmortem existence; and, of course, to provide premortem security for his widow. Since Israelite law did not provide for the widow to inherit the property of her husband, the danger of alienating the ancestral holding, the *naḥālāh*, does not seem to have been an issue as far as this stipulation was concerned, quite apart from the fact that the brothers are residing together, in the same household. It is obvious that this procedure would work only if certain conditions were fulfilled, namely, that a brother or next of kin (*go'ēl*, "redeemer" in Hebrew) was available, and that this person had no (understandable) economic or psychological objections to performing this "redemptive" task. To encourage him to do so, the widow enlisted the local elders, and if they failed to talk him into it, he was subjected to a ritual of public humiliation.[31] The stories of Tamar, Judah's daughter-in-law (Genesis 38), and Ruth (chap. 4) show to what lengths a young widow might be driven to secure compliance with the levirate custom, thus preserving her husband's line and securing her own future at the same time.

Little need be added about other variations in the practice of marriage during the heyday of the monarchy in Israel. The story of Sarah and Hagar (Genesis 16 and 21) exemplifies the practice of designating a surrogate childbearer in the event of infertility, a practice also attested in Mesopotamia. Polygamy was countenanced, authorized as it was by such unimpeachable examples as Abraham, Isaac, Jacob, and Moses. It continued to be countenanced down to the time of the Mishnah, which allowed those who could afford it to have as many as five wives (*m. Ketub.* 10:5; *m. Ker.* 3:7), and eighteen for kings (*m. Sanh.* 2:4). The essential requirement was wealth; the husband had to be able to pay the marriage fees of two or more wives and support them. The enactment in Deuteronomy 21:15–17 stipulates that the husband may not set aside the rights of primogeniture in favor of a younger son born of the preferred spouse. The problems endemic to polygamous or, more commonly, bigamous unions can easily be imagined and in fact are amply illustrated in narratives of interspousal rivalry—Rachel and Leah, Hannah and Peninnah, for example. Understandably, therefore, the practice fell into desuetude outside of the royal circle.[32]

Divorce

When we speak of divorce, it is particularly important to appreciate the limitations of our sources. There is no legislation bearing directly on marital dissolution. Deuteronomy 24:1–4 used to be interpreted in some quarters as a divorce law, on account of Jerome's misunderstanding of the syntax of this long sentence in his Vulgate translation,[33] and the text provided an important biblical source of rabbinical law on divorce.[34] But the law simply states that a man who has divorced his wife may not take her back after she has survived a second husband or been divorced by him. The occurrence of what appears to be standard terminology suggests, notwithstanding, that a firm legal tradition did exist: The divorced woman receives a severance document (sēper kĕrîtût), perhaps accompanied by the simple statement "You are not my wife" (Hos. 2:4 [ET 2:2]); she then becomes the gĕrûšâ, "the dismissed one," and is sent away (verbal stem šlḥ).[35]

While it no doubt happened occasionally that a woman who could afford to do so simply left her husband (e.g., Judg. 19:1–2; Jer. 3:6–7), it seems that only the husband could initiate divorce proceedings. The custom that obtained in the Jewish settlement on the island of Elephantine in Upper Egypt during the Persian period, according to which either partner could divorce, may therefore derive from local Egyptian custom rather than from Palestinian-Israelite practice.[36] Our sources have little to say on possible restrictions on the husband's right to divorce or on legal entitlements of the divorced woman. The law in Deuteronomy 24:1–4 referred to a moment ago speaks of the husband divorcing his wife after finding something improper, indecent, or at least objectionable in her. The Hebrew term used at this point, 'erwat dābār, has given rise to a great deal of discussion to which I do not propose to add.[37] It was probably chosen precisely because it was vague, ill-defined, and nonrestrictive. The Deuteronomic law concerning an accusation of premarital unchastity brought by a husband against his wife (22:13–21) might suggest that some such reason was required for divorce, that the male partner could not divorce "for any reason whatsoever," as argued by the Hillelites (cf. Matt. 19:3). But the intent behind the accusation seems rather to have been financial gain, or at least avoidance of financial loss, by securing the return of the mohar from the woman's father, or at least avoiding having to return the dowry and having to make a substantial severance settlement. Financial arrangements attending divorce are specified in other ancient Near Eastern laws (e.g., the Code of Hammurabi 137–40); they may have been specified in the *sēper kĕrîtût* handed to the divorced wife (Deut. 24:1, 3; Isa. 50:1; Jer. 3:8), but if so, we are not told what they were.[38]

It needs to be said, once again, that the legal material dealing with marriage and divorce gives us a very partial and to that extent misleading picture of the relevant social realities. It highlights the economic aspects of familial relations. It also serves to remind us that there was much less emphasis on sexual mores in *themselves* than there is in our contemporary western culture. Unfortunately, however, the context for an adequate understanding of these laws and norms is for the most part missing. Unlike the scholars who have given us a history of private life in ancient Rome and Byzantium,[39] we have absolutely no inscriptions and no iconographic material bearing on married life in Israel of the biblical period. To make matters worse, there is very little narrative confirmation of or overlap with the situations assumed to exist in the laws. Much, too much, therefore, is left to our imagination, but we must make the most of what we have.

Family Roles, Relations, and Conflicts

Children

Since the raison d'être of the family in Israel, as elsewhere, was the procreation and nurture of children, we begin our survey of this microcosm of roles, expectations, and relations with the child. Philippe Ariès proposed that the discovery of childhood as a distinct phase of life is a relatively recent event. He argued that for most of recorded history, in most cultures, small children—minors—were practically invisible; where they appear in literature and image, they are represented as scaled-down adults; and in our western culture, we have to wait for the late sixteenth or early seventeenth century for boys to emerge as the first "specialized children."[40] After viewing representations of children in ancient Egyptian and Greek funerary art, we may have some reservations about this conclusion. With respect to children in Israel during the time of the kingdoms, however, Ariès's thesis is at least consistent with the custom of identifying the child with reference to the father— for example, Saul son of Kish, Micaiah son of Imlah—and it may serve to remind us that practically no provision was made for the legal protection of minors. Moreover, the laws and norms that speak of children generally refer to young adults, and the same is true of most of the admonitions regarding intergenerational, familial relations in the proverbial literature.

We can get some idea of the rather vague and ill-focused conception of childhood from the relevant vocabulary. The most common Hebrew terms, which appear in English as "child" or "youth," are *yeled* and *na'ar*. The former can refer to the fetus (Ex. 21:22), a newborn baby (the Hebrew children, including Moses, saved from death in Egypt), a young child who can still be carried in the arms (Ishmael, the widow's son resuscitated by Elijah), a page at court (Daniel's companions), or a young man in general (Rehoboam's companions, 1 Kings 12:8–14). Some special and somber occurrences may be noted: an apparent case of sexual abuse (Gen. 21:9), child prostitution (Joel 3:3 [4:3]), infanticide, and cannibalism (Lam. 4:10). The term *na'ar* also can refer to infants (Moses again, Ichabod grandson of the priest Eli) and to the young in general (Ishmael, Isaac, etc.), including those still very immature (e.g., the son of Gideon who was afraid to kill), as well as *nĕ'ārîm* such as Shechem, who was capable of rape (Gen. 34:19). Joseph, a seventeen-year-old *na'ar*, is the only young person whose actual age is given (Gen. 37:2). Absalom, presumably some years older, is always referred to by David as a *na'ar*. The term also serves to designate military personnel (Gen. 14:24; Judg. 8:20; 1 Sam. 21:5–6), civil servants (e.g., 1 Kings, 20:14–15; Esth. 2:2; 6:3, 5; Isa. 37:6), and servants in general (as the French *garçon* does for "waiter"); perhaps also cultic officials (Ex. 24:5; 33:11; 1 Sam. 1:24, 27). It therefore functions more as a designation of status and office than simply of age.[41]

Most of the other terms occurring here and there in the narrative and prophetic literature are equally unspecific. The young person who collected Jonathan's arrows at target practice (cf. our term *ball boy*) is described as a *na'ar*, a *na'ar qāṭān* (little boy), and an *'elem* (boy, youth). This last term (fem. *'almāh*) occurs only in 1 Samuel 20—22 and where Saul asks about David the young giant-killer in 1 Samuel 17. We must also note *baḥûr*, "adolescent," often occurring in tandem with *bĕtûlâ*, "a young woman of marriageable age" (Deut. 32:25; Isa. 62:5; Amos 8:13), but also, like *na'ar*, in military contexts (Jer. 11:22; Ezek. 23:6, 12; Amos 2:11). The terminology for periods of the life cycle is therefore very fluid.

It is also consistent with Ariès's thesis that we do not find a clear consciousness of childhood as a distinct life phase; and in fact, no biblical source alludes to childhood or youth in the abstract before Koheleth, who speaks of the days of youth (*yaldût*, Eccl. 11:9–10). The kind of cataloging we find in Jeremiah 6:11 is quite accidental: in a typical Jeremiad, he foresees divine vengeance visited on infants (*'ôlāl*), youths (*baḥûr*), husbands and wives, old folk (*zāqēn*), and the really old (literally, "full of days"). But we do find the very early years of life well covered. For the period from birth to weaning, generally about three years,[42] there are three terms (*'ôlēl, 'ôlāl, yônēq*), all derived from two verbal stems with the meaning "suck" or "suckle." Once past this stage (a passage that many, perhaps most, would not have survived), the child is a *gamûl* (fem. *gĕmûlâ*), "a weaned child" (Isa. 11:8) or simply a *yeled* or *na'ar*. The savage side of Near Eastern society in antiquity may be gauged from the statistic that twenty-two of the thirty occurrences of these three terms for infants refer to their being violently destroyed.

On the birth and nurture of children, our information is not abundant. We do not know, for example, whether it was a regular practice for the father to acknowledge paternity by taking the child on his knees, as is perhaps hinted at in Job 3:12 ("Why did the knees receive me?" [author's translation]). More likely, something of the kind occurred only where there were grounds for doubt, as with the practice attested in the Hammurabi Code of simply pronouncing the phrase "my children."[43] Women probably gave birth in a sitting position, as was common everywhere, with or without the help of a midwife (*mĕyalledet*, Gen. 35:16–17; Ex. 1:15). The charming narrative of the Hebrew midwives outwitting an irascible but befuddled Pharaoh (Ex. 1:15–22) may indicate a connection between midwifery and practical wisdom (cf. the French *sage-femme*) of the kind exemplified by the wise women of Tekoa and Abel of Bethmaacah (2 Samuel 14 and 20).[44] It also seems to have been the mother's prerogative to name the child (e.g., Gen. 29:32–35;30: 6–13; 1 Sam. 1:20; 4:21). Newborn children would either be breast-fed by the mother or handed over to a wet nurse (*'iššâ mĕneqet, 'omēn*, Ex. 2:7; Num. 11:12) for a period of three years or more. Isaiah 28:9–10 may imply that the process of learning the letters of the alphabet by rote (*ṣav lāṣāv, ṣav lāṣāv, qav lāqāv, qav lāqāv*), and therefore the child's education, began immediately after weaning.

Priestly law called for circumcision on the eighth day after birth (Lev. 12:3), but the timing was probably an innovation introduced in the Babylonian diaspora as a distinctive mark of ethnic identity. In its original form, circumcision was essentially an apotropaic and initiatory prenuptial ritual, as is also apparent in some early narratives: for example, the proposed matrimonial alliance with the Schechemites (Genesis 34) and the strange incident involving Moses, Zipporah, and their son at the caravanasary in the wilderness (Ex. 4:24–26). During the period with which we are concerned, it does not seem to have been very significant.

Near Eastern legislation gives little attention to protecting the interests of small children. There are laws governing the payment of nurses and the legal consequences of an accident to the child while under a nurse's care and also providing for the care of small children in extraordinary circumstances, for example, while the father is a prisoner of war and therefore absent indefinitely. The Code of Hammurabi sets restrictions on the father's freedom to disinherit children, requires explicit acknowledgment of paternity in certain cases, and has a series of laws on adoption, including penalties for the rejection of adoptive parents, presumably by a somewhat older child.[45] Practically none of this is replicated in Israelite legislation.

The Law about Miscarriage

The fact that children were a valuable resource, together with the high incidence of child mortality, explains why the laws have nothing to say about abortion and infanticide. All the more surprising, therefore, that most of the legal collections from the ancient Near East, including those of the Sumerian cities, Babylon, the Hittites, the Assyrians, and the Israelites, contain a law regulating injury to a pregnant woman that leads to a miscarriage. The Covenant Code version (Ex. 21:22–23) may be translated literally as follows:

> When men fight and injure a pregnant woman so that her children come out but there is no serious harm, he [the one responsible] shall be fined according as the woman's husband imposes on him, and he shall pay as the assessors determine. But if serious harm follows, you shall give a life for a life. (author's translation)

The assumption is that the injury was not premeditated and is therefore a civil tort rather than a criminal case. The parallel Near Eastern laws deal not with injury sustained during a brawl but with a blow inflicted by one person, one would suppose deliberately, though only the Sumerian laws distinguish between accidental and deliberate action. The offending party, significantly, is never the woman's husband. In each case, the one responsible must compensate for loss of the fetus, not because the latter was thought to enjoy legal rights but because children were a valuable economic resource. Only the Hittite laws fix the penalty according to the stage reached in the pregnancy—ten shekels for the tenth month, five for the fifth. The "serious harm" ('asôn) referred to in the Israelite law presumably means the death of the woman; in this case the penalty, in all the relevant laws, is much more severe, involving application of the *lex talionis*. It is interesting to note that the Old Greek version (LXX) translates the obscure *'asôn* with *exeikonismenon [paidion]*, meaning "fully formed [child]," representing a certain shift of focus from the mother to the fetus.[46]

Young Adults

Most of the legal stipulations, norms, and admonitions dealing with children in the Hebrew scriptures are concerned with young adults who are still members of the paternal household and therefore under the jurisdiction of the paterfamilias. The latter's authority was extensive but not absolute. The law contemplates the case of a father selling a daughter into slavery (Ex. 21:7), but the situation was clearly one of extreme crisis, in which a parent's only recourse was to amortize unpaid debts by means of the indentured service of members of his household. This was a not uncommon occurrence and remained so for centuries, as we may see from the complaint about social abuses addressed to Nehemiah (Neh. 5:1–5). Genesis 38:24 might also suggest that Judah is condemning his daughter to death for getting pregnant out of wedlock. But we have no assurance that the narrator is interested in legal verisimilitude, and we know of no penalty of death by burning for sexual misconduct. With the imposition of the state apparatus and the establishment of a central and local judicial system, the discretionary power of the paterfamilias was, in any case, considerably reduced.

One example of this curtailment is the Deuteronomic law concerning an ungovernable son (Deut. 21:18–21). It stipulates that the young adult who is unresponsive to parental discipline and seriously disrupts the order of the household is to be brought before the town elders. To satisfy the requirement of at least two witnesses (Deut. 17:6; 19:15), both parents must be present. Their testimony leads, presumably after some form of investigative process, to the public execution of the delinquent by stoning. The extremely casual formulation of this "law," which fails to require any proof from the plaintiffs or provide any recourse or appeal for the defendant, makes it extremely improbable that it was ever implemented, at least not in this form; and our suspicions are further aroused by some striking parallels with the didactic literature on child-parent relations in the formulation of the law (e.g., the accusation of gluttony and drunkenness added for good measure; cf. Prov. 23:21).[47]

The Decalogic command to honor father and mother (Ex. 20:12; Deut. 5:16) should be taken with its negative counterpart that condemns the cursing—that is, repudiating—of parents (Ex. 21:17; Lev. 20:9; Deut. 27:16). What was at stake here was the fundamental order, well-being, and even survival of the household. The law about the ungovernable son, discussed above, may be taken—and was probably offered—as one illustration of the breakdown of that order. Another would consist in striking a parent, an act that carried the death penalty in Israel (Ex. 21:15) and the amputation of a hand in the Hammurabi Code (195). Frequent appeals to the Old Testament in support of "family values," which have led in the past to the execution of minors for striking or cursing parents,[48] make it advisable to repeat that these norms have in mind young or middle-aged adults still resident within the paternal household.

Not very different in form are the exhortations and denunciations addressed to the same category and age group in the didactic literature. Among the worst offenses are violent abuse of aged parents, robbing them or, worse, putting them out in the cold (Prov. 19:26; 20:20; 28:24). But the honoring of parents involves the good estate of the household and clan at a deeper and more explicitly religious level. The literature of the ancient Near East testifies to the importance of proper burial on one's own land. In the Aqhat text from the Late Bronze Age, Ugarit king Daniel laments the lack of a son who will perform filial duties for him. He lists such things as patching his roof, washing his clothes, cleaning him up and taking care of him when he is drunk, and so on, but the most important is to set up the stelae of his ancestral spirits and free his spirit from the underworld (cf. 2 Sam. 18:18).[49] The postmortem honoring of parents is therefore essential for the survival of the kinship group on its own land in its totality. Failure to perform this duty will result, by virtue of the lex talionis, in being subject to the same fate, namely, to be without rest among one's own or, worse, to lie unburied. This is what I take to be the meaning of the threat addressed to the abusive son that "your lamp will go out in utter darkness" (Prov. 20:20). In another collection it is stated more clearly still:

> The eye that mocks a father
> and scorns to obey a mother
> will be pecked out by the ravens of the valley
> and eaten by the vultures.
>
> (Prov. 30:17)[50]

Strategies of Marriage
and Inheritance

The severity of these norms and of the threats that reinforce them testifies to the crucial importance of perpetuating the household, which,
as a total unit including persons, livestock, and land, is encapsulated in
the *name* of the paterfamilias. In normal situations, continuity was assured through primogeniture. The firstborn son would generally inherit
the bulk of the estate, including title to the patrimonial plot of land
(*naḥălāh*), with the remainder distributed among younger siblings
(Deut. 21:17; cf. 2 Kings 2:9).[51] The wording of the stipulation in
Deuteronomy 21:15–17, according to which this custom could not be
waived in favor of a younger son born of a preferred wife, suggests that
the father made the appropriate dispositions, where possible in writing,
on a specific and solemn occasion. Other children, male and female, inherited a share of the estate. Contrary to the common practice in the ancient Near East, there seems to have been no legal provision for a widow
to succeed to her husband's estate other than recourse to levirate marriage (Deut. 25:5–10), discussed earlier, though we have noted that
some nevertheless did so. It is therefore hardly surprising that widows
and their children are mentioned so often as in need of protection and
charity.

Since patrimonial domain had to be passed on intact to the next generation, a patrilineal system such as that of ancient Israel required alternative arrangements if the head of a household had no son. In this
situation, as noted earlier, a daughter could inherit subject to the
proviso that she married within the paternal clan (Num. 27:1–11;
36:1–12). If the paterfamilias had neither son nor daughter, his brother
would be first in line; then a paternal uncle; and in the last resort, the
nearest of kin in the clan (Num. 27:7–11).

That the options did not end there can be deduced from the stories
about Israel's ancestors in Genesis 12—50. There is, of course, the
problem of the date of composition, more in question today than ever,
and the connected question of the social realities that the stories reflect.
Since the narrative chain deals with the fortunes of a family (in the
broad sense) through four generations, the issue of inheritance can be
expected to loom large; and since all the ancestresses are initially infertile, a certain amount of ingenuity on the part of the lead players can be
anticipated. At the very beginning of the story, the close association of
Lot with Abraham (Gen. 11:27, 31; 12:4–5; 13:1), together with the

failure of Sarai to give birth to a child (11:30), may imply that Abraham already thought of his nephew as his heir by adoption, in keeping with well-attested practice in the Near East. If so, it didn't work out, and uncle and nephew went their separate ways (13:2–13). It seems that Abraham then planned to make one of his household slaves his heir by adoption (Gen. 15:1–3), an option also attested as an acceptable alternative elsewhere in the culture area (e.g., Nuzi on the Upper Euphrates) and perhaps not unknown in Israel (1 Chron. 2:34–35; Prov. 17:2). After this, too, was ruled out, Sarai, still infertile, offered Abraham her slave-woman Hagar, with the idea that a son born of this union would be Abraham's legal heir and legatee (Gen. 16:1–4). This practice of obtaining an heir through a proxy wife appears in numerous contracts from Mesopotamia throughout its history.[52] Eventually, of course, Abraham and Sarah beat the odds and produced a son, thus enabling the direct line to continue.

It is rather surprising that adoption, attested in numerous contracts from the Old Babylonian to the Achaemenid period and in Sumerian, Babylonian, and Assyrian law codes,[53] does not seem to have been much in vogue in Israel and is not the object of legislation, either biblical or postbiblical. Alleged adoptive acts in the narrative lack the kind of formulaic terminology that would clearly identify them as such. Moses the foundling becomes the "son" of Pharaoh's daughter (Ex. 2:10), but this may be the author's way of representing what he took to be an Egyptian practice. Jacob may have adopted his grandsons Ephraim and Manasseh (Gen. 48:5–6, 15–16), as may Joseph his grandchildren (Gen. 50:23). Perhaps the clearest instance is Mordecai taking the orphaned Esther, his cousin, as his daughter (Esth. 2:7), though this too may reflect a local custom, in this case from the Iranian diaspora.

We should note in passing the type of marriage by means of which the ancestors perpetuated their line. According to one tradition (Gen. 20:12), Abraham married his sister, daughter of his father but not his mother, a relationship dangerously close to incest and of a kind forbidden in the ritual law (Lev. 18:9; 20:17; Deut. 27:22). Isaac married his cousin's daughter Rebekah (Gen. 24:15, 24, 47), which was somewhat more in keeping with convention. Jacob married his maternal uncle's daughter Rachel, the closest relationship outside of ego's lineage and the proper balance between endogamy and exogamy (Gen. 28:2, 5; 29:9–10). Cross-cousin marriage of this kind, the preferred type in many societies though forbidden in several states in the United States, seems to mark the optimum, the stage of social maturity at which the ancestral lineage could segment, and consequently, Israel as an ethnos came into existence.[54]

Let us add that a reading of these beguiling stories in Genesis with an eye to the interconnected relations of filiation, siblingship, and affinity may lead us to reflect that the privatized, nuclear family of our contemporary urban culture has flourished at the expense of a richly textured, multigenerational, and multirelational milieu for the nurture of children and social life in general. If we find in much of the family history in the Hebrew Bible relatively little emphasis on displays of emotion, the impression should be balanced by an awareness of supportive societal structures no longer available to most of us, the absence of which may have something to do with our well-advertised social ills. The society reflected in these stories took its toll on the individual and especially on certain groups—not least women—but it had something to offer in compensation.

Gender Distinction

Throughout our sources, we detect an anxiety to preserve clear distinctions in gender roles and between the respective spheres in which male and female operate. This hardly requires detailed proof-texting, but we may recall Samuel's response to the popular request for a king, in which the tasks assigned to those conscripted into the royal service are very clearly gender-related (1 Sam. 8:10–18). The insistence on distinctiveness, which is ubiquitous in ritual legislation (e.g., the prohibition against sowing a vineyard with two kinds of seed, plowing with two different species of animal, or wearing clothes made of wool and linen, Deut. 22:9–11), can no doubt be construed as part of an overall taxonomic system, a kind of cosmology reflecting a cosmic order in which everything is created "according to its kind" (Gen. 1:1–2:4). But it is also, I suspect, an aspect of societal attitudes generally characteristic of the culture area to which Israel belonged. It comes to particularly clear expression in gender roles within and beyond the family and in the emphasis on gender distinction.

We may assume, to begin with, that most forms of sexual behavior familiar to us today were also familiar, or at least not unknown, in Iron Age Israel. The prohibition of cross-dressing (Deut. 22:5), the kind we presume took place in saturnalian rites as a deliberate reversal of gender roles, is diagnostic of the anxiety to preserve distinctions and contrasts with the widespread tolerance of such practices in other societies. Homosexual relations between males (lesbians are not mentioned) are defined as abominable and subject to the death penalty (Lev. 18:22; 20:13). This is even more severe than the Assyrian law according to which the offending party is sodomized and castrated but not put to death;[55] and it is a chastening thought that in the United Kingdom, the death penalty for homosexual acts, derived ultimately from Old Testament law, was repealed only a little over a century ago. The prohibition notwithstanding, male prostitutes functioned in the Jerusalem temple precincts throughout the entire history of Judah, resisting successive efforts to dislodge them.[56] Bestiality, familiar throughout history in most rural communities, is also condemned as a particularly gross form of mixing and confusing categories (Ex. 22:18 [22:19]; Lev. 18:23; 20:15–16; Deut. 27:21).

Priestly definitions of the degrees of consanguinity and affinity within which marriage was prohibited (Lev. 18:6–18; 20:11–21) were also dictated by anxiety to make a clean distinction between Israel and its more permissive neighbors; this is apparent from the context in which the exclusions are presented (Lev. 18:1–5, 24–30; 20:22–24). While these regulations are not particularly severe—they permit marriage with niece or cousin, for example—had they been in effect, they would have ruled out the marriages of many of the great figures from the past, including Abraham, Moses' parents, Jacob, and Judah. Abraham's marriage with the daughter of his father but not his mother (Gen. 20:12) would be excluded (Lev. 18:9; Deut. 27:22); Amram, father of Moses, married his maternal aunt (Ex. 6:20), also forbidden (Lev. 18:14); Jacob's marriage with his wife's sister would have been illicit (Gen. 29:30; Lev. 18:18), as would Judah's marriage with his daughter-in-law (Genesis 38; cf. Lev. 18:15).[57] It is also of interest to note that the menstrual taboo is attached to these restrictions on sexual relations (Lev. 18:19). Whatever its original rationale, the sequestration of the woman during her menses and after childbearing (forty days for a male child and eighty for a female child, Lev. 12:1–8) served to perpetuate her essentially private status and justify her exclusion from public office, including the cult.[58]

Gender Roles within Marriage

When we come to talk about gender roles within marriage, and specifically the roles of women, we have to bear in mind that, contrary to what a spate of recent publications may have led us to believe, there is no "Old Testament view of women" but rather a plurality of views determined by variables such as epoch, literary genre, and social class.

Quite simply, the Old Testament is not an entity capable of generating any *one* view of women. In what might be called Israel's "heroic age," for example, a wife could be won by deeds of valor, as Othniel won Achsah (Josh. 15:15–19; Judg. 1:11–15), or a woman might, exceptionally, play a prominent role in the public arena—generally that of conflict—as did Deborah and Jael, the latter declared "most blessed of women" after immobilizing the Canaanite leader with a tent peg through his head (Judges 4–5). We would expect the *Weltanschauung* of the royal court and of the peasantry to reflect back to us significantly different understandings of gender roles.

At the same time, Israel shared certain suppositions about gender relations with all Near Eastern and Levantine societies in antiquity, suppositions that have come to be encapsulated in the vague and unsatisfactory term *patriarchy*. Many of these will be apparent from what has been said so far on the hierarchical household and its ethos. A social unit organized according to patrilineal descent has to import women, since it needs their reproductive capacities for its own self-perpetuation. In a certain real sense, therefore, women remain outsiders to the group. We should add that gender disparity was powerfully reinforced by the belief that the man contributed, by insemination, all that was necessary for the generation of children. At that time and long after—in fact, until the discovery of the female ovum in 1827—the woman was regarded as a purely passive receptacle for the production of a child.[59]

Women as Daughters,
Sisters, Wives, Mothers

We come now to the place of the woman within the household. A daughter was under the authority of her father or ward until she married, at which time she passed under the authority of another male, her husband. If the father died before she married, she would be under the protection of a brother or other close male relative, as the case might be. The woman's sexuality was therefore always in function of the dominant patrilineal system. We have already seen some examples of how clearly these jurisdictions were defined and with what severity and jealousy the rights inherent in them were protected as an important point of male honor. The daughter as prospective bride was a valuable commodity, but only as long as she remained *virgo intacta* (Deut. 22:13–21, 28–29). This was a matter not so much of sexual ethics as of economics and of honor, her own and that of the household of origin. The man who raped a young unmarried woman would therefore have had reason to fear being hunted down and killed by one of her male relatives, even if he agreed to marry her (e.g., Dinah and her brothers, Genesis 34; Tamar, Absalom, and Amnon, 2 Samuel 13). In spite of some "texts of terror"—the gang rape of the young woman in Judges 19:24 being a particularly gruesome example—daughters were therefore not expendable, and we hear of no exposure of newborn females, a custom prevalent in ancient Greece and Rome. In fact, the only case of exposure in the Hebrew Bible is that of the male Hebrew infants in Egypt (Exodus 1).

At that time, and for long afterward, a girl was considered marriageable in her early teens. We could apply to ancient Israel the old Arab proverb that the only things a man should do quickly are bury the dead, serve a guest, and marry off a daughter. During those few years of childhood and early adulthood, the daughter's education consisted in acquiring the skills that would fit her for her role in a new household, which would be a replica of the household of origin. The women on whom our sources report exhibit an invincible desire for marriage and children, not because they were ideologically naive and unenlightened but because they had few, if any, other options. The examples of Lot's daughters, Judah's daughter-in-law, and Ruth illustrate how far some young women were prepared to go to achieve their goal, which was, basically, to survive.

It is difficult to gauge the emotional quality of wife-husband relations from our sources. This is, of course, in good part a function of the sources themselves, but there are also important social coordinates and determinants. Both spouses would have been much closer to their respective families of origin than is generally the case today. So, for example, when Samson's wife was trying to worm the answer to his riddle out of him, he asked her why he should tell her when he had not even told his parents (Judg. 14:16). We note, too, Laban's concern for his daughters even after they had been married off (Gen. 31:50), which is also a feature of Bedouin family life. The fact that the young woman generally had no say in the choice of a partner, the constant proximity of members of the husband's household of origin, and, not least important, the lack of private space must have discouraged emotional warmth and intimacy.

The husband's discretionary power over the wife was considerable but not absolute. If things went badly wrong she could return to her household of origin, if they could afford to support her. The Levite's girlfriend from Bethlehem did that, and exceptionally, the Levite tried to coax her back with tender words (Judg. 19:1–3). By custom, and perhaps by law, wives were entitled to food, clothing, and the exercise of marital rights (Ex. 21:10). Like Sarah preparing food for guests in her tent (Gen. 18:6, 9), married women occupied the private domain and involved themselves with the well-known, traditional roles, including such things as processing flax to make linen clothes and preparing food. (With respect to cooking, the only recorded exception to this female monopoly was Gideon, who was something of a fast-food specialist; see Judg. 6:19.) Women would also have worked periodically in the fields, orchards, and vineyards, as Mediterranean women still do. In managing the household, they would have had to deploy considerable managerial skills, though perhaps not quite up to the standards of the 'ēšet ḥayil ("capable wife"? "woman of substance"?) of Proverbs 31:10–31. In addition, there were certainly others who, like Rebekah or Bathsheba, played a dominant role in the public arena. We shall see more of these later.

In the inevitable round of tensions, power plays, and trade-offs within the small world of the household, the woman had leverage primarily as mother of her children, especially her male children. Her role in childrearing meant that she was the one most responsible for the internalization of the group ethos and for what passed for education in general; hence the frequent allusions in the aphoristic and didactic literature to the mother's instruction (e.g., Prov. 1:8; 6:20; 23:22–25; 31:1–9). In our sources, the topos of the mother-son bond occurs with some frequency and lets us see how this special relationship could be exploited to counter, in some measure, the authority of the paterfamilias; one thinks of Rebekah teaming up with Jacob (Genesis 27) and Bathsheba tirelessly promoting Solomon's (very shaky) claim to the throne (2 Samuel 11; 1 Kings 1—2). The subversive potential of the woman as mother, actual or prospective, is particularly apparent in the matter of cult practice. A female outsider to the kinship group would very likely introduce the children to an alien cult; hence the resistance to marriage with women outside the kinship group that keeps cropping up throughout the history (e.g., Ex. 34:16; Deut. 7:3–4; Proverbs 1—9).

Family Religion

Religion in Ordinary Time

The specifically religious aspect of the social life of the household in Iron Age Israel—domestic religion, in other words—appears at first sight to be impenetrable to the contemporary historian. Much of the information provided in the narrative and legal material presupposes the religious orthodoxy and orthopraxy either of the literati who drafted the Deuteronomic program or of the official state priesthood. Both constructed the past in their own image, implying either that people thought and behaved in the religious sphere as the authors believed they should or that they were condemned for engaging in religious practices that were a normal and accepted part of social life at the time. The Deuteronomists, for example, condemn the cult of the Canaanite mother goddess (e.g., Deut. 16:21) and denounce its practitioners (e.g., 1 Kings 15:3; 18:19; 2 Kings 21:7; 23:4–7), yet it is tolerably clear that it survived as an important feature of popular religion down into the second temple period. Relevant archaeological data (buildings, artifacts, inscriptions, etc.) are also hard to come by, in part because much has not survived but also because archaeologists have paid scant attention to the private life of small groups.[60]

The festivals marking the high points of the agrarian year, as set out in the Gezer almanac,[61] would presumably have been celebrated at one of the regional sanctuaries or "high places" (bāmôt) before these were abolished or eclipsed by the state cult. These festivals (principally Pesaḥ-Maṣṣot, Shavuot, Sukkot) have been thoroughly studied and need occupy us no further. The celebration of Sabbath and new moon festivals would also have helped break up the monotony of the daily round (e.g., Isa. 1:13; Amos 8:5).

More important, since more intimately associated with the kinship structure, was the annual clan sacrifice and meal. As an important affirmation of solidarity among living and dead members of the clan (mišpāḥāh), presence at this event was mandatory, at least for adult males. The importance of sacrificial ritual as emblematic of kinship unity and a means of verifying and controlling membership in the clan or phratry is well attested. In ancient Rome, for example, membership in a particular gens was established not so much by birth as by aptitude for participation in the annual sacra gentilicia. Annual sacrifices of this kind served to legitimate and sustain a social order based on patrilineal descent; to provide a public, observable verification of clan membership; and to confirm hierarchical status within the group by a graded distribution of portions or "cuts" of the sacrificial animal. It was also taken for granted that forebears or ancestors, those already "gathered to their people," participated.[62]

In his magisterial work The Religion of the Semites, William Robertson Smith affirmed the existence of the annual clan sacrifice in Israel while admitting it was more a matter of inference than of evidence.[63] The clearest example is the *zebaḥ hayyāmîm* (annual sacrifice) at which David's presence was required by his kinsfolk, the fellow members of his *mišpāḥāh*. It coincided with the new moon, lasted at least two days, and involved a meal shared in common (1 Sam. 20:5–6, 28–29). Saul's anger on hearing that David had skipped attendance at court to participate in this event was no doubt fueled by awareness that such "gatherings of the clans" could also serve as occasions for plotting revolt. We do not hear of ancestors as participants or of a cult being offered to them, but given the historian's rejection of the cult of the dead in any shape or form, we would not expect to.

We noted earlier an important and somewhat neglected reason for the inalienability of ancestral land, namely, that it had also to serve as burial site. The social life of the patrilineal descent group and its persistence through time were for this reason inextricably bound up with ownership of real estate. Naboth's refusal to give up his ancestral heritage has already been mentioned. The wise woman of Tekoa feared that both she and her surviving son would be cut off from "the heritage of God" (*naḥălat 'ĕlohîm*), which perhaps has the same meaning (2 Sam. 14:16).[64] The old prophet of Bethel predicts that his prophetic visitor from Judah will not be buried in the ancestral grave (*qeber 'ăboteykā*, 1 Kings 13:22), a sad fate indeed for a man of God. As death approached, it was important for Abraham to own, rather than hold in fief, a parcel of land in which he and other family members would be buried (Gen. 23:1–20; 25:8–10; 35:29; 49:33; 50:7–14). Customary law governing inheritance was also dictated by the need to perpetuate the name of the deceased paterfamilias, which in effect meant the continuation and extension through time of the kinship group. The command to honor father and mother therefore extended beyond the moment of the parent's death. It included, in the first place, the obligation of burying the parent in the ancestral plot and seeing to the accompanying rituals of mourning. These rituals included laments, self-lacerations, and shaving part of the hair, the last two proscribed by Deuteronomic and Priestly orthodoxy (Deut. 14:1–2; Lev. 19:27–28; 21:5), which of course did not mean that they did not happen.[65] In burying Jacob, Joseph provided a perfect model of filial *pietas* in this respect (Gen. 50:1–14). It was also necessary to set up a marker or monument, the quality and size of which were obviously dictated by what the survivors could afford. (To this day, funerary monuments serve as indicators of socioeconomic status.) The death of the paterfamilias and the accompanying ritual must therefore have been one of the most profound *religious* experiences in the life of the individual household.

Ancestor Cult

Dead kinsmen, especially those long dead, joined the ranks of the shades (*rĕpā'îm*)[66] and in some obscure sense entered into the sphere of divinity, reflected in occasional references to dead ancestors as *'ĕlohîm*, "divinities."[67] In this respect Israelite beliefs differed little, if at all, from those of the entire culture area.[68] We recall how, on seeing the ghost of Samuel, the witch of Endor explained, "I see divine beings [*'ĕlohîm*] coming up from the underworld" (1 Sam. 28:13; author's translation). What kind of cult was offered to or on behalf of forebears is difficult to determine, since state orthodoxy proscribed rituals of this kind in the belief that they subtracted from the official Yahweh cult; which perhaps helps to explain the emphasis in temple hymnography on postmortem oblivion (e.g., Ps. 6:5; 88:4–6). We may find a clue in Absalom's setting up his own monument since he had no son to invoke or keep in remembrance his name (*hazkîr šĕmî*, 2 Sam. 18:18). In Mesopotamia the invoking of the name (*šuma zakāru*) was an essential part of the funerary ritual (*kispu*), which included the offering of food and pouring of a water libation for the dead; and similar ceremonies are attested elsewhere in the Near East and Levant. With what frequency and on which occasions these rites were observed during the time of the kingdoms we do not know. Reference in Jeremiah 16:5–9 to the "house of mourning" and the "house of feasting" (*bêt marzēaḥ, bêt mišteh*) in connection with funerary rites suggests a parallel with the *marzēaḥ* funerary meal attested at Ugarit and in many other centers down into the Greco-Roman period. This appears to have been initially a kind of wake at which the living celebrated the departed members of the clan while assuaging their sorrow, relieving the tensions of everyday life, and reinforcing the kinship bond with the help of strong drink. They no doubt thought of it as a religious experience, and perhaps that is all that matters.[69]

The *tĕrāpîm* stolen by Rachel as she prepared to leave her father's house (Gen. 31:19, 34–35) have been widely understood to be household gods, similar to the *lares* and *penates* of the Romans. Elsewhere they are represented as idolatrous objects, which could be used for purposes of divination. The *tĕrāpîm* that Michal put in David's bed to cover his escape was apparently a life-sized and anthropomorphic object

(1 Sam. 19:11–17), probably larger, therefore, than the one on which Rachel sat while Laban searched her tent. There may have been some association with the veneration of ancestors, but this is by no means certain.[70] Cult objects found in domestic contexts—for example, incense stands, small altars, model sanctuaries—suggest that the more substantial households, at least, had their own domestic shrines at which familial rituals were carried out under the direction of the paterfamilias. The most numerous class of finds is, however, the small clay figurine of a nude female representing one of the native goddesses, most likely Asherah, wife of El and patroness of fertility (*dea nutrix*). Hundreds of these cult objects have been found in numerous locations, including more than three hundred in one site alone in the proximity of the Jerusalem temple.[71] Here, at any rate, is one instance where archaeological data can be aligned with evidence in biblical texts. Sporadic attempts to impose Yahwism as the official and exclusive national cult routinely failed to dislodge the worship of the goddess, principally Asherah, from the prominent place in the life of the people that it had occupied from earliest times. From this point of view, the restoration of the goddess cult by Manasseh (ca. 687–642 B.C.E.) looks like a conservative reaction to the "Yahweh alone" ideology, and one that survived both the Josian reform and the fall of Jerusalem, which happened shortly thereafter. The goddess cult was, understandably, especially popular with women and is defended by them in one of the very few places where a biblical author allows the voices of women to be heard on the subject of religion (Jer. 44:15–19).[72]

We may conclude by saying that popular and domestic religion in Israel during the time of the kingdoms was more a natural function of the social life of the household unit than a matter of personal choice or conviction, as we generally imagine it to be with us. It was a world in close communion with the dead, whose ghosts had to be laid to rest and who could intercede on behalf of the living—an anticipation, therefore, of the Roman Catholic veneration of saints. Cults were also offered to the local manifestation of Yahweh, El, or Baal,[73] and no doubt also to "the queen of heaven" (Jer. 7:18; 44:17–19, 25), especially at critical moments of the individual's life cycle and of the group's generally precarious existence. While much of this activity took place within the household, the more important occasions would have required attendance at one of the local sanctuaries or "high places" (*bāmôt*), which the representatives of the state cult attempted repeatedly, and with limited success, to abolish.

Family Values and Deviance

We can get some sense of the prevalent ethos of Israelite and Judean society under the monarchy from laws and narratives datable to that time. We note, for example, how a strong sense of corporate liability persisted and was applied in cases in which the perpetrator of a criminal act escaped detection (Deut. 21:1–9), even after the principle of personal responsibility had won general acceptance. We hear of things that are "not done in Israel," for which the term *nĕbālâ* ("outrage," rather than "folly") is used. With one exception (Josh. 7:15), all recorded instances have to do with serious sexual offenses.[74] Many other actions—a proportionately higher number, in fact, than in other Near Eastern law codes—were subject to the death penalty, though we have practically no way of knowing to what extent these death penalty laws were implemented.

These are the extreme cases; on the regulation of conduct within the parameters of legal sanctions and the blood feud, our best source of information is the corpus of didactic material contained in the book of Proverbs. The collection as a whole reached its final form only at a considerably later time, but it would be generally agreed that at least the two longest compilations of aphorisms (Prov. 10:1–22:16; 25:1–29:27) reflect views current in a particular segment of society under the monarchy. The heading to the second of these (25:1) informs us that they were copied by Hezekiah's men, one of several indications of literary activity in Judah at that time, namely, the early seventh century B.C.E.[75] We must add, however, that the two compilations prescribe ethics and etiquette for young males from well-to-do families and destined for public service, and therefore they cannot be taken to reflect ethical consensus in the society as a whole. They may nevertheless give us an idea of what, in these socially elite circles, was considered the appropriate manner of running a household, irrespective of whether families succeeded or even aspired to live up to the proposed ideal.

Great emphasis is placed on control, hierarchy, subordination to authority. On familial roles and the conduct appropriate to each of them there are no surprises. Children of all ages are to be docile to parents. In training children to take their place in society, parents must use strict discipline. "If I strike you, my son, you will not die," the father reassures his offspring as he thrashes him, echoing a common topos in this kind of literature (cf. Prov. 23:13).[76] Slaves, too, must be dealt with firmly, on the same principle (Prov. 29:19). Hard work and good husbandry are the keys to success (Prov. 12:10–11; 13:23; 27:23–27; 28:19). In both Judean and Egyptian aphoristic writings, the sluggard is the butt of satire. "There is a lion outside!" he cries, and so he stays in bed (Prov. 22:13; 26:13). If you wish to be wealthy—a thoroughly commendable goal—you need to be a shrewd businessman, avoiding borrowing and never standing surety for someone else's debts (Prov. 13:11; 17:18; 22:7; etc.). And for the son who chooses to disregard all of this sage advice, there is always the ultimate threat of being disinherited (Prov. 11:29; 17:2).

For most modern readers, one of the most depressing features of this aphoristic instruction is its consistently negative attitude toward women, an attitude that reaches the nadir of irrationality in the writing of Jesus ben Sira in the early second century B.C.E. ("Better is the wickedness of a man than a woman who does good," Sir. 42:14.) Leaving aside the usual admonitions to avoid the company of women outside one's own circle (e.g., Prov. 22:14), we note the frequent recurrence of the motif of the quarrelsome and contentious wife (Prov. 19:13; 21:9, 19; 25:24; 27:15). That this reflects a level of exasperation on the part of the head of the household whose efforts at control are less than completely successful is confirmed by the author's positive portrayal of good wives as obedient, submissive, and frugal (Prov. 12:4; 19:14; etc.). While serving as an allegorical counterpart to the woman called Wisdom (ḥokmâ) in the first nine chapters, the petit bourgeois portrait of the ideal wife at the end of the book (Prov. 31:10–31) displays an ideal, or perhaps (as the initial rhetorical question suggests) an unattainable, male fantasy of the perfect spouse, who does her husband proud and brings up a clutch of perfectly adorable children while engaged in a daunting range of managerial tasks.

This sententious and heavy-handed kind of teaching was, needless to say, the product of a particular social class with a very limited and sclerotic view of human relations. It moved mechanically and unreflectively on the teacher-disciple, father-son axis. Even when viewed benevolently, women were outsiders, part of the environment that had to be controlled. And indeed, in a certain sense the married woman always remained an outsider vis-à-vis the household into which she had been imported. Teaching of this kind, which placed so much weight on self-control, social maintenance, and property rights, reflected—in a form distorted by its class ethos—some of the basic structures of the household but filtered out the emotional quality of the relationships that sustained it, and much else besides.

The Family and the State

The Emergence and
Consolidation of the State

Our present purpose fortunately does not require us to survey the extensive literature of the last several years on the process by which a state system emerged in Iron Age Israel. We saw at the beginning of the study that archaeological data indicating state organization, in the form of such giveaway clues as settlement patterns, public works, and luxury items, are sparse indeed before the eighth century B.C.E. The biblical record, in contrast, describes in considerable detail administrative measures taken two centuries earlier, under Solomon, to set up a state system (1 Kings 3—11), and experience teaches that this information should not be dismissed out of hand simply because archaeological support is currently lacking.

The first stage was the construction, with the help of forced labor, of a palace and temple. Both were relatively complex institutions, requiring a corps of bureaucrats, lay and clerical, to staff them. At this point the historian appends a list of these bureaucrats (śārîm), including priests, scribes, the majordomo of the palace, military personnel, and supervisors of the corvée (1 Kings 4:1–6); the list can be filled out with other biblical references and titles appearing on seals and bullae from a somewhat later time.[77] Solomon also is credited with an impressive military buildup (1 Kings 4:26; 10:26–29), the fortification of the major cities in the kingdom (9:15–19), and trade ventures as far away as the Arabian Peninsula and the East African coast (9:26–10:25; the visit of the queen of Sheba, a favorite theme of the Midrash, is probably based on a trade mission of relatively modest proportions). These projects placed a heavy burden of taxation and services on the population as a whole, leading to the secession of the central and northern regions after Solomon's death (1 Kings 12:1–15).

The most far-reaching of Solomon's administrative measures was the division of the kingdom into twelve districts, primarily for fiscal purposes, and these naturally would also have had their administrative staffs supported at the public expense (1 Kings 4:7–19). It is of possible significance for our theme that these divisions do not correspond to tribal territories, since, on the assumption that a twelve-tribal system was in place at that time, the intent would have been to redirect allegiance from the kinship and tribal structure to the state. About half a century after Solomon's death, Jehoshaphat, the first Judean king to accept the division of the kingdom as a fait accompli, replicated Solomon's measure in the much smaller territory of Judah.[78]

Assuming this situation, we go on to ask, first, what effect the centralization of political and economic power and religious authority had on the kinship structure in general and the household unit in particular, and second, whether the state officialdom pursued a deliberate policy toward the family.

The Impact of the
State System on the Family

The process of political, economic, and military centralization, even though never fully carried through, had a direct and negative impact on the typical rural household. The upkeep of court and temple and the personnel who served them and the maintenance of any army, often including mercenaries, meant a heavy burden of taxation. It is explicitly stated that the division of the kingdom into twelve administrative districts was aimed at facilitating tax collection (1 Kings 4:7–19), and the same purpose was served by David's census (2 Sam. 24:1–9). We are unfortunately not well informed on the taxation system in force under the monarchy. Tax liability was paid in bullion (coinage came into use only in the Persian period), produce, and labor. Amos refers to exactions of wheat (Amos 5:11) and the king's mowings (7:1), and Samuel's warning about the implications of choosing a king, referred to earlier, mentions a levy of 10 percent of the yield of wheat and grapes (1 Sam. 8:15). The Samaria ostraca and the *lmlk* (*lammelek,* "for the king") seal impressions on jar handles provide further illustration of the flow of goods from the countryside to the court in both kingdoms.[79]

The landowning peasant was also at the mercy of military adventurism, originating either in his own land or elsewhere. Beginning with the Assyrian campaigns to the west in the mid-eighth century B.C.E., rulers in both kingdoms were obliged to buy off foreign aggressors with huge indemnities, which, of course, had to be squeezed out of the property-owning population (2 Kings 15:19–20; 18:14–15; 23:33–35). This was in addition to the burden of military service and forced labor. The establishment of a national cult center also represented a significant drain on resources, including livestock. The standard form of support was tithing, a theme in which the authors of the Deuteronomic law had a practically compulsive interest,[80] but other contributions, not all voluntary, were expected (see Kings 12:5 [12:4]; 22:4). We must also assume that clergy were tax-exempt, as they were in other Near Eastern countries. The well-known prophetic outbursts against the contemporary cults (e.g., Isa. 1:10–17; Amos 5:21–24) had therefore little to do with predilection for a spiritual as opposed to a materialistic religion, the standard view until recently, and a great deal to do with an institution that legitimated and was itself an integral part of an oppressive economic system.

Households and their families were already in a precarious situation, due to the vagaries of climate—frost in winter, to which olives are particularly susceptible; irregular rainfall or a sequence of two or three dry years, not uncommon in Palestine in either ancient or modern times. State impositions would have driven those unable to produce a substantial surplus—certainly the majority—to take out loans in order to get by. We have no information on rates of interest in Iron Age Israel, but in Babylon the minimum interest for produce was 33.3 percent per annum, while in the Jewish settlement at Elephantine on the Upper Nile, it was as high as 60 percent, and double for late payment.[81] The laws forbade interest on loans made to fellow Israelites (Ex. 22:25–27; Lev. 25:35–38; Deut. 23:19–20), but the person of the debtor and his family members could be seized to amortize the debt by indentured service (1 Sam. 22:2; 2 Kings 4:1–7). In addition, pledges could be taken even from the poorest (Ex. 22:26–27; Deut. 24:6, 10–13; Amos 2:8). An inscription found at Meṣad Hashavyahu near Yavneh-Yam in Israel, from the seventh century B.C.E., records the petition of a farm laborer addressed to the local military governor, complaining that a certain Hoshaiah had confiscated his cloak, very likely for nonpayment of a debt.[82] By that time, there must have been many in the same situation as this anonymous plaintiff.

For the rural household, the worst aspect of state encroachment was the threat it posed to possession of their inherited plot of land. Patrimonial domain was theoretically inalienable, but the ruler needed land both as a source of revenue and to reward or placate retainers by making land grants. Land not covered by customary Israelite law could be purchased, as David obtained freehold for the site of a sanctuary in Jerusalem from a Jebusite (2 Sam. 24:18–25) and Omri purchased the hill of Samaria, presumably from a Canaanite, for the site of his new capital (1 Kings 16:24). Wars and rebellions also provided occasions for confiscating land, as occurred when David took over Saul's estates, disposing of them as he saw fit (2 Sam. 9:7; 12:8; 16:4; 19:30). If the

Naboth incident (1 Kings 21:1–16), discussed earlier, is any guide, the
ruler also exercised the right to acquire land by vacant possession,
though Ahab initially, if grudgingly, respected Naboth's refusal to sell
based on customary law.

Increasing control of the judicial process by the state made it easier
to circumvent legal custom or even to change the law regarding land
tenure. Isaiah's complaint about iniquitous decrees that rob the poor of
their right (Isa. 10:1–4) indicates that something of the sort did happen, especially when it is taken in tandem with the same prophet's de-
nunciation of those who "join house to house" and "add field to field"
(Isa. 5:8; cf. Micah 2:2). In the case of insolvency, one could also take
over the usufruct of a plot of peasant land as a pledge, leaving the owner
with nominal title to the property, or ownership could be transferred
by adoption, a fiction attested in the Nuzi tablets from northern Mesopotamia in the mid-second millennium B.C.E. The net result was the
erosion, by enclosure and foreclosure, of peasant freehold—and therefore of the kinship and family structure dependent on it—and the corresponding development of royal and aristocratic estates (latifundia) attested in later sources, biblical and nonbiblical.[83]

Raison d'État and the Family

A degree of political and economic centralization is an inevitable
concomitant of statehood and can be expected to generate resentment
at the local level, quite apart from the kind of abuses we have been describing. In the kingdoms of Israel and Judah, however, state centralization implied a deliberate policy of redirecting allegiance from the lineage to the state and to that extent undermining the kinship structure,
especially at the level of the clan. A selective survey of the legal and
quasi-legal material in Deuteronomy 12—26 will enable us to explore
the implications of this policy for the Israelite family.

The Deuteronomic law begins, in chapter 12, by insisting frequently,
even redundantly, on the centralization of worship, especially sacrifice,
and the prohibition of local cults—high places (bāmôt), monuments to
male and female deities (maṣṣēbôt, 'ăšērîm), and even local manifesta-
tions of the national deity, Yahweh.[84] These measures were part of a
comprehensive centralization of political and economic power, including the necessary support for the temple clergy, who were essentially
state officials. The insistence on coming to the state sanctuary (for obvious reasons, Jerusalem is not named) to eat the family sacrificial meal

takes aim at the annual clan sacrificial meal discussed earlier, one of the most powerful means of sustaining the cohesion of the lineage group. The Deuteronomic requirement that adult males are to present them-selves three times a year at the national shrine (Deut. 16:16–17) is dic-tated by the same strategy of directing allegiance away from the large kinship units, and the same can be said for the "nationalization" of the three agrarian festivals (Deut. 16:1–15).

We should also consider the implications of the prohibition of the cult of the dead, especially dead ancestors. The prohibition extended to necromancy, meaning commerce with the dead by conscripting the services of a specialist (usually female) who commands the ghosts (ba'ălôt 'ôb) Deut 14:1; 18:11;26:14).[85] The intent was to loosen the spiritual bonds of kinship in general, and especially the link between kinship and land tenure, by removing one of the principal reasons for inalienability, namely, the ancestral plot (naḥălāh), as locus of ancestral burial and attendant rites. I suggested earlier that the insistence in sev-eral psalms on postmortem oblivion may be viewed as indirectly op-posing the older, more traditional, and more popular view according to which relations with the world of the dead were of central importance.

Leaving aside the specifically religious aspects, the intent of much of the Deuteronomic legislation to undermine the traditional lineage sys-tem is so apparent that it is surprising how few have commented on it.[86] The setting up of a local and central judiciary (16:18–20; 17:8–13) and the reservation of some cases to the latter (e.g., false witnessing, 19:16–21) inevitably restricted the judicial competence of the head of the household. Several laws also limited his discretion in dealings with members of the household, for example, in matters concerning inheri-tance and the disciplining of children (21:15–17, 18–21). Moreover, he no longer had the option of blocking the marriage of a daughter to the man who had raped her (22:28–29; cf. Ex. 22:16–17). We note at several points in the Deuteronomic laws how the role of the elders (zĕqēnîm) has been taken over by the state-appointed judges or magis-trates (šopĕṭîm).[87] There were also laws limiting in equal measure the role of the go'ēl, the avenger of a kinsman's blood. These include the es-tablishment of sanctuary for manslaughter (19:1–13) and procedures involving elders, together with state-appointed lay and clerical magis-trates, in the event of a homicide the perpetrator of which remained un-detected (21:1–9).

At different periods of history, ancient and modern, political and ec-clesiastical authorities have had a stake in controlling the exercise of the sexual function because of its obviously crucial role in matters of inheritance and title to property. It seems to be particularly important for states in the process of formation or consolidation to subvert the solidarity of local kinship and residential nexuses; and since the strength of the bond between individual spouses is in inverse proportion to the strength of bonds in the wider kinship group, one way of undermining group connections is for the state to use its legislative power to strengthen the nuclear family unit.[88] A noticeable feature of the familial law of Deuteronomy is the severity with which it protects the exclusive union of wife and husband, including the death penalty for adultery (22:22). The law governing palingamy (second marriage) is also relevant, whether its primary purpose was to discourage divorce in the first place or, more probably in my opinion, to protect the second marriage of the woman by ruling out the possibility of her return to the original husband (24:1–4). Even the granting of a year's exemption from military service for the newly wedded husband (24:5; cf. 20:7) is significant in this respect, namely, in pointing to a strategy of strengthening the nuclear family unit while undermining the larger lineage network of which it was a part.

The Effect of State
Centralization on the Family

To judge by the protest directed against it, the process we have been describing was getting underway by the eighth century B.C.E. and continued to the end of Judean independence. Because of the well-known uncertainty about the date, function, and composition of the Deuteronomic program, the social impact of state encroachment is more difficult to assess. The breakup of households as a result of insolvency would have swelled the ranks of the mobile underclass of day laborers living a hand-to-mouth existence. Many of these would have drifted to the cities, while others would have taken the more profitable but riskier option of brigandage. We recall that David recruited a following from assorted fugitives, including those on the run from creditors (1 Sam. 22:2), and Nabal, the loutish husband of Abigail, complained about slaves breaking away from their masters (1 Sam. 25:10). In some respects the slave ('ebed) would have been better off than the day laborer (śākîr), since he or she was a valuable economic asset that could be traded off. In any case, the chronically marginal classes of people, including slaves and resident aliens (gērîm), would have been among the first to lose the protection of an economically endangered household, but younger sons would also have been especially vulnerable.

The Deuteronomic covenant features a curse on those who deprive widows and their children of their rights (Deut. 27:19), but it is not clear what these rights were. It seems, in fact, that widows were commended to public charity and the "social security system" of the triennial tithe (Deut. 14:29; 26:12–13) precisely because no legal provision was made for them to inherit their husbands' property. In general, there were few economic niches for women who had been deprived of the protection afforded by the household of either orientation or procreation. For obvious social reasons, these women did not have the advantage of mobility enjoyed by their male counterparts; hence we hear of itinerant "men of God" but not of "women of God." Since women were not employed in the national cult,[89] the only options we know of were prostitution and witchcraft,[90] though one might discover or activate the talent necessary to be recognized and consulted as a "wise woman" (2 Sam. 14:1–20; 20:14–22).

It would be simplistic to conclude that the disintegration of the household when faced with the invasive power of state institutions was entirely a bad thing. Especially in its judicial capacity, the state provided a balance and corrective to the potentially arbitrary exercise of patriarchal domination within the extended and multiple family unit. The experiences of child abuse and spouse abuse in our contemporary societies should suffice to justify the monopoly or at least control of physical coercion by the state. In any event, as sociologist Max Weber argued,[91] the process was irreversible. Large landholdings were more stable and efficient and could be taxed more easily than small holdings, and the household was not in other respects the ideal productive unit. A natural desire on the part of household members for mobility and for a career in one of the developing urban centers may also have been a factor in the unit's disintegration, after education became available outside of the household.

Before leaving our topic, we observe how the *bêt 'āb* served as a model for different kinds of voluntarist associations that exhibited the same combination of authoritarian structure and emotional bonding. We might think of religious communities today (e.g., Franciscans, Dominicans) in some respects as fictive extended kinship groups, under a paterfamilias (father abbot or prior) and behaviorally and economically self-regulating. In the early history of Israel, we hear of prophetic-ecstatic conventicles (*bĕnê hannĕbi'îm*, literally "sons of the prophets") that exhibited some of these characteristics. Since the members were not celibate, we find them living in clusters or compounds of individual families (2 Kings 4:1–7), as economically interdependent units (e.g., 2 Kings 4:38–41; 6:1–7) under the direction of a "father" (2 Kings 2:12; 13:14; cf. 1 Sam. 10:12). If our sources were more forthcoming, we should probably find that groups such as the Nazirites and Rechabites, the latter under the authority of their "father" Jehonadab/Jonadab (2 Kings 10:15–16; Jer. 35:6), were similarly organized. An example of a different kind would be the craft guild for which the term *family* (*mišpāḥāh*) was used (1 Chron. 2:55; 4:21), which also may have referred to its president as "father" (*'āb,* 1 Chron. 4:14). In Mesopotamia the member of the guild was a "son" (*māru, aplu*), one member referred to another as "brother" (*aḫu*), and the president was the "chief" (*aklu, rabu*) and in some cases the "father" (*abu*).[92]

How far the erosion of the household unit would have gone, and what would have emerged from this process of state encroachment if it had been allowed to continue uninterrupted, we do not know. We do know that the social organization of the commonwealth established in postdisaster Judah during the Persian period was of a quite different kind: the twelve-tribal idea persisted as an ideal down into the Roman period, but the basic unit (the *bēt 'ābôt*), the divisions, and the unit names were completely different.[93] At this point, however, the Israelite family enters a new chapter of its history.

NOTES

I wish to thank Andrew McGowan, Jerome Neyrey, and Jean Porter for reading earlier drafts of this chapter and making valuable suggestions.

1. For archaeological data pointing in this direction, see David W. Jamieson-Drake, *Scribes and Schools in Monarchic Judah: A Socio-Archeological Approach* (Sheffield: Almond Press, 1991). The conclusions reached call for caution, since the archaeological record is patchy and incomplete. William V. Harris, *Ancient Literacy* (Cambridge, Mass.: Harvard University Press, 1989), 45–64, provides a useful analogy in dealing with archaic Greece.
2. *ANET,* 284–85.
3. Lawrence E. Stager, "The Archaeology of the Family in Ancient Israel," *BASOR* 260 (1985): 1–35; John S. Holladay, Jr., "Religion in Israel and Judah under the Monarchy: An Explicitly Archaeological Approach," in *Ancient Israelite Religion,* ed. Patrick D. Miller, Jr., Paul D. Hanson, and S. Dean McBride (Philadelphia: Fortress Press, 1987), 249–99.
4. On the eighth- to seventh-century B.C.E. papyrus discovered in a cave at

Muraba'at, see John C. L. Gibson, *Textbook of Syrian Semitic Inscriptions,* vol. 1: *Hebrew and Moabite Inscriptions* (Oxford: Clarendon Press, 1971), 31–32.

5. On these Hebrew kinship terms, see Francis I. Andersen, "Israelite Kinship Terminology and Social Structure," *BT* 20 (1969): 29–39; C. H. J. de Geus, *The Tribes of Israel* (Assen and Amsterdam: Van Gorcum, 1976), 133–64; Niels Peter Lenche, *Early Israel: Anthropological and Historical Studies on the Israelite Society before the Monarchy* (Leiden: E. J. Brill, 1985), 245–85; J. D. Martin, "Israel as a Tribal Society," in *The World of Ancient Israel,* ed. R. E. Clements (Cambridge: Cambridge University Press, 1989), 95–118. On the tribal structure in general, see J. Helm, ed., *Essays on the Problem of Tribe* (Seattle: University of Washington Press, 1967); and R. M. Keesing, *Kinship Groups and Social Structure* (New York: Holt, Rinehart & Winston, 1975). The triadic kinship division is also that of Émile Durkheim, *De la division du travail social,* 6th ed. (Paris: Libraire Félix Alcan, 1932), 149–57. Geoffrey Cowling, "The Biblical Household," in *Wünschet Jerusalem Frieden. Beiträge zur Erforschung des Alten Testaments und der antiken Judentums,* ed. M. Augustin and K. D. Schunck (Frankfurt: Peter Lang, 1988), 179–92, takes issue with practically all the assumptions about kinship with which biblical scholars, including those cited in this note, work. Specifically, he does not accept that *bayit* is identical with *bêt 'āb* or that the latter refers to a household. Some of his observations are well taken (e.g., that membership of the *bayit* is not exclusively a matter of kinship), but his objections do not seem particularly persuasive.

6. On these expressions, see A. Alfrink, "L'Expression *šākab 'im 'ăbôtāyw,*" *OTS* 2 (1943): 106–18; idem, "L'Expression *ne'ĕsap 'el 'ammāyw,*" *OTS* 5 (1948): 118–31; G. R. Driver, "Plurima Mortis Imago," in *Studies and Essays in Honor of Abraham A. Newman,* ed. Meir Ben-Horin, (Leiden: E. J. Brill, 1962), 128–43.

7. Stager, "Archaeology of the Family," 15, 18; and, rather differently, Y. Shiloh, "The Population of Iron Age Palestine in the Light of a Sample Analysis of Urban Plans, Areas, and Population Density," *BASOR* 239 (1980):25–35.

8. A not unrepresentative view on life expectancy in antiquity would be that of Thomas Carney, *The Shape of the Past* (Lawrence, Kans.: Coronado Press, 1975), 88: "In preindustrial society, however, probably a third of the live births were dead before they reached the age of six. By sixteen something like 60% of these live births would have died, 75% by twenty-six, and 90% by forty-six. Very few—3% maybe—reached their sixties. . . . A man who reached forty could well be in atrocious physical shape. . . . Even the elite, whose health and medical welfare were well looked after, suffered grievously from disabilities and infirmities from their forties on." Carney's rather somber view of life in antiquity as nasty, brutish, and especially short is somewhat exaggerated, and his statistics call for caution; there are just too many variables and imponderables. Suffice it to note that in Athens, for

example, public arbitrators had to be at least sixty years old, and Solon's laws forbade attendance at funeral ceremonies to women under the age of sixty; and also Psalm 90:10, which pegs the normal life span at seventy.

9. They rest on Sabbath (Deut. 5:12–15; cf. Ex. 20:10; 23:12) and rejoice with the other members of the household at the festivals—a recurring topos in Deuteronomy (12:7, 12, 18; 14:26; 15:20; 16:11, 14; 26:11).

10. For the texts, see Gibson, *Hebrew and Moabite,* 5–20, 71–83.

11. Leviticus 25:23. Ownership of the land by the deity is expressed in such practices as the offering of the firstfruits, tithing, sabbatical and jubilee years; see K. H. Henery, "Land Tenure in the Old Testament," *PEQ* 86 (1954):5–15; G. von Rad, "The Promised Land and Yahweh's Land in the Hexateuch," in *The Problem of the Hexateuch and Other Essays* (Edinburgh and London: Oliver & Boyd, 1966), 79–93; Walter Brueggemann, *The Land* (Philadelphia: Fortress Press, 1977); Joseph Blenkinsopp, "Yahweh and Other Deities: Conflict and Accommodation in the Religion of Israel," *Interpretation* 40 (1986):354–66; Christopher J. H. Wright, *God's People in God's Land* (Grand Rapids: Wm. B. Eerdmans Publishing Co., 1990).

12. On the Naboth incident, see, in addition to the commentaries, Francis I. Andersen, "The Socio-Juridical Background of the Naboth Incident," *JBL* 85 (1966:46–57; Davie Napier, "Inheritance and the Problem of Adjacency: An Essay on 1 Kings 21," *Interpretation* 30 (1976):3–11; and R. Bohlen, *Der Fall Nabot* (Trier: Paulinus, 1978).

13. On the test case of the daughters of Zelophehad, see, in addition to the commentaries, Z. Ben-Barak, "Inheritance by Daughters in the Ancient Near East," *JSS* 25 (1980):22–33; Katherine Doob Sakenfeld, "Zelophehad's Daughters," *Perspectives in Religious Studies* 15 (1988):37–47.

14. On widows as charter members of the *personae miserae* class, see F. C. Fensham, "Widow, Orphan and the Poor in Ancient Near Eastern Legal and Wisdom Literature," *JNES* 21 (1962):129–39; G. W. Coats, "Widow's Rights: A Crux in the Structure of Genesis 38," *CBQ* 34 (1972):461–66; and H. A. Hoffner, " '*almānāh,*" *TDOT,* 1:287–91.

15. On the jubilee, see Robert North, S.J., *Sociology of the Biblical Jubilee* (Rome: Pontifical Biblical Institute, 1954); Edward Neufeld, "Socio-Economic Background of *Yōbēl* and *Šemiṭṭā,*" *Rivista degli Studi Orientali* 33 (1958):53–124; Niels Peter Lemche, "The Manumission of Slaves—the Fallow Year—the Sabbatical Year—the Jobel Year," *VT* 26 (1976):38–59; Christopher J. H. Wright, *God's People in God's Land: Family, Land and Property in the Old Testament* (Grand Rapids: Wm. B. Eerdmans Publishing Co., 1990), 119–28, 143–51; and Raymond Westbrook, "Jubilee Laws," in *Property and the Family in Biblical Law* (Sheffield: JSOT Press, 1991), 36–57.

16. Consult Julius Lewy, "The Biblical Institution of DERÔR in the Light of Akkadian Documents," Eretz Israel 5 (1958):21–31; Raymond Westbrook, "Redemption of Land" and "The Price Factor in the Redemption of Land," in *Property and the Family,* 58–68, 90–117.

17. See W. J. Woodhouse, *Solon the Liberator* (New York: Octagon Books, 1965); Edwin M. Yamauchi, "Two Reformers Compared: Solon of Athens and Nehemiah of Jerusalem," in *The Bible World: Essays in Honor of Cyrus H. Gordon,* ed. G. Rendsburg, R. Adler, M. Arfa, and N. H. Winter (New York: KTAV Publishing House, 1980), 269–92.

18. An interesting point made by Stager, "Archaeology of the Family," 12; for these activities in general, see Oded Borowski, *Agriculture in Iron Age Israel* (Winona Lake, Ind.: Eisenbrauns, 1987).

19. As claimed by Amihai Mazar, *Archaeology of the Land of the Bible 10,000–586 B.C.E.* (New York and London: Doubleday, 1990), 489–91, 507–13.

20. Encounter at a well is, of course, a familiar literary topos, e.g., Gen. 24:11–27; 29:1–12; Ex. 2:15–20; John 4:1–38.

21. The most recent discussion of this issue, with bibliographical references, is Eckart Otto, "Town and Rural Countryside in Ancient Israelite Law: Reception and Redaction in Cuneiform and Israelite Law," *JSOT* 57 (1993): 3–22.

22. E.g., Alexander Rofé, "Family and Sex Laws in Deuteronomy and the Book of the Covenant," *Henoch* 9 (1987):131–59.

23. E.g., Code of Hammurabi 164; see Raymond Westbrook, "The Dowry," in *Property and the Family,* 142–64; and cf. K. Grosz, "Bridewealth and Dowry in Nuzi," in *Images of Women in Antiquity,* ed. A. Cameron and A. Kuhrt (Detroit: Wayne State University Press, 1983), 193–206.

24. Anthony Phillips, "Another Look at Adultery," *JSOT* 20 (1981):3–25, emphasizes that the intent of the accusing husband is the recovery of the *mohar* rather than simply to divorce his bride.

25. Phillips, "Another Look at Adultery"; also M. Tsevat, *"bᵉtûlāh," TDOT* 2:340–43; and Karen Engelken, *Frauen im Alten Israel* (Stuttgart: W. Kohlhammer, 1990), 19–25. Gordon J. Wenham, *"Bᵉtulah: 'A Girl of Marriageable Age,'" VT* 22 (1972):326–48, argued that the *bᵉtûlîm* consisted of a cloth or garment stained with menstrual blood, the absence of which was taken by the husband as an indication that his bride was pregnant before her marriage to him. But since he would have had to wait about a month to be sure, or even plausible, how could he then assert that impregnation had taken place before marriage? For a similar line of argument, see, most recently, Carolyn Pressler, *The View of Women Found in the Deuteronomic Family Laws* (Berlin and New York: Walter de Gruyter, 1993), 22–31. She takes the view that the "tokens" consisted in hymenal blood; this makes more sense, but then what evidence could the parents produce in refutation of the husband's allegation?

26. In addition to the commentaries, see Michael Fishbane, "Accusations of Adultery: A Study of Law and Scribal Practice in Num 5:11–31," *HUCA* 45 (1974):25–45; Herbert C. Brichto, "The Case of the *Sota* and a Reconsideration of Biblical 'Law,' " *HUCA* 46 (1975):55–70; Tikva Frymer-Kensky, "The Strange Case of the Suspected Sotah (Numbers 5:11–31)," *VT* 34 (1984):11–26.

27. E.g., Gen. 12:10–20; 20:3; 39:9; 2 Samuel 11—12; Jer. 3:8; 5:7–8; 23:10, 14; 29:23; Ezek. 16:32, 38; 23:45; Hos. 3:1; 4:13–14; 7:4. On adultery in the ancient Near East and the Levant in general, see W. Kornfeld, "L'Adultère dans l'orient antique," *RB* 57 (1950):92–109; Jack Goody, "A Comparativist Approach to Incest and Adultery," *British Journal of Sociology* 7 (1956):286–305; Anthony Phillips, *Ancient Israel's Criminal Law* (New York: Schocken Books, 1970), 119–29; idem, "Another Look at Adultery," *JSOT* 20 (1981):3–25; Henry McKeating, "Sanctions against Adultery in Ancient Israelite Society, with Some Reflections on Methodology in the Study of Old Testament Ethics," *JSOT* 11 (1979):57–72; Robert Gordis, "On Adultery in Biblical and Babylonian Law—A Note," *Judaism* 33 (1984):210–11; M. J. Giovannini, "Female Chastity Codes in the Circum-Mediterranean: Comparative Perspectives," in *Honor and Shame and the Unity of the Mediterranean*, ed. D. D. Gilmore (Washington, D.C.: American Anthropological Association, 1987), 61–74; Alexander Rofé, "Family and Sex Laws in Deuteronomy and the Book of the Covenant," *Henoch* 9, 2 (1987):131–59; Arnold A. Anderson, "Law in Old Israel: Laws Concerning Adultery," in *Law and Religion*, ed. Barnabas Lindars (Cambridge: James Clarke & Co., 1988), 13–19; and Raymond Westbrook, "Adultery in Ancient Near Eastern Law," *RB* 97 (1990):542–80.

28. The Middle Assyrian laws also make no distinction between town and countryside in the case of an unmarried virgin (Tablet A 55; *ANET* 185); the case of a married or betrothed woman may have been the subject of the previous law, no longer legible (54). Cf. the distinction in the Hittite law 197 between a location in the mountains and in a house in the city (*ANET,* 196).

29. Herbert C. Brichto, "Kin, Cult, Land and Afterlife—A Biblical Complex," *HUCA* 44 (1973):1–54. Theodore J. Lewis, "The Ancestral Estate (NḤLT 'LHYM) in 2 Samuel 14–16," *JBL* 110 (1991):597–612, stresses the importance of perpetuating the names of deceased ancestors, also known as *'ĕlohîm,* and invoking them in funerary rites.

30. On levirate marriage, see Millar Burrows, "Levirate Marriage in Israel," *JBL* 59 (1940):23–33; D. Thompson and T. Thompson, "Some Legal Problems in the Book of Ruth," *VT* 18 (1968):79–99; R. G. Abrahams, "Some Aspects of Levirate," in *The Character of Kinship*, ed. Jack Goody (Cambridge: Cambridge University Press, 1973), 163–74; E. W. Davies, "Inheritance Rights and the Hebrew Levirate Marriage," *VT* 31 (1981):138–44, 157–68; idem, "Ruth IV 5 and the Duties of the go'el," *VT* 33 (1983):231–34; Raymond Westbrook, "The Law of the Biblical Levirate," in *Property and the Family*, 69–89.

31. C. M. Carmichael, "A Ceremonial Crux: Removing a Man's Sandal as a Female Gesture of Contempt," *JBL* 96 (1977):321–36.

32. Some have found traces of uxorilocal (the wife's domicile) marriage in the Hebrew Bible, e.g., in the Samson story (Judges 13—16), but the evidence does not persuade. A. F. L. Beeston, "One Flesh," *VT* 36 (1986):115–17,

explains Gen. 2:24 in the light of the Arab custom by which, exceptionally, a man is incorporated by marriage into the clan ("flesh") of his wife.

33. In the Hebrew, the main clause—and the main point—occurs only in v. 4: given the situation as described in vv. 1–3, the first husband may not remarry the woman. In the Vulgate, the main clause begins *scribet libellum repudii* ("he shall write a bill of divorce"). The issue of palingamy (second marriage) is discussed by R. Yaron, "The Restoration of Marriage," *JJS* 17 (1966):1–11, with a response by G. J. Wenham, "The Restoration of Marriage Reconsidered," *JJS* 30 (1979):36–40; see also T. R. Hobbs, "Jeremiah 3:1–5 and Deuteronomy 24:1–4," *ZAW* 86 (1974):23–29; and J. Carl Laney, "Deut 24:1–4 and the Issue of Divorce," *Bibliotheca Sacra* 149 (1992):3–15.

34. See Ben-Zion Schereschewsky, "Divorce in Later Jewish Law," *EncJud* 6 (1971):125–35.

35. The *sēper kĕrîtût* is mentioned at Deut. 24:1, 3; Isa. 50:1; Jer. 3:8; priests may not marry a widow or a *gĕrûšâ* (Lev. 21:7, 14; 22:13; Ezek. 44:22). As in the Elephantine contracts, the formula "I hate [i.e., divorce] my wife" may have been used in some periods (cf. use of the stem *śn'*, "hate," in Deut. 21:15–17; 22:13–21; 24:1–4; cf. Jer. 3:1–4, 8).

36. On the three divorce contracts extant from Elephantine (Jeb), see Bezalel Porten, *Archives from Elephantine: The Life of an Ancient Jewish Military Colony* (Berkeley and Los Angeles: University of California Press, 1968), 208–10, 261–62.

37. The impossibility of a literal translation ("nakedness of a thing") indicates idiomatic usage; it occurs elsewhere only in Deut. 23:15 [ET 23:14], with reference to feces or other unclean matter in the camp.

38. Needless to say, a great deal has been written on the biblical texts touching on divorce, most of it with reference to certain well-known New Testament texts; for a brief overview, see Robert W. Wall's article "Divorce," in *ABD* 2 (1992):217–19; and the short articles in *EncJud* 6 (1971): 122–37.

39. Paul Veyne, ed., *A History of Private Life*, vol. 1: *From Pagan Rome to Byzantium* (Cambridge, Mass., and London: Belknap Press of Harvard University Press, 1987).

40. Philippe Ariès, *Centuries of Childhood: A Social History of Family Life* (New York: Vintage Books, 1962), 58.

41. As argued by H. P. Stähli, *Knabe, Jüngling, Knecht: Untersuchungen zum Begriff N'R im Alten Testament* (Frankfurt: Peter Lang, 1978); see also J. Macdonald, "The Status and Role of the Na'ar in Israelite Society," *JNES* 35 (1976):147–70; S. Ben-Reuven, "*Bēn* in Contrast to *yeled* and *na'ar* in the Bible," *Beth Mikra* 28 (1982/83):147–49 (Hebrew). According to Franz Dummermuth, "Josua in Ex. xxxiii, 7–11," *TLZ* 19 (1963):161–68, *na'ar* can also have the meaning "cultic ecstatic" and in this sense describes the function of Joshua in the oracle tent in the wilderness.

42. That Samuel was weaned at the age of three is perhaps suggested by the three-year-old bull (1 Sam. 1:24 LXX) offered by Hannah. On breast-feeding, see

Mayer I. Gruber, "Breast-Feeding Practices in Biblical Israel and in Old Babylonian Mesopotamia," *JANESCU* 19 (1989):61–83 (reprinted in idem, *The Motherhood of God and Other Studies* [Atlanta: Scholars Press, 1992], 69–107).

43. Code of Hammurabi 170–71 (*ANET,* 173). That the children of Machir ben Manasseh were "born on Joseph's knees" (Gen. 50:23) may, however, signify adoption rather than acknowledgment. It is unclear whether Bilhah's bearing a child on Rachel's knees (Gen. 30:3) signifies assistance in · labor or a claim that the child legally belongs to Rachel, rather than to the surrogate mother.

44. On midwifery in antiquity, including Israelite antiquity, see J. Towler and J. Bramall, *Midwives in History and Society* (London: Croom Helm, 1986); and Victor H. Matthews and Don C. Benjamin, *Social World of Ancient Israel* (Peabody, Mass.: Hendrikson, 1993), 67–81.

45. See Eshnunna 32–34 (*ANET,* 162); Code of Hammurabi 14, 29, 137, 168–71, 185–93 (*ANET,* 166–67, 172–75); Middle Assyrian laws 53 (Tablet A; *ANET,* 185); Hittite laws 171, 200(B) (*ANET,* 195, 197).

46. See further my treatment of the text in Joseph Blenkinsopp, *The Pentateuch* (New York: Doubleday, 1992), 202–3. From the extensive and growing bibliography on Ex. 21:22–23 I mention only recent papers by Stanley Isser, "Two Traditions: The Law of Ex 21:22–23 Revisited," *CBQ* 52 (1990):30–45; and Eckart Otto, "Town and Rural Countryside in Ancient Israelite Law: Reception and Redaction in Cuneiform and Israelite Law," *JSOT* 57 (1993):7–18.

47. In addition to the commentaries, see Elizabeth Bellefontaine, "Deuteronomy 21:18–21: Revisiting the Case of the Rebellious Son," *JSOT* 13 (1979):13–31; David Marcus, "Juvenile Delinquency in the Bible and the Ancient Near East," *JANESCU* 13 (1981):31–52; and Phillip R. Callaway, "Deut. 21:18–21: Proverbial Wisdom and Law," *JBL* 103 (1984):341–52.

48. It appears that two children were executed in keeping with these Old Testament laws during the mercifully short period of Calvinist theocratic rule in Geneva.

49. Aqhat A i 22–35 (*ANET,* 150); more accessibly in Michael D. Coogan, *Stories from Ancient Canaan* (Philadelphia: Westminster Press, 1978), 32–47. See A. van Selms, *Marriage and Family Life in Ugaritic Literature* (London: Luzac & Co., 1954), 100–105; John F. Healey, "The *Pietas* of an Ideal Son in Ugarit," *Ugarit-Forschungen* 11 (1979):353–56; and Theodore J. Lewis, *Cults of the Dead in Ancient Israel and Ugarit* (Atlanta: Scholars Press, 1989), 53–71. Note, too, how Absalom erected his own stela, since he had no son to keep his name in remembrance (*lĕhazkîr*) by reciting it in a cultic context (2 Sam. 18:18).

50. On posthumous honor due to a parent, see Brichto, "Kin, Cult, Land and Afterlife," 1–54; Lewis, "Ancestral Estate," 597–612; see also the reference to invoking the gods (*ilāniya*) and the dead (*mētēya*) in recently discovered wills from Late Bronze Emar in Syria; and John Huenergard, "Biblical Notes on Some New Akkadian Texts from Emar," *CBQ* 47 (1985):428–34.

51. The context of Zech. 13:8 suggests "two-thirds" rather than "a double share" for Hebrew pî šĕnayim, though this has been contested by E. W. Davies, "The Meaning of Pî Šĕnayim in Deuteronomy 21:17," VT 36 (1986):341–47.

52. References and discussion in John Van Seters, Abraham in History and Tradition (New Haven, Conn., and London: Yale University Press, 1975), 68–71, 87–95.

53. Van Seters, Abraham in History and Tradition, 69–74, 78–91; Samson Kardimon, "Adoption as a Remedy for Infertility in the Period of the Patriarchs," JSS 3 (1958):123–26; Shalom M. Paul, "Adoption Formulae: A Study of Cuneiform and Biblical Legal Clauses," Maarav 2 (1980):173–85; and M. Malul, "Adoption of Foundlings in the Bible and Mesopotamian Documents: A Study of Some Legal Metaphors in Ezekiel 16:1–7," JSOT 46 (1990):97–126; from the comparativist viewpoint, see Jack Goody, "Adoption in Cross-Cultural Perspective," Comparative Studies in Society and History 11 (1969):55–78; and "Strategies of Heirship," Comparative Studies in Society and History 15 (1973):2–20.

54. On the issue of marriage customs in Genesis 12—50, I am indebted especially to Mara E. Donaldson, "Kinship Theory in the Patriarchal Narratives: The Case of the Barren Wife," JAAR 49 (1981):77–87; and Robert A. Oden, "Jacob as Father, Husband and Nephew: Kinship Studies and Patriarchal Narratives," JBL 102 (1983):189–205. Also worth consulting are Nathaniel Wander, "Structure, Contradiction, and 'Resolution' in Mythology: Father's Brother's Daughter Marriage and the Treatment of Women in Gen 11–50," JANESCU 13 (1981):75–99; Terry J. Prewitt, "Kinship Structures and the Genesis Genealogies," JNES 40 (1981):87–98; Naomi Steinberg, Kinship and Marriage in Genesis: A Household Economics Perspective (Minneapolis: Fortress Press, 1993). On cross-cousin marriage in general, see R. F. Murphy and L. Kasdan, "The Structure of Parallel Cousin Marriage," in Marriage, Family and Residence, ed. P. Bohanan and J. Middleton (Garden City, N.Y.: Natural History Press, 1968), 185–201.

55. Middle Assyrian laws Tablet A 20 (ANET, 181).

56. 1 Kings 14:24; 15:12; 22:47 (22:46); 2 Kings 23:7; cf. Deut. 23:18–19 (23:17–18). The arguments of Elaine A. Goodfriend, "Prostitution (OT)," ABD 5 (1992):505–10, following M. Gruber, "The qodes in the Book of Kings and in Other Sources," Tarbiz 52 (1983):167–76, against the practice of male cult prostitution in Judah, are forced and unconvincing, not least her interpretation of "You shall not bring the fee of a female prostitute or the price of a 'dog' into the house of Yahweh your God" (Deut. 23:19 [ET 23:18]), involving a literal understanding of "dog" (keleb).

57. In addition to the (few and far between) commentaries on Leviticus, see Karl Elliger, "Das Gesetz Leviticus 18," ZAW 67 (1955):1–25; Susan Rattray, "Marriage Rules, Kinship Terms and Family Structure in the Bible," SBL Seminar Papers 26 (1987):537–44.

58. See T. Buckley and A. Gottlieb, eds., *Blood Magic: The Anthropology of Menstruation* (Berkeley: University of California Press, 1988).

59. I am indebted to my colleague Jerome Neyrey for bringing this to my attention. On the broader social and political implications of emotional male-female attachments, see the interesting paper of William J. Goode, "The Theoretical Importance of Love," *American Sociological Review* 24 (1959):38–47. Needless to say, a vast amount continues to be written on the treatment of women in the Hebrew Bible. I mention only, among the more recent publications, Athalya Brenner, *The Israelite Woman* (Sheffield: JSOT Press, 1985); Esther Fuchs, "The Literary Characterization of Mothers and Sexual Politics in the Hebrew Bible," *Semeia* 46 (1989):151–66; and G. I. Emmerson, "Women in Ancient Israel," in Clements, *World of Ancient Israel,* 371–94.

60. William G. Dever, "Material Remains and the Cult in Ancient Israel: An Essay in Archaeological Systematics," in *The World Shall Go Forth: Essays in Honor of David Noel Freedman in Celebration of his Sixtieth Birthday,* ed. C. L. Meyers and M. O'Connor (Winona Lake, Ind.: Eisenbrauns, 1983), 571–87; idem, *Recent Archaeological Discoveries and Biblical Research* (Seattle and London: University of Washington Press, 1990), 119–66; "Religion in Israel and Judah," 249–99.

61. *ANET,* 320; Gibson, *Hebrew and Moabite Inscriptions,* 1–4.

62. See note 6, above.

63. William Robertson Smith, *The Religion of the Semites: The Fundamental Institutions* (2d ed., 1894; reprint, New York: Schocken Books, 1972), 275–77—a book that can still be read with pleasure and profit. On sacrifice as a way of determining membership in the kin group, see the fine comparativist study by Nancy Jay, "Sacrifice, Descent and the Patriarchs," *VT* 38 (1988):52–70; and her *Throughout Your Generations Forever: Sacrifice, Religion and Paternity* (Chicago: University of Chicago Press, 1992). The same subject is dealt with in Joseph Blenkinsopp, "Deuteronomy and the Politics of Post-Mortem Existence," *VT* 45.7 (1995):1–16.

64. See Lewis, "Ancestral Estate."

65. See Roland de Vaux, *Ancient Israel: Its Life and Institutions* (London: Darton, Longman & Todd, 1961), 56–61, who, however, denies the existence of a cult of the dead in ancient Israel; presumably he took the term *cult* in the Roman Catholic liturgical sense of acts and words addressed to either God or the saints (*latreia* and *douleia,* respectively); B. Lorenz, "Bemerkungen zum Totenkult im Alten Testament," *VT* 32 (1982):229–34; R. E. Cooley, "Gathered to His People: A Study in the Dothan Family Tomb," in *The Living and Active Word of God: Essays in Honor of Samuel J. Schultz,* ed. M. Inch and R. Youngblood (Winona Lake, Ind.: Eisenbrauns, 1983), 47–58.

66. On the rĕpā'îm (shades), see Conrad L'Heureux, "The Ugaritic and Biblical Rephaim," *HTR* 67 (1974):265–74; W. J. Horowitz, "The Significance of the Rephaim," *Journal of the Northwest Semitic Languages* 7 (1979): 37–43; and Mark S. Smith, "Rephaim," *ABD* 5 (1992):674–76.

67. The dead are called *'ĕlohîm* at 1 Sam. 28:13; 2 Sam. 14:16; and Isa. 8:19–20. Note also the *'ĕlohîm* to whom the Israelites sacrificed at Shittim (Num. 25:2), who are called *mētîm* at Ps. 106:28.

68. Miranda Bayliss, "The Cult of the Dead Kin in Assyria and in Babylonia," *Iraq* 35 (1973):115–25; Marvin Pope, "The Cult of the Dead at Ugarit," in *Ugarit in Retrospect,* ed. G. D. Young (Winona Lake, Ind.: Eisenbrauns, 1981), 159–79; John Huenergard, "Biblical Notes on Some New Akkadian Texts from Emar," *CBQ* 47 (1985):428–34; and Theodore J. Lewis, *Cults of the Dead in Ancient Israel and Ugarit* (Atlanta: Scholars Press, 1989).

69. On the *marzēah* at Elephantine and elsewhere, see Porten, *Archives from Elephantine,* 179–86; a more popular account is provided in Philip J. King, *Amos, Hosea, Micah—an Archaeological Commentary* (Philadelphia: Westminster Press, 1988), 137–61.

70. Genesis 31:19, 34–35; Judg. 17:5; 18:14, 17–18, 20; 1 Sam. 15:23; 19:13, 16; 2 Kings 23:24; Ezek. 21:26 (21:21); Hos. 3:4; and Zech. 10:2.

71. In addition to the references in note 60, above, see Mazar, *Archaeology of the Land of the Bible, 501–2.*

72. On the syncretic cult in Israel in general, see Morton Smith, *Palestinian Parties and Politics That Shaped the Old Testament* (New York and London: Columbia University Press, 1971). In recent years the goddess cult in Israel has received a great deal of attention, especially after the provisional publication of the graffiti from Kuntillet 'Ajrud in the Sinai. See Zeev Meshel, "Kuntillet 'Ajrud," *ABD* 4 (1992):103–9; and John Day, "Asherah," *ABD* 1 (1992):483–87.

73. On the existence of local Yahweh cults, see P. Kyle McCarter, Jr., "Aspects of the Religion of the Israelite Monarchy: Biblical and Epigraphic Data," in Miller et al., eds., *Ancient Israelite Religion,* 137–55.

74. Genesis 34:7; Deut. 22:21; Judg. 19:22–26; 2 Sam. 13:12; and Jer. 29:23.

75. Biblical tradition also credits Hezekiah with the composition of a psalm (Isa. 38:9). According to the tractate *Baba Batra* (*b. B. Bat.* 15a), Hezekiah and his colleagues also wrote (i.e., copied) Proverbs, the Canticle, Koheleth (Ecclesiastes), and Isaiah. The highest concentration of inscribed material also dates from this period: ostraca from Arad, Hurvat Uza, Tell Qasile, Meṣad Hashavyahu, and Jerusalem; the famous Siloam inscription; seals, seal impressions, and a great number of stamped jar handles.

76. E.g., Aramaic Instruction of Ahiqar, practically identical; see *ANET,* 428.

77. Titles on seals and bullae include *na'ar* and *'ebed* (page, servant), *'al habbayit* (majordomo of the palace), *śar hā'îr* (governor of the city), *bēn hammelek* (member of the royal family). See Mazar, *Archaeology of the Land of the Bible,* 455–58, 518–20; Nahman Avigad, *Hebrew Bullae from the Time of Jeremiah: Remnants of a Burnt Archive* (Jerusalem: Israel Exploration Society, 1986); idem, "The Contribution of Hebrew Seals to an Understanding of Israelite Religion and Society," in Miller et al., eds., *Ancient Israelite Religion,* 195–208.

78. I take the view, widely accepted, that the catalog of Judean cities in Josh.

15:21–62 reflects the administrative reforms of Jehoshaphat (2 Chron. 17:2, 12–13;19:4–11). It appears from his list that Judah was divided into four main districts, two of which were, on account of their size, subdivided into four and five regions respectively. Jerusalem, with its palace and temple under direct royal administration, brought the total up to twelve.

79. On the ostraca, see note 10, above; also Klaus A. D. Smelik, *Writings from Ancient Israel* (Edinburgh: T. & T. Clark, 1991), 116–31. On the seal impressions, consult L. H. Herr, *The Scripts of Ancient North-West Semitic Seals* (Missoula, Mont.: Scholars Press, 1978); Mazar, *Archaeology of the Land of the Bible*, 455–58; Avigad, *Hebrew Bullae.*

80. Deuteronomy 12:6, 11, 17, 26; 14:22–26; 16:16–17; 18:3–5; 26:1–4.

81. G. A. Barrois, "Debt, Debtor," *IDB* 1 (1964):809–10; and for Elephantine, Porten, *Archives from Elephantine*, 77–80.

82. Gibson, *Hebrew and Moabite Inscriptions*, 26–30; Smelik, *Writings from Ancient Israel*, 93–100.

83. Indirectly in 1 Chron. 27:25–31; 2 Chron. 26:10; 32:28–29; directly in the Zeno papyri and Josephus. See Hans Bartke, "Die Latifundien in Juda während der zweiten Hälfte des achten Jahrhunderts v. Chr.," in *Hommages à André Dupont-Sommer*, ed. A. Caquot and M. Philonenko (Paris: Adrien-Missionneuve, 1971), 235–54.

84. Deuteronony 12:5–8, 11–12, 13–14, 17–18, 26–27; 16:21–22.

85. On the relevant texts in Deuteronomy, see Lewis, *Cults of the Dead*, 90–104.

86. At the risk of sinning by omission, I may mention Max Weber, *Ancient Judaism* (1917–1919; reprint, New York: Free Press, 1952), 61–70; and the unfortunately little read contribution of Antonin Causse, "La Crise de la solidarité de famille et de clan dans l'ancien Israël," *RHPR* 10 (1930): 24–60; idem, "Les Prophètes et la crise sociologique de la religion d'Israël," *RHPR* 12 (1932): 94–140; idem, *Du groupe ethnique à la communauté religieuse. Le Problème sociologique de la religion d'Israël* (Paris: Alcan, 1938). Commendable also is the study of Naomi Steinberg, "The Deuteronomic Law Code and the Politics of State Centralization," in *The Bible and the Politics of Exegesis*, ed. David Jobling, P.L. Day, and G. T. Sheppard (Cleveland: Pilgrim Press, 1991), 161–70.

87. The state-appointed judiciary is of great importance in Deuteronomy and is listed before other organs of statecraft, including the monarchy (Deut. 16:18–20; 17:8–13). In such issues as undetected homicide, witnessing, and the infliction of physical punishment (Deut. 19:15–20; 21:1–9; 25:1–3), we see it taking over functions previously discharged by the elders.

88. Y. A. Cohen, "Ends and Means in Political Control: State Organization and the Punishment of Adultery, Incest and the Violation of Celibacy," *American Anthropologist* 71 (1969):658–87.

89. I leave aside the much-debated matter of cult prostitutes (*qĕdēšôt*) and the hypothesis that Solomon's temple employed female singers, the latter based precariously on a reading of Amos 8:3 as *šārôt hēkāl*, "singers"

(rather than "songs") of the "temple" (rather than "palace"). The literature is reviewed by Phyllis Bird, "The Place of Women in the Israelite Cultus," in Miller et al., eds., *Ancient Israelite Religion*, 397–419.

90. First Samuel 28:3–25; in a slightly improved text, the witch of Endor is called a *ba'ălat 'ôb*, literally, "a mistress who commands the spirits or ghosts." See also Ezek. 13:17–23.

91. Max Weber, *Economy and Society*, translation of 4th German ed. of 1956 (Berkeley and Los Angeles: University of California Press, 1978), 1: 356–84.

92. Apart from the second temple Levitical guilds, little seems to have been written on guilds in Israel, no doubt because there is little to write about; but see Samuel Klein, "Die Schreiberfamilien: 1 Chronik 2 55," *Monatschrift für Geschichte und Wissenschaft des Judentums* 70 (1926):410–16; I. Mendelsohn, "Guilds in Ancient Palestine," *BASOR* 80 (1940):17–21; and for Mesopotamia, I. Mendelsohn, "Guilds in Babylonia and Assyria," *JAOS* 60 (1940):68–72; and Alfred O. Haldar, *Associations of Cult Prophets among the Ancient Semites* (Uppsala: Almqvist & Wiksell, 1945), 126–30; D. E. Weisberg, *Guild Structure and Political Allegiance in Early Achaemenid Mesopotamia* (Baltimore: Johns Hopkins University Press, 1967).

93. In Ezra-Nehemiah, one of our principal sources for the Achaemenid period, duodecimal symbolism is detectable, but apart from the reference to the province as "Judah and Benjamin" (cf. "Judea and Samaria" as an ideological construct in modern Israel), tribal names are absent, and the *bêt 'ābôt* (Ezra 1:5; 2:68; 3:12; 4:2–3; 8:1–29; 10:16; Neh. 8:13) is quite different from the preexilic *bêt 'āb*; on which see the study of Joel Weinberg, "Das Bêit 'Abôt im 6-4 Jh. v.u.Z.," *VT* 23 (1973):400–414.

3

Marriage, Divorce, and Family in Second Temple Judaism

JOHN J. COLLINS

The second temple period covers a span of some six hundred years, during which the Jewish people, like all peoples of the eastern Mediterranean, underwent great cultural upheavals. The Babylonian exile involved the demise of the monarchy, the interruption and reorganization of the temple cult, and the impoverishment of the population as a whole. The Hellenistic age brought exposure to a new culture and saw the rise of new forms of association, such as those we find attested in the Dead Sea Scrolls. It also brought increased urbanization, with the multiplication of Hellenistic cities, inhabited mainly by Gentiles,[1] and the growth of Jerusalem, which was sparsely populated in Nehemiah's time, to a city of some eighty thousand people at the turn of the era.[2] The failure of the rebellions against Rome in 66–70 and 132–135 C.E. again reduced the land to poverty. Jerusalem was destroyed. Thereafter Jewish life in the land of Israel, which is reflected in the rabbinic corpus, was village life, as it had been in early Israel. Throughout this period, an ever increasing proportion of the Jewish people lived outside the land of Israel in a far-flung diaspora.

Continuity and Change

Even if we leave aside the Greek-speaking Diaspora of the Hellenistic age, where the cultural innovation was greatest, it is clear that second temple Judaism entails considerable diversity. There was also considerable continuity. Throughout this period, the Jewish population of the land of Israel was predominantly rural and engaged in agriculture.[3] For much of this period, Jerusalem was the only significant Jewish city.[4] Even Jerusalem was a small town by modern standards, and we should not suppose that its residents were completely isolated from the surrounding countryside.[5] The impact of Hellenistic mores was most conspicuous in the upper classes, such as the Tobiads in the period before the Maccabean revolt[6] and the family of Herod in the Roman era. There were always powerful conservative and traditional forces in Jewish society, and these forces eventually prevailed in the rabbinic tradition. This later tradition is often suggestive of how life might have been in the second temple period. It would be a great mistake, however, to take the Mishnah or the Talmud as a normative description of Jewish life in the period before the fall of Jerusalem.

The Ancestral Household

The political changes in the governance of Judaea in the second temple period are well documented. It is much more difficult to find evidence of social changes at the level of the individual household. Much has been written in recent years about the emergence after the exile of a new structure, the *bêt 'ābôt*, or "fathers' house," as distinct from the traditional *bêt 'āb* or "father's house."[7] The term *bêt 'ābôt* appears some sixty-five times in Ezra-Nehemiah-Chronicles, as against six times in the Deuteronomic History. It refers to large units of eight hundred to one thousand adult males and appears to take the place of the traditional clan (*mišpāḥāh*) rather than of the "father's house."[8] One function of these groups was genealogical; they established lines of continuity, whether real or fictitious, with preexilic Israel. In Ezra 2:59–63, we read of people who came up from the exile "though they could not prove their families or their descent, whether they belonged to Israel." Priests who could not establish their genealogies were excluded from the priesthood as unclean. The *bêt 'ābôt* were actual structures of the postexilic community and not mere notional constructs. We often read of the "heads" of these houses, notably in the context of Ezra's reform (Ezra 10:16). Joel Weinberg supposes that this structure compensated for the breakup of families and clans by unifying a number of families that were related, either fictionally or genuinely. He refers to the *bêt 'ābôt* as "collectives" and attributes to them "a conscious solidarity based on communal ownership of lands."[9] In fact, we have no evidence about the nature or basis of their solidarity, except that it involved a supposed common ancestry. While the *bêt 'abôt* were undoubtedly important in postexilic Judaean society, they shed no light on the life of the individual households in this period.

Unfortunately, we have virtually no evidence about family life in rural villages in the second temple period proper. When we get such accounts in the rabbinic period, however, the picture that emerges is rather similar to that of the ancestral household in ancient Israel, at least insofar as it involves an extended family.[10] Married children still moved in with the groom's parents. We read of a bêt ḥătānût, or "wedding chamber," built on the roof to accommodate the newlyweds.[11] Widows and divorced women still returned to their fathers' houses. Widows sometimes had special rooms set aside for them (bĕt 'almānût) in the rabbinic period. In the apocryphal book of Judith from the Hellenistic period, Judith "set up a tent for herself on the roof of her house" even though she remained at her own house (8:5). Often the different components of the extended family had separate but adjacent houses around a courtyard. Servants lived with the family as members of the household. This formation of the extended family presumably persisted throughout the second temple period, at least in villages and rural areas. A nuclear family was more likely to be separated from its relatives in an urban setting or in a context of exile; Tobias, son of Tobit, had to make a long journey to find a bride from his "father's house." Even in the most urban contexts of antiquity, links with kin and community remained strong. The family was never so "nuclear" as it is in the modern West. Nonetheless, the role of the extended family in Jewish antiquity should not obscure the primary place of the nuclear family of parents and their children throughout ancient Israelite and Judaean history. Responsibility for the raising of children rested primarily with the biological parents, and support of aged parents was primarily the moral responsibility of their children.

The Case of Ruth

Since the book of Ruth is often dated to the postexilic period,[12] some note should be taken of it here, although there is no consensus about its time of origin. The ostensible setting of the book is in the time of the Judges, and the society it describes is simple and agrarian. The case for a postexilic date rests mainly on the importance attached to the fact that Ruth is Moabite. Since marriage with foreign women was a contentious issue in postexilic Judah, the book has been construed as a protest against narrow ethnocentrism.[13]

Even if the book was written after the exile, the society it describes may reflect an earlier time. In fact, the picture of marriage and family that we find in Ruth contrasts sharply with most of what we consider in the following pages. The story assumes that when a woman was widowed, it was normal for her to return to her parents' house (here called her "mother's house" rather than her father's). Ruth elects to stay with her mother-in-law, Naomi, instead. She is bound to Naomi by loyalty, not by legal obligation. Her marriage to Boaz is brought about by unconventional means. Ruth goes to Boaz when he is asleep and "uncovers his feet" (a euphemism for his genitals). The episode has sexual connotations, even though the narrative is discreet.[14] The marriage is formalized in conjunction with a property transaction. Boaz declares in the presence of witnesses that he has acquired from the hand of Naomi all that belonged to her husband and her sons, as well as Ruth the Moabite to be his wife, to maintain the dead man's name. The witnesses affirm the arrangement with a blessing. There is no question of written documents, but the transaction is in conformity with custom and has the force of law.

The primary emphasis of the story, however, is not on legal obligation but on fidelity and kindness, the bonds that impel the members of a rural community to look out for one another's welfare. There is no marriage contract between Ruth and Boaz, and no provision is made for divorce. The available evidence for actual marriages in second temple Judaism has quite a different character.

Marriage

In contrast to the story of Ruth, our primary evidence for marriage and family life in second temple Judaism is legal in character. It consists of archives of legal documents, admittedly in very limited quantity. This evidence comes from the Jewish military colony at Elephantine in Upper Egypt in the fifth century B.C.E. and from the caves near the Dead Sea from the early second century C.E. The evidence is not necessarily typical of second temple Judaism. The marginal character of the Elephantine community should be obvious. Also, the archives may give an unduly legalistic impression, since they lack narrative context. Nonetheless, it is primary documentary evidence, unfiltered by editors. Since the literary sources of the Hebrew Bible have a heavily theological character, stamped with the views of the sages who transmitted them, the primary, unedited evidence of the papyri is especially welcome.

The Elephantine Contracts

We have seven marriage contracts from Elephantine, three of them practically complete.[15] Three of the seven contracts concern two figures whose archives are preserved, so that we get a broader view of

their family history. One is the archive of a woman named Mibtahiah,
who was a member of a prominent family. Her nephew Jedaniah, son
of her brother, was leader of the Jewish community in the last decade
of the fifth century. Mibtahiah was married three times, and partial doc-
umentation survives from each of her marriages. The archive of her documents spans a period of sixty years and includes a fragmentary document of betrothal (C 48) and a marriage contract (C 15). The other
archive pertains to a man named Ananiah son of Azariah, priest of the
god YHW, who was married to an Egyptian slave-girl (K 2).[16]

These marriage contracts provide a clear view of the legal steps involved in the constitution and dissolution of marriage at Elephantine.
Four steps can be distinguished in the constitution of marriage.[17]

1. The groom requests the hand of the bride from the
   person who has authority over her, normally the father, or the master in the case of a slave-girl.
2. He declares solemnly, "She is my wife and I am her
   husband." The formula typically concludes with the
   words "from this day and for ever" (K 2, C 15) or
   "from this day for ever" (K 7, K 14). This formula
   does not imply that the marriage is indissoluble,
   since the contract goes on to provide for divorce; it
   means only that no term to the contract is envisaged.
3. He pays a *mohar*, or "bride-price," to the person with
   authority over her.
4. The contract is drawn up. The contract specifies the
   contents of the bride's dowry. It also provides for the
   dissolution of marriage. The names of witnesses are
   appended.

These marriage contracts underline the legal and economic aspects
of marriage. The contract was formally an agreement between the
groom and the person with authority over the bride. The contracts
contain no expression of the bride's assent, even though she has the
power to initiate divorce and so her consent is de facto required. It
should be borne in mind that early marriage was the norm in antiquity.[18] The Talmud praises the man who arranges his children's marriage just before they attain puberty (*Yebam.* 62b). That way it was easier to ensure that girls were virgins when they married. But marriage

contracts were settled with the father or person in authority even when the bride was mature. Even when Mibtahiah provided her own dowry, as she appears to have done in the case of her third marriage,[19] the *mohar* was paid to her father.

It is clear that the legal forms did not always accurately reflect current mores. The *mohar* was routinely included with the wife's dowry, to be returned to her in the event of divorce. The formal recipient received no benefit from it. The main purpose of the contract was to record the dowry, which would revert to the wife in the event of divorce. It also specified any unusual arrangements—e.g., Mibtahiah's marriage contract with her second husband, an Egyptian named Ashor, specified that she would inherit his property if he died childless. The contract was given to the bride and passed into her archive.

The Contractual View of Marriage

Perhaps the most noteworthy aspect of these contracts from a modern viewpoint is precisely the consistent view of marriage as a contract. The witnesses are human, not divine.[20] It is assumed that the arrangement can be terminated at will by either party, without necessarily entailing moral culpability. Marriage is a pragmatic instrument for securing rights to property and inheritance. Bonds of affection and religious obligation were undoubtedly factors in Jewish marriages in this period and indeed are sometimes in evidence,[21] but they were not adequate safeguards of the rights of husbands, wives, and children, which are enshrined in these legal documents.

The importance of marriage contracts was recognized from an early time in the great urban cultures of the ancient Near East.[22] The Code of Hammurabi 128 declares, "If a seignior acquired a wife, but did not draw up the contracts for her, that woman is no wife." The Laws of Eshnunna 27–28 insist that the status of wife depends on the existence of a formal contract between the husband and the wife's parents. Marital status was not attained by cohabitation.

Whether marriage contracts were in use in preexilic Israel and Judah is a matter of dispute. There is no direct evidence for marriage contracts in the Hebrew Bible, and some scholars conclude that the written marriage contract was not the common practice in preexilic Judaea.[23] Others point to the fact that the bill of divorce is cited (Deut. 24:1; Isa. 50:1; Jer. 3:8) and that written deeds of sale were in use in the Babylonian period (Jer. 32:8–12).[24] M. J. Geller has argued that the parallels between the Elephantine papyri and Hosea 1—3 show that Hosea was alluding to juridical clauses from contemporary contracts and that the Elephantine Jews were following legal conventions in use in eighth-century Israel.[25] The formula for divorce is the same in both contexts ("You are not my wife and I am not your husband"), and marriage agreements involve a payment in silver and a clause forbidding the wife to have relations with anyone except her husband. Oddly enough, we have no bill of divorce from Elephantine, although the use of such documents can probably be inferred.[26] A contractual view of marriage, with clearly defined rights and obligations, does not necessarily require a written document, and there is no reference to any such document in the book of Hosea. The use of written documents is much more likely in the postexilic period, especially among returnees from the exile who had become familiar with Babylonian custom. References to the "bill of divorce" appear from the time of Deuteronomy (late seventh century). The evidence of Elephantine also strengthens the likelihood that written contracts were in use in Judah in the Persian period.[27]

The written marriage contract certainly became standard in later Judaism. In the book of Tobit, the betrothal and marriage of Tobias to his kinswoman Sarah is carried out impromptu on the day of Tobias's arrival. Her father Raguel takes Sarah by the hand and gives her to Tobias, saying, "Take her to be your wife in accordance with the law and decree written in the book of Moses" (Tobit 7:12). But he then calls her mother and tells her to bring writing material, and he writes out "a copy of a marriage contract, to the effect that he gave her to him as wife according to the decree of the law of Moses" (7:13). The document envisaged would seem to fall far short of the careful legal instruments preserved at Elephantine, but the fact that a written document was required even in such a hasty union between relatives shows how standard it had become.[28] It is not clear what "decree of the law of Moses" is envisaged. Perhaps it was the command given at creation in Genesis 1:28 or 2:24, or perhaps it is a more general appeal to Jewish tradition. We find a similar appeal in the Roman period, in a contract from Murabba'at (p Mur 20)—"according to the law of Moses"—and in the marriage contract of the woman Babatha from Naḥal Ḥever.[29] In the Cairo Genizah documents from the early Middle Ages, the phrase "according to the Law of Moses and Israel" is standard at the end of the bill of divorce.[30]

The Contracts from
the Dead Sea Region

We now have a number of marriage contracts from the early second century C.E. that throw important light on the period between the Bible and the Mishnah.[31] Four such documents were found at Murabba'at, two in Aramaic (p Mur 20 and 21) and two in Greek (p Mur 115 and 116). There is also a bill of divorce in Aramaic.[32] Three marriage deeds were found at Naḥal Ḥever in the Babatha archive: one in Aramaic, relating to the second marriage of the woman Babatha, and two in Greek, one relating to the marriage of Babatha's stepdaughter Shelamzion and one recording the marriage of Jesus son of Menahem and Salome.[33] A further Greek contract from Naḥal Ḥever (XHev [Se gr] 2) has now been published.[34] Another document refers to a divorce of another woman named Shelamzion.[35]

The Aramaic contracts are very similar in form to the later Jewish marriage document, or K^etubbāh.[36] They record a declaration of intent by the husband: "You shall be my wife according to the law of Moses" (p Mur 20.3; p Yadin 10.5). There is no reciprocal declaration by the woman. The contracts continue with a promise by the husband to support his wife and with a record of the amount of mohar owed to the woman. Babatha's contract continues, "And if you are taken captive, I will redeem you from my house and from my estate, and I will take you back as my wife, and I owe you your ketubba money" (i.e., the price of redemption will not be deducted from the money owed to the wife). This is in accordance with the Mishnah, which insists, "If she was taken captive, he must ransom her" (m. Ketub. 4:9). The corresponding passages in p Mur 20 and 21 are damaged; the editor, J. T. Milik, erroneously restored references to divorce in both cases, but the undamaged evidence of Babatha's contract is decisive.[37] The contracts go on to make provision for male and female children and for the wife in the event of widowhood, again in accordance with the Mishnah (m. Ketub. 4:10–12). Sons would inherit the money owed to the mother. Daughters were to be supported in the home until marriage. The provision for widowhood in Babatha's contract reads as follows: "If I go to my eternal home before you, you will dwell in my house and be provided for from my house and from my estate until the time that my heirs wish to give you your ketubba money" (lines 15–16). According to the Mishnah, the people of Jerusalem and Galilee used to write that the wife could remain in the house as long as she remained a widow, but the people of

Judaea gave the heirs the right to evict her if they paid her k*etubbāh* money (*m. Ketub.* 4:12). Babatha's contract conforms to Judaean practice, which is not surprising, since her husband was from Engedi near the Dead Sea.

On the whole, the contracts from Murabba'at and Naḥal Ḥever show that the Palestinian type of contract, known from rabbinic sources and the Cairo Genizah, was already in use in the early second century C.E.[38] While the provisions for divorce were not written into this type of contract, divorce is attested in other documents from this period.

The Greek contracts do not record the words of the husband's declaration but report the transaction in the third person. These contracts make no reference to "the law of Moses and the Jews," as the Aramaic contracts do. They resemble the Aramaic contracts in their concern for the economic aspects of the marriage, but they differ in their specific focus. Whereas the Aramaic contracts record the bride-price, or *mohar,* that the husband is obliged to pay in the event of divorce, the Greek contracts are acknowledgments of the dowry brought in by the wife.[39] It seems, then, that the proto-rabbinic type of contract attested in the Aramaic documents was not yet normative for all Jews. Both types of contract, however, are concerned for the economic well-being of the wife. This concern remains central to the well-documented development of Jewish marriage contracts in later tradition.[40]

Minority Views and Practices

The pragmatic, contractual view of marriage is typical of ancient Israel and Judah and, indeed, of the entire ancient Near East. We find an exception to this idea in the Hebrew Bible in the words of the prophet Malachi (2:14), who says that God is witness to the contract or covenant (bĕrît) of marriage and who gives the institution a more idealistic character.[41] Malachi, however, was a reformer, arguing against the current understanding of marriage. We consider his views in more detail when we turn to the subject of divorce. The use of marriage as an analogy for the covenant between God and Israel (Hosea 2; Ezekiel 16) may have contributed to a more solemn view of marriage but does not presuppose it.[42] The pragmatic view of marriage prevails in Ben Sira and in the rabbinic literature.[43]

It should also be noted that marriage could be initiated in a less formal way, and that the marriage contract sometimes ratified a de facto union. When Ananiah son of Azariah married the Egyptian slave-girl

Tamut at Elephantine (K 2), the couple already had a child. This situation is not uncommon in Egyptian marriage contracts. There are two examples at Elephantine. It has been inferred that the marriage contract was required only "to fix the property rights of the parents and children and thus need not have been drawn up until a child was born."[44] This, however, is exceptional in the Jewish papyri. It is simplest to suppose that Ananiah and Tamut had been living together, or at least had sexual relations, before they formalized their marriage.

A similar situation is attested in the Babatha archive from Naḥal Ḥever. P Yadin 37 states that "Jesus son of Menahem . . . has taken Salome . . . to live with her, as also before this time." The editor, Naphtali Lewis, suggests that the bride must have been an orphan or a minor during the period of premarital cohabitation, but he also notes the analogy with the "unwritten marriages" known from Greco-Egyptian papyri, where couples lived together as man and wife without a formal contract.[45] The assumption that this marriage conformed to rabbinic Halakhah is gratuitous.[46] In fact, the Mishnah acknowledged that "in three ways is a woman acquired . . . through money, writ, and intercourse" (m. Qidd. 1:1).[47] Normal practice required all three ways, but it is apparent that not all were always implemented. The Mishnah makes provision for situations where there was no written contract (m. Ketub. 4:7) and notes that in Judaea, "he who eats at his father-in-law's, not in the presence of witnesses, does not have a virginity claim, because he is intimate with her" (m. Ketub. 1:5).[48] The examples from Elephantine and Naḥal Ḥever do not necessarily show that the practice of unwritten marriage was approved by Jewish religious authorities, only that the practice was known, as it has been known in most, if not all, societies.

The Mohar Bride-Price

The mohar (the Akkadian terhatum) and the dowry occupy a pivotal place in the contracts of both the Persian and the Roman periods and are standard features of Babylonian marriage contracts from the second millennium. The payment of the mohar, or "bride-price," has often led to the view that marriage was analogous to a sale and purchase, but this view has been widely rejected.[49] Originally, the bride-price was paid to the bride's father or to the person in authority over her. Westbrook plausibly explains it as a price paid for the transfer of this authority to the husband.[50] In the Elephantine contracts, however, the mohar is added to the dowry, and the fact that it is still paid to the father or person in authority is no more than a legal formality. By rabbinic times, the groom did not actually have to provide the *mohar* but only to promise it. It became payable only in the event of divorce, and it came to be known as the *k^etubbāh*, or "written document." This reform was credited to Rabbi Simeon ben Shetach in the first century B.C.E.[51] The classic text is found in *b. Ketub.* 82b:

> Thus it was taught: Formerly they used to write [in the *ketubah*] two hundred [*zuzim*] for a virgin and one hundred [*zuzim*] for a widow, but [men] used to grow old and not take wives. They decreed that they would deposit it [the *mohar*] in her father's house, but when he [her husband] became angry with her he would say, "Go to your *ketubah*." They decreed to deposit it in her father-in-law's house; wealthy women converted [the *mohar*] into pots of silver and gold, and poor women into chamber pots, but when [her husband] became angry, he said to her, "Take your *ketubah* and go." Until Simeon b. Shetach came and decreed that [her husband] write for her [in her *ketubah*], "All my possessions are security for your *ketubah*."

This passage describes three stages in the history of the *mohar*. First, it was paid to the bride's father and he retained it. Second, the *mohar* was converted into utensils and added to the dowry. This stage is reflected in the Elephantine papyri.[52] Finally, Simeon ben Shetach ruled that the *mohar* would be paid only in case of divorce.[53]

Throughout the second temple period, the *mohar* was mainly a contribution to the wife's security in the event of a divorce. Babatha's marriage contract constitutes the first documentary evidence for the *mohar* being conceived as standing debt.[54] Simeon ben Shetach's reform dispensed with the fiction of a payment to the bride's father and was considered to provide a greater deterrent to divorce than had the previous arrangements.

At Elephantine, the *mohar* for a virgin was double that paid for a widow or divorcée, and this remained true in the Talmud. This custom can be explained partly in economic terms. A widow or divorcée would presumably have had a dowry and *mohar* from her previous marriage. Undoubtedly, the *mohar* also had symbolic significance. A high value was placed on virginity for reasons of purity. This is apparent in the law regulating the marriage of a high priest: "He shall marry only a woman who is a virgin. A widow, or a divorced woman, or a woman who has been defiled, a prostitute, these he shall not marry. He shall marry a virgin of his own kin, that he may not profane his offspring among his kin" (Lev. 21:13–15).

While the dowry remained the property of the wife, a large dowry could enhance the attractiveness of a prospective bride. Several writers warn against marrying a woman for her money. Ben Sira deems it "hard slavery and a disgrace if a wife support her husband" (Sir. 25:21–22, author's translation). The Talmud predicts that "he who takes a wife for the sake of money will have unworthy children" (*Qidd.* 70a). Eventually, the rabbis limited the size of a dowry to 10 percent of the father's possessions (*Ketub.* 53a). But no such regulation was in force in the second temple period. The book of Tobit has Raguel give his daughter half of all his possessions at the time of her marriage to Tobias (Tobit 10:10).[55] In this fictional case, however, the two families are closely related, and Raguel has no other child to whom he might leave his possessions.

Divorce and Polygamy

Divorce

The Jewish documents from the Persian and the Roman periods regard divorce as a routine, unexceptional development[56] and also furnish several examples of marital separation. The reform of the *mohar* arrangement by Simeon ben Shetach was an attempt to make divorce more costly and less attractive to the husband, with the implication that the frequency of divorce was sometimes perceived as a problem.

No reason was required for the initiation of divorce at Elephantine. The contracts simply specify that, "to-morrow or another day," if X should stand up in the congregation and say, "I hate my wife/husband," certain financial obligations are entailed. There were, however, some circumstances that would lead directly to divorce. One was adultery on the part of the wife: "Yehoyishma will not have the authority to have intercourse with another man except Ananiah, but if she does, it is divorce; they will enact for her the law of divorce" (K 7:33–34). (It should be noted that adultery does not entail the death penalty in the Elephantine contracts, biblical law notwithstanding. Similarly, Proverbs 6:32–35 assumes that the penalty was vengeance by the wronged husband, who had the option of accepting or refusing monetary compensation.)[57] When the wife is divorced, "she may go wherever she wishes" (K 7:24). The contracts do not prohibit extramarital intercourse by the husband, but we do find stipulations that he not take a second wife. Ashor, Mibtahiah's second husband, declared, "I shall have no right to say I have another wife besides Miphtahiah and other children than the children whom Miphtahiah shall bear to me" (C 15:31–32).[58] Polygamy was legal, but a prudent woman could protect herself against it by the marriage contract.

While divorce could be obtained at will by either party, it was not to be taken lightly, for it had well-defined economic consequences. The contracts do not envisage "no-fault" divorce by mutual consent. One party had to take the initiative. If the wife initiated the divorce, she had to pay divorce money (kesep śin'â). If the husband initiated the proceedings, he normally had to pay divorce money (K 2:8; 7:22); at the least, he forfeited the mohar (C 15:27).[59] Some contracts took steps to ensure that if one party was at fault, that party bore the responsibility in the divorce proceedings. So K 7 provides that if the woman commits adultery or if the man takes a second wife, "divorce it is." In short, by violating certain terms of the contract, a person might have been deemed to have initiated a divorce. Regardless of who took the initiative, the wife retained the possessions she brought with her. The amount of the divorce money was not great. In one case the divorce money required of a woman was about the price of a woolen garment (K 2). The most weighty consideration for the husband was that he would have to return the dowry.[60] The divorced woman had to leave the matrimonial home, but her right to remarry was explicitly granted.

Custody of the children is not discussed in the Elephantine papyri. This is also true of Egyptian[61] and Babylonian marriage contracts. The Code of Hammurabi 137 clearly stipulates that if a husband divorces a wife who has borne him children, "they shall return her dowry to that woman and also give her half of the field, orchard, and goods in order that she may rear her children." If the wife is guilty of "neglecting her house and humiliating her husband," however, she may be divorced without compensation. Presumably the children remain with the father in that case, but the law is not explicit.[62] The Laws of Eshnunna 59 specify that "if a man divorces his wife after having made her bear children and takes [ano]ther wife, he shall be driven from his house and from whatever he owns." Neither the later Babylonian contracts[63] nor the Jewish contracts envisage a situation where the man leaves the home. In the notorious case of the divorce of foreign wives in the course of Ezra's reform, the women were sent away "with their children" (Ezra 10:44).[64]

The Aramaic contracts from the Roman era do not address the subject of divorce, but we have documents relating to divorce from

Murabba'at and Naḥal Ḥever. A bill of divorce preserved in p Mur 19 specifies for the divorced woman that she may marry "any *Jewish* man that you wish," a restriction that was neither imposed nor observed at Elephantine. Nothing is said about the support of children. While we have no clear case of child-support payments to a divorced wife, we have a somewhat analogous situation in the Babatha archive. There we find that after the death of Babatha's first husband, the money for the support of their son was held in trust by two guardians. The payment of this money became the subject of litigation.[65] The concept of support payments was evidently known, but we remain uncertain about the actual arrangements for children in the event of divorce.

The Hebrew Bible never legislates for divorce but clearly presupposes that it may occur. Deuteronomy 24:1–4 mentions two cases in which a man might divorce his wife: if she did not find favor in his eyes because he found "something objectionable ['erwat dābār] about her," and simply if he "hates" her. The precise connotation of both expressions is debated. The phrase 'erwat dābār means "some improper or indecent behavior."[66] It is reasonable to suppose that this provision bears some analogy to the Code of Hammurabi 141–43, which allows a man to divorce his wife *without a settlement* if he can show that she was "neglecting her house and humiliating her husband." A similar principle is enunciated in the Mishnah, with greater specificity as to the offenses:

> These are they that are put away without their Ketubah: a wife that transgresses the Law of Moses and Jewish custom. What [conduct is such that it transgresses] the Law of Moses? If she gives her husband untithed food, or has connexion with him in her uncleanness, or does not set apart dough-offering, or utters a vow and does not fulfill it. And what [conduct is such that it transgresses] Jewish custom? If she goes out with her hair unbound, or spins in the street, or speaks with any man. (*m. Ketub.* 7:6; H. Danby, *The Mishnah* [Oxford: Oxford University Press, 1933], 255)

We should not suppose, however, that there was an unbroken tradition on this matter. Deuteronomy 24:1 was invoked in a famous debate between the houses of Shammai and Hillel in the first century B.C.E. The Shammaites attempted to restrict the man's power of divorce to cases of adultery, but the school of Hillel ruled that divorce was permitted "even if she spoiled a dish for him, for it is written, 'Because he has found in her indecency in *anything*' ('erwat dābār, Deut. 24:1)" (*m. Git.* 9–10). Rabbi Akiba went further: "Even if he found another fairer than her, for it is written, 'And it shall be if she finds no favour in his eyes . . .' (Deut. 24:1)."[67] Neither Hillel nor Akiba, however, exempted the man from paying the divorce settlement in these cases, and it is also not apparent that Deuteronomy 24 implies any such dispensation.[68]

The second expression in Deuteronomy 24, "to hate" (śānē'), is simply a technical term for divorce and should be translated "repudiate" rather than "dislike."[69] To say "I hate my wife/husband" serves as a formula of divorce. The technical sense is confirmed by the expressions "the law of hatred" (dîn śin'ā) and "money of hatred," that is, divorce money (kesep śin'ā).

Raymond Westbrook has disputed this common view that "hate" in the papyri is synonymous with divorce. He argues that the verb to hate is only an abbreviated version of a longer formula, "hate and divorce."[70] He points to a number of Akkadian parallels for this expression, as well as an Elephantine contract (K 2:21–22) in which the formula for divorce is "I hate you. I will not be your wife." Westbrook argues that the last phrase is the operative formula for divorce and that "hate" gives the motivation. "The motivation appears to turn what might otherwise be an innocent act into a guilty one, and we therefore feel justified in applying the terminology of modern criminal law: it is the *mens rea,* the 'guilty mind,' which is a necessary constituent of the offense." In the context of marriage, "the verb 'hate' therefore expresses the fact that the divorce in this case is for purely subjective reasons, and the financial penalties, whether by contract or under the general law, will apply."[71]

In Westbrook's view, then, Deuteronomy 24 envisages two quite distinct legal situations. In the first, the husband divorced the wife on grounds of indecency and had to pay no divorce money. In the second, the divorce was for subjective reasons, and the divorce payments were required. On this interpretation, the distinction between justifiable and arbitrary divorce that we find in the Code of Hammurabi and in *m. Ketub.* 7 is also presupposed in the biblical texts.

While Westbrook's argument is attractive in some respects, it is not persuasive. The verb *to hate* in the context of divorce, in either Akkadian or Hebrew, cannot be restricted to divorce for purely subjective reasons. None of the examples that Westbrook cites requires this interpretation. For example, the Laws of Eshnunna 30 read, "If a man hates his city and his master and flees . . ." (cf. Code of Hammurabi 136). The point is not that he fled his city because of aversion but that he repudiated it for whatever reason. (The Laws list no circumstances in which a man is justified in leaving his city and his master.) The very fact that the verb *to hate* can stand alone in the context of divorce shows that it has become a technical term, and this is confirmed by its use in the expressions "law of hatred" and "silver of hatred." Consequently, it is not at all clear that there is any significant difference in Deuteronomy between divorcing a wife because of "some offense" and repudiating her for no stated reason. It should be noted that the expression "gratuitous hatred" is found in medieval contracts in the Cairo Genizah to specify repudiation that is not warranted by an offense on the part of the wife.[72]

The papyri, as we have seen, envisage a few situations that are deemed to institute divorce (adultery on the part of the wife, taking a second wife on the part of the husband). These actions shift the financial liability for the divorce and so are somewhat analogous to the offenses that cause the wife to forfeit her *ketubah* in the Mishnah. But the situation in the papyri is very different from that of the Mishnah. Not only are the offenses that institute divorce few and weighty, but the laws apply equally to husband and wife. The Murabba'at papyri make no mention of circumstances that would cause the *ketubah* to be forfeited. The Mishnah, in multiplying the justifications for divorce without compensation, departed significantly from the legal tradition of second temple Judaism, as it is attested in the papyri, and tilted the scales in favor of the divorcing male.

The Right of Women to Divorce

The right of women to initiate divorce is assumed at Elephantine, even in the case of a slave-woman. This right is not given in the Bible and has been attributed to Egyptian influence.[73] E. Lipiński, however, points out that divorce by the woman appears in Egyptian law only in the Persian period, and he suggests that it reflects Semitic influence.[74] Scattered examples are found in documents from the nineteenth century B.C.E. on. Lipiński attributes the custom to a West Semitic tradition, but some of the examples he cites are Babylonian.[75] These examples, however, are exceptional in Babylonian law. A woman could not divorce her husband at will but only if she could demonstrate that he was at fault.[76] One group of Old Babylonian contracts specifies that if the wife divorces the husband, she incurs the death penalty, which would seem to negate her right to divorce effectively. Another group prescribes penalties that are more in line with those imposed on the husband.[77] Westbrook concludes that "divorce by the wife is a practical impossibility even when theoretically valid" in the Old Babylonian laws.[78] The neo-Babylonian laws provide only for divorce by the husband. The Elephantine papyri are exceptional in routinely granting the woman the right to divorce, and this custom must be seen in the context of Egypt in the Persian period.

Whether the practice at Elephantine has any significance for the province of Judah in the second temple period has been much disputed.[79] The Bible never excludes the possibility of divorce by the wife, but neither does it ever envisage it, and so most commentators have assumed that no such right existed. Mishnaic law is unambiguous: "A woman is divorced irrespective of her will; a man divorces of his own accord" (m. Yebam. 14:1). The Mishnah also recognizes that a woman may have a right to a divorce under certain circumstances, and that she can appeal to the courts to require her husband to grant her a divorce.[80] She does not, however, have the power to divorce her husband directly.

Yet there is some evidence that Jewish women did, on occasion, divorce their husbands, and not merely ask them for a divorce. Josephus mentions two instances of divorce initiated by women in the Herodian household—once by Salome, Herod's sister (Ant. 15.7.10 §259), and once by Herodias, Agrippa's daughter (Ant. 18.5.4 §136)—but he says that these divorces were "not in accordance with Jewish law." The conduct of the Herodian nobility is not a reliable guide to Jewish custom. Josephus himself was twice divorced. He married his first wife under Roman custody at the end of the war, but he writes that she "left me" (apēllagē) when they were released and he followed Vespasian to Rome (Vit. 414–15). It would appear that this divorce was at the wife's choice, but the account is too elliptic to warrant any conclusions about the process.[81] Josephus took the initiative in the divorce of his second wife, "being displeased at her behavior" (Vit. 426). References to divorce by the wife in the New Testament (Mark 10:11–12; 1 Cor. 7:10–11) are usually taken to reflect a Gentile context.[82]

More controversial evidence for Jewish practice is now available from Naḥal Ḥever. The main document in question is p Ṣe'elim 13. A woman named Shelamzion acknowledges the receipt of seven items from Eleazar, "who was formerly her husband and who received a bill of divorce from her" (the passage is apparently addressed to Eleazar).[83] The document is dated to "the third year of the freedom of Israel under the command of Simon bar Kosiba, the prince of Israel," so its Jewish character is not in doubt. The Aramaic can also be translated as "who received a bill of divorce from him"; in this case we have to posit a very abrupt change of addressee: "You, male, who were formerly her husband, and you, female, who received a writ of divorce from him."[84]

While there are abrupt changes from second to third person in the document, this reading is undeniably awkward. The interpretation of the passage remains in dispute.

A second disputed passage occurs in the Greek marriage contract of Shelamzion stepdaughter of Babatha to Judah Cimber. This contract provides that he "shall redeem this contract for his wife Shelamzion whenever she may demand it of him, in silver secured in due form, at his own expense interposing no objection." The most obvious situation in which a wife might demand the redemption of her *ketubah* is the case of divorce. This provision can be reconciled with Mishnaic law, insofar as the wife asks the husband for a divorce rather than simply divorces him, but it does not restrict her right to ask for a divorce to any special circumstances.

The law later formulated in the Mishnah, which gave only husbands the right to divorce, was known in the period between the Jewish revolts of 66–70 and 132–135 C.E., as can be seen from Josephus. Whether it was normative among all Jews at this time is uncertain. The Aramaic papyrus we have cited may be read as implying the wife's right to divorce, but it constitutes only slight and ambiguous evidence. If it is so read, we still have no way of knowing how widely the wife's right to divorce was recognized.[85] The instance documented in the papyrus may have been exceptional, but we must also reckon with the possibility that what Josephus calls Jewish law was only the position of the Pharisees, and that some other strands of Judaism had a different tradition.[86]

Polygamy

We have noted that some of the marriage contracts from Elephantine specifically guard against bigamy on the part of the husband. Polygamous marriages were permitted in the Bible, with several illustrious precedents, from Abraham to Solomon. They remained legal in the second temple period.[87] Josephus, in his account of the marriages of Herod and his relatives, adds, "For it is our ancestral custom that a man have several wives at the same time" (*Ant.* 17.14; *BJ* 1.477). Justin Martyr raises the practice as a charge against the Jews in his *Dialogue with Trypho* 141. The Mishnah allowed a man to have as many as five wives if he could afford it (*m. Ketub.* 10:5; *m. Ker.* 3:7) and permitted eighteen for kings (*m. Sanh.* 2:4). Polygamous marriages are attested among people in high places, such as the sons of Herod. Polygamy was finally

declared illegal among Jews by the emperor Theodosius I in 393 C.E.
Despite the legal situation, however, it is generally assumed that monogamy was the norm throughout the second temple period.[88]

This assumption has now been put in doubt by the Babatha archive
from Nahal Hever. Babatha was married twice. Her first marriage ended
with the death of her husband. Her second husband died in 130 C.E.,
and Babatha became the owner of several palm groves that belonged to
him. She became involved in litigation, however, with her late husband's family about some of the property. One summons related to this
case is especially interesting: "In the presence of witnesses . . . Babatha
daughter of Shimeon of Maoza summoned Miriam daughter of Beianos
of En-gedi to go forth together with her to Haterius Nepos the governor
wherever he may be present; since you [Miriam] plundered everything
in the house of Yehudah son of Eleazar Khthusion *my and your husband.*
. . ." Miriam replied, "I warned you not to approach the property of my
husband . . . you have no claim against the said Yehudah my husband
regarding the property." If Miriam had been divorced, Babatha would
most certainly have pointed this out and not referred to "my and your
husband." We have here, then, clear evidence of bigamy, in a fairly remote rural area, among people of moderate means.[89]

While Babatha was not a poor woman, she was still illiterate, and her
social standing was far removed from that of the Herods and their ilk.
Babatha remains a single instance and does not warrant any generalization about the extent of polygamy in second temple Judaism, but the
practice was evidently not so restricted as had been supposed. The
bigamy of her second husband, Yehudah, entailed some economic advantage. Babatha had her own property and on one occasion lent her
new husband three hundred denarii. After his death, however, we find
the rival wives involved in litigation. There can be no doubt that
polygamy always entailed the risk of marital discord.

A Prophetic Critique

The marriage contracts from Elephantine and Nahal Hever provide
an important background to the developing debates on divorce and
monogamy in second temple Judaism. Divorce figures prominently in
two texts from the Persian period. In Ezra 9–10, Ezra obliges Jews who
had married foreign women to divorce them and send them away with
their children. Ezra seems to have gone beyond Deuteronomic law in
this action,[90] but the incident is exceptional and is not indicative of nor-

mal attitudes toward divorce, except insofar as it assumes that divorce is permissible. The second text, Malachi 2:10–16, has been more influential in shaping attitudes toward divorce, especially in Christian circles. The passage in Malachi is translated as follows in the NRSV:

> Have we not all one father? Has not one God created us? Why then are we faithless to one another, profaning the covenant of our ancestors? Judah has been faithless, and abomination has been committed in Israel and in Jerusalem; for Judah has profaned the sanctuary of the LORD, which he loves, and has married the daughter of a foreign god. May the LORD cut off from the tents of Jacob anyone who does this—any to witness or answer, or to bring an offering to the LORD of hosts.
>
> And this you do as well: You cover the LORD's altar with tears, with weeping and groaning because he no longer regards the offering or accepts it with favor at your hand. You ask, "Why does he not?" Because the LORD was a witness between you and the wife of your youth, to whom you have been faithless, though she is your companion and your wife by covenant. Did not one God make her? [Or: Has he not made one?] Both flesh and spirit are his.[91] And what does the one God[92] desire? Godly offspring. So look to yourselves, and do not let anyone be faithless to the wife of his youth. For I hate divorce, says the LORD, the God of Israel, and covering one's garment with violence, says the LORD of hosts. So take heed to yourselves and do not be faithless.

This passage bristles with problems, many of them textual, and we cannot attempt a full exegesis here.[93] While the NRSV translation is distinctive in some respects, it is typical in its implication that Yahweh hates divorce and condemns it utterly. Malachi, so understood, is in sharp contrast not only to practice at Elephantine but also to Ezra and Deuteronomy and to much of later Jewish tradition.

The passage addresses two related but distinct transgressions (cf. v. 13: "this you do as well" [or: secondly]). In the first instance, Judah is said to have married the daughter of a foreign god. Scholarship is sharply divided on the nature of this offense. One school of thought takes the daughter of a foreign god to mean a goddess.[94] This interpretation is not required by the expression "daughter of a foreign god,"[95] but the phrase does carry implications of syncretism and idolatry. The more usual view is that the passage refers to marriage with foreign women, a phenomenon well known in the Persian period.[96] Those who married foreign women were likely to give some acknowledgment to their wives' cults and gods.[97] Yet the Jews who were guilty of this had not abandoned the cult of Yahweh; otherwise they would not be concerned at the loss of one to bring an offering to the Lord of hosts. The offense is syncretism rather than outright apostasy.

The second half of the passage (Mal. 2:13–16) deals more directly with problems of marriage and divorce. Here we are told that God refuses to accept the offerings of the Judaeans "because the LORD was a witness between you and the wife of your youth, to whom you have been faithless, though she is your companion and your wife by covenant." Some scholars have denied that there is any reference to human marriage here. F. F. Hvidberg argues that "Yahweh is himself very nearly 'the wife of youth,' with whom Judah had a covenant."[98] A. Isaksson is bolder and says that "it is really Yahweh himself who is given these designations."[99] B. Glazier-McDonald argues that "the wife of your youth" and "the wife of your covenant" refer to both a divorced human wife and Yahweh.[100]

Even if we accept the possibility that Malachi could reverse the usual gender roles by casting Yahweh as wife, this line of interpretation would seem to be precluded by the statement that Yahweh is witness "between you and the wife of your youth" (Mal. 2:14).[101] There can be little doubt that the reference is to the breakup of actual marriages. Indeed, even if the passage were meant to refer metaphorically to the cult of Yahweh, the metaphorical statement must still be intelligible on the primary, literal level. Hosea's metaphor of marriage between God and Israel was conventional in its view of the adulterous wife. At the very least, Malachi is breaking with convention in denouncing the unfaithful husband. In contrast, in Proverbs 2:17 it is the "strange woman" (Hebrew; NRSV, "loose woman") who "forsakes the partner of her youth and forgets her sacred covenant."

In view of the reference to the daughter of a foreign god in the preceding passage, it is commonly argued that the prophet was condemning his contemporaries for divorcing their Jewish wives in order to marry foreign women.[102] There is no actual evidence, however, that this was the case. If it were, we might expect the prophet to mention it first, before the daughter of the foreign god, since such divorces would have paved the way for the idolatrous marriage. It is more likely, however, that the problem of divorce is linked to the idolatrous marriage only as another instance of faithless behavior.[103] It is noteworthy that the prophet does not call for the divorce of the daughter of a foreign god or give explicit sanction to divorce in any context.

The explicit mention of divorce in Malachi 2:16 is beset with textual difficulties, and the verse is possibly corrupt. The phrase usually rendered "for I hate divorce" reads *kî śānē' śallah* in the Masoretic text. The grammatical forms of *śānē'* and *śallah* are problematic. The verb *śallah*, "send," is usually taken as an infinitive, with the force of an abstract noun. The traditional interpretation appears to take *śānē'* as a verbal adjective used as a participle, with an implied first-person pronoun; so, "I hate."[104] But there is no first-person pronoun in the context. D. L. Petersen avoids this problem by translating "divorce is hateful."[105] Alternatively, the word *śānē'* can be construed as a third-person perfect, "he hated/hates," with an indefinite subject.[106] By minor emendation, *śallah* can be repointed as a piel perfect, "he sent away" (*śillah*). The problems of this phrase are already reflected in the ancient versions. Some Greek manuscripts read, "But if you hate and send away . . . ," others, "But if you hate, send away!" (taking *śallah*, quite grammatically, as an imperative). The *Scroll of the Minor Prophets* from Qumran supports the latter Greek reading,[107] thereby permitting, or even urging, divorce. In fact, this interpretation has broad support in the ancient versions (Vulgate, Targum) and in traditional Jewish interpretation (Talmud, Rashi, Kimchi, Maimonides).[108] Nonetheless, it is difficult to reconcile with the remainder of the verse, which refers to covering one's garment with violence and ends with a warning against faithlessness.[109] Malachi clearly intended to condemn divorce. The ancient Hebrew text in the *Scroll of the Minor Prophets* must be read as a correction of the text preserved by the Masoretes, attempting to clarify its sense and reconcile it with Jewish tradition.

We have seen already that the verb *śānē'*, "to hate," is commonly used in contexts of divorce and indeed is often taken as a synonym for divorce in the Elephantine papyri. In light of this observation, the NRSV translation "I hate divorce" is almost certainly wrong. Rather, we should translate, with Westbrook, "For he has hated, divorced . . . and covered his garment in injustice."[110] The subject is indefinite. The force of the statement is that one who "hates and divorces" is openly unjust. This statement clarifies the "faithless" action against the wife of youth in Malachi 2:14.

In accordance with his theory that the verb *to hate* indicates divorce for purely subjective reasons, Westbrook argues that the passage in Malachi refers to divorce *without justification:* "The criticism is not of divorce as such, but divorce for 'hate,' where the husband follows his own inclination and the wife has done nothing to deserve such a fate."[111]

Hugenberger follows this interpretation and argues that Malachi is condemning not divorce in general but only "divorce because of aversion,"
where the divorce is not warranted by any transgression on the part of
the wife.[112] We have seen, however, that Westbrook's attempt to restrict
the verb "to hate" to "divorce because of aversion" is unsuccessful. "To
hate" in this context is simply a technical term for divorce, for whatever
reason. The expression in Malachi, then, should be translated "for one
repudiates, divorces . . . and covers his garment with violence." Malachi
states no exceptions and makes no distinction between divorce that is
justified and that which is not.

It is possible, of course, that Malachi assumed distinctions that he did
not make explicit. Prophets are not lawyers and are not wont to make
fine distinctions. (Amos's sweeping dismissal of the sacrificial cult
comes to mind as an analogy.) Perhaps all we can safely infer from
Malachi's enigmatic text is that he viewed the practice of divorce in his
day as excessive and unjust. The concern of the prophet, however, is
very different from that of the law codes and marriage contracts. He is
not attempting to balance rights and obligations in a realistic and pragmatic way but to articulate an ideal and denounce its betrayal.

It is also possible that the statement "he repudiates, divorces . . ." is
a secondary addition to the text of Malachi.[113] This might explain the
awkwardness of the sudden use of the third person. If this is so, Malachi
may have been condemning the marital infidelity of husbands (a striking position in itself) rather than divorce. In this case, however, we
would have to say that the glossator was more daringly original than the
prophet, and this would be very unusual. It may be that the redactor
was only making more explicit the abuses the prophet had in mind.

Malachi's understanding of marriage is obscured by the state of the
text of 2:15, which ranks as one of the most difficult verses in the Hebrew Bible. The Hebrew literally reads, "And not one did, and had a
remnant of spirit."[114] The NRSV takes the "one" as a reference to God:
"Did not one God make her?" The more usual interpretation, however,
takes "one" as the object: "Did he (God) not make one?"[115] On this interpretation, there is an implied reference to Genesis 2:24, which says
that man and wife become "one flesh." If this reading of the passage is
accepted, then šě'ār, "remnant," should most probably be repointed as
šě'ēr, "flesh": "Has he not made one, which has flesh and spirit?"[116] The
text is too uncertain to warrant a confident conclusion, but many commentators see an allusion to Genesis here. The remainder of the verse,
"And what does one seek? Godly offspring," can also be seen against a

background in Genesis.[117] In Genesis 1:28 the only injunction laid on the primal couple is to "be fruitful and multiply, and fill the earth," and this verse looms very large in the later Jewish understanding of marriage. On this interpretation, Malachi sees the goal of marriage in procreation. Extramarital relations are not constructive toward this goal. (Cf. Prov. 5:16: "Should your springs be scattered abroad, streams of water in the streets?") Divorce is counterproductive.[118]

Genesis and the Theological Understanding of Marriage

While the interpretation of Malachi 2:15 remains quite uncertain, there is no doubt that both the Priestly theology of Genesis 1 and the Yahwist theology of Genesis 2—3 were conducive to an ideal of monogamy. Both texts speak of one man and one woman. Neither envisages the dissolution of the union. Neither was a legal, prescriptive text, and they entailed no prohibition of divorce or polygamy. But in the postexilic period, these texts were prominently displayed at the beginning of the Torah, and we should expect that they would have had an effect on the formation of religious ideals, if not always on practice.

In fact, Genesis is used in various ways in second temple Judaism. The command to increase and multiply was taken very seriously in rabbinic Judaism. The rabbis even specified the number of children required to fulfill the commandment and warned that "if a man married a woman and lived with her ten years and she bore no child, it is not permitted for him to abstain."[119] This emphasis, however, is not found in the literature of the period between the Bible and the Mishnah. Ben Sira does not mention procreation as the purpose of marriage but says that "he who acquires a wife gets his best possession, a helper fit for him and a pillar of support" (Sir. 36:29–30; cf. Gen. 2:20). A similar emphasis is found in a wisdom text called 4QSapiential Work A from Qumran: "Walk together with the helpmeet of your flesh according to the statute engraved by God that man should leave his father and his mother . . . and that they should become one flesh."[120] This ideal falls some way short of the companionate marriage of modern times, but it acknowledges that companionship had a place in marriage, however patriarchal the society. (Contrast the view, found in the New Testament in 1 Tim. 2:15, that women are saved through childbearing.)

The patriarchal assumptions of Ben Sira are all too evident in his reading of the Adam and Eve story. He is the first to contend that "in a woman was sin's beginning, on account of her we all die" (Sir. 25:24). He follows this with the advice: "Allow water no outlet, and be not indulgent with an erring wife. If she walks not by your side, cut her away from your flesh with a bill of divorce" (25:25–26). These comments must be seen in the context of Ben Sira's general view of women and of family relationships, a subject to which we return below. For the present, suffice it to note that the influence of Genesis did not always lead to a rejection of divorce or to an appreciation of equality in marriage.

Adam and Eve are invoked more positively as a paradigm of marriage in Tobit 8:5–7, in the prayer of Tobias on his wedding night:

> Blessed are you, O God of our ancestors. . . .
> You made Adam, and for him you made his wife Eve
>   as a helper and support.
> From the two of them the human race has sprung.
> You said, "It is not good that the man should be alone;
>   let us make a helper for him like himself."
> I now am taking this kinswoman of mine,
>   not because of lust,
>   but with sincerity.
> Grant that she and I may find mercy
>   and that we may grow old together.

The prayer is noteworthy for its disavowal of lust on the wedding night and the emphasis on enduring companionship. Sarah, wife of Tobias, had already had seven husbands, all of whom were killed by a demon on their wedding night. The text preserved in the Vulgate at 6:17 draws the inference: "The fiend has power over such as go about their marrying with all thought of God shut out of their hearts and minds, wholly intent on their lust"; and it adds that Tobias and Sarah observed a three-day abstinence, to show their control of their desires.[121] The Latin text is undoubtedly at some distance from the original Aramaic of Tobit, but the specific disavowal of lust is already moving in this direction and has no basis in the text of Genesis.

Purity and Asceticism

The sexual relations of Adam and Eve were a matter of some controversy in antiquity. Rabbinic materials generally assume that the initial sexual union took place in the Garden of Eden. Christian sources tend to place it after the Fall and expulsion.[122] But there are also some di-

vergent Jewish traditions on the subject, preserved in the Pseud-
epigrapha.[123] *Second Baruch* 56:6, written at the end of the first century
C.E., lists the conception of children and the passion of parents among
the consequences of Adam's transgression. We may suspect Christian
influence on this work, which is preserved not in its original language
but in Syriac translation. A more typically Jewish scruple is found in the
book of *Jubilees* 3, which dates from the second century B.C.E. There we
read that Adam "knew" his wife as soon as she was brought to him (v.
6), but Eve had to wait eighty days before she was brought into the garden, "for it is holier than any place on earth" (v. 12).[124] It appears, then,
that Adam and Eve do not have sex in the garden, according to *Jubilees,*
for reasons of purity. This kind of restriction on sexual activity is also
typical of the mind-set of the sect whose writings are preserved in the
Dead Sea Scrolls.[125]

The first explicit prohibition of polygamy in Jewish tradition is found
in the scrolls, in a sectarian rule book. The *Damascus Document* (CD)
denounces the followers of a rival teacher because

> they shall be caught in fornication twice by taking two wives in
> their lifetime, whereas the principle of creation is, male and female
> he created them. Also those who entered the Ark went in two by
> two. And concerning the prince it is written, He shall not multiply
> wives to himself; but David had not read the sealed book of the
> Law which was in the ark. (CD 4:20–5:2; author's translation)

The precise interpretation of this passage has been much disputed. Various scholars have taken it to forbid not only polygamy but also divorce
and remarriage.[126] The logic of the biblical verses cited would seem to
be directed against polygamy rather than against remarriage,[127] but the
expression "in their lifetime" would also seem to exclude divorce, or at
least remarriage while the first wife was alive.[128]

A related passage in the *Temple Scroll* clearly allows remarriage after
the death of the first wife in the case of the king. There the Deuteronomic restriction on the king against taking many wives is elaborated:
"He shall take for himself a wife from his father's house, from his father's
clan. And he may not take any other woman in addition to her, but she
alone shall be with him all the days of his life. And if she dies, he shall
take for himself another from his father's house, from his clan" (11
QTemple 57:16–19).[129] While this passage allows the king to remarry
after the death of his wife, it does not permit divorce: "she alone shall
be with him all the days of his life."[130] Yet the existence of divorced

women is acknowledged in 11QTemple 54:4. J. Baumgarten concludes that "the king as a role model for moral behavior was subject to supererogatory restrictions limiting him to one wife during her lifetime; divorcing her would not free him as it would a commoner to marry another."[131] In the *Damascus Document,* at least the ban on polygamy is extended to all the people.[132] While CD is not explicit on the question of divorce, the practice is probably excluded by the principle that men may not take two wives in their lifetime.[133] The strand of Judaism represented by these documents, then, broke clearly with prevalent Jewish tradition in holding that polygamy and divorce were forbidden by implication in several passages of the Torah.

This innovation is in accordance with the strict interpretation of marital law that is characteristic of these documents. Whereas Leviticus 18 prohibited union between uncle and niece, CD extends the prohibition to nephews and aunts (CD 5), since "although the laws against incest are written for men, they also apply to women." The same prohibition is found in the incest laws in column 66 of the *Temple Scroll.* The so-called messianic rule prescribes that a man "shall not [approach] a woman to know her by lying with her before he is fully twenty years old, when he shall know [good] and evil" (1QSa 1:10–11). In contrast, rabbinic tradition regarded twenty as the *terminus ante quem* for marriage.[134] The *Damascus Document* and the *Temple Scroll* also share a prohibition against sexual relations within "the city of the sanctuary."[135] The laws of CD include a provision that apparently forbids intercourse during pregnancy.[136] Most intriguing is a fragment of the *Damascus Document* (D^e, 4Q270) that prescribes a penalty for the man who "approaches to fornicate [zĕnût] with his wife in violation of the law." Such a person must "depart and return no more." The nature of the offense is unclear. It may refer to relations during menses, which are specifically denounced in CD 5:6–7. Alternatively, Baumgarten suggests that the code presupposes a rule of abstinence, of whatever duration, for married members of the sect.[137]

Celibacy and
the Dead Sea Sect

It is generally assumed, with good reason, that the Dead Sea Scrolls were the library of an Essene community.[138] The accounts of the Essenes preserved by Josephus, Philo, and Pliny all emphasize that they lived a celibate life. Josephus (*BJ* 2.8.2 §§120–21) says that they turn aside from pleasures as an evil, and regard self-control and not succumbing to the passions as a virtue. Marriage they regard with contempt, but in adopting other persons' children who are still pliable for learning, they consider them as their own kin and mold them according to their customs. They do not reject marriage and the propagation that comes from it, but they guard themselves against the licentious allurements of women and are persuaded that not one of them keeps her pledge to one man.[139]

He grants, however, that

there is another order of Essenes, who have the same views as the rest in their way of life, customs, and laws, but are at variance in their opinion of marriage. For they think that those who do not marry cut off the most important part of life, namely genealogical succession; and further, if all were to hold the same opinion, the whole race would die out very quickly. They put their wives to the test, however, for a three-year period, and marry those who, having three periods of purification, give proof that they are able to bear children. They do not have intercourse with them during pregnancy, demonstrating that they marry not for self-gratification but for the necessity of children. (BJ 2.8.13 §§160–61)

Philo says flatly that "no Essene takes a wife" (Hypothetica 11.14) and explains the custom in terms of "shrewdly providing against the sole or principal obstacle threatening to dissolve the bonds of communal life." Pliny claims that the Essenes near the Dead Sea lived "without women" and marvels that "for thousands of centuries a race has existed which is eternal, yet into which no one was born" (NH 5.17.4 §73).

None of these can be accepted as a firsthand account of the Essenes. All three authors were dependent on sources that described various Jewish groups for the benefit of Hellenistic readers, and the accounts bear the imprint of Greek philosophical debates.[140] Scholars have noted that the statements of Josephus are considerably more nuanced than those of Philo and Pliny. There is some tension, if not outright contradiction, between his statements that the Essenes regard marriage with contempt and that they do not reject marriage and the propagation that comes from it. H. Stegemann has argued that the notion of Essene celibacy originated in the source used by Josephus, Philo, and Pliny and that the author of this source was unfamiliar with the reality of Jewish life and erred in assimilating the Essenes to Greek models.[141] The impression that the Essenes were celibate could have arisen from the fact that women were excluded from many of their solemn gatherings. The account of the "second order" of Essenes preserved by Josephus might then be close to the reality of the entire sect. It is certainly easier to reconcile the second order with the Dead Sea Scrolls than to find evidence of outright celibacy in the Hebrew and Aramaic sources.

The issue of celibacy has become something of an embarrassment to those who identify the Dead Sea sect as Essenes.[142] The scrolls never require celibacy, and there are regulations for married life in the *Damascus Document* and the messianic rule of 1QSa. The presence of some female skeletons in the Qumran cemetery has not been satisfactorily explained, although it is often noted that the female skeletons hitherto excavated were not found in the main part of the cemetery.[143] There is no mention of women and children, however, in the *Community Rule* (1QS), the rule of the *yaḥad,* or "commune," that is most often identified as the Qumran community. Yet even there, we find that the blessings of those who walk in the way of light include fecundity (*pĕrût zera',* 1QS 4:6–8), and while this expression may be used in a figurative sense, it also admits of an interpretation in terms of procreation. The *Pesher on Psalm 37* (4Q171 3:1), speaks of "those who return to the wilderness, who will live for a thousand generations in safety; to them will belong all the inheritance of Adam and to their seed forever." It is reasonable to assume that those who return from the wilderness are the same as "those who observe the law, who are in the council of the *yaḥad*" in the same document (2:15). In the *Hôdāyôt* (*Thanksgiving Hymns*) 4:14 (formerly numbered 17:14–15), we also read of people who will "inherit all the glory of Adam and abundance of days." God will preserve them "that their seed may be before thee forever."

If the references to seed in these passages and in 1QS 4 are taken literally, they require a marrying community. It is possible, however, that the language is used figuratively and that the reference is to the later generations of the community, not to their genealogical descendants.[144] Moreover, many scholars object that the law-centered community could not have ignored the commandment in Genesis to increase and multiply.[145] An ideal of celibacy would seem to be alien to Judaism, at least Judaism as represented by the rabbinic corpus. The Mishnah declares emphatically that "no man may abstain from keeping the law *Be fruitful and multiply* unless he already has children" (*m. Yebam.* 6:6). The Talmud records the opinion of Rabbi Eliezer that "he who does not engage in propagation of the race is as though he sheds blood" (*b. Yebam.* 63b).

But if the Dead Sea Scrolls fail to provide direct corroboration for celibacy in a Jewish context, they provide abundant indications of a mind-set that was conducive to sexual abstinence. This mind-set was rooted in the Levitical concern for purity. According to Leviticus 15:18, sexual intercourse renders both man and woman impure; they are required to bathe and remain impure until the evening. Certain situations where purity was essential required temporary abstinence.[146] One such situation was the ritual preparation for a military campaign (cf. 1 Sam. 21:2–7). This situation may have some relevance to the Qumran covenanters, insofar as they were preparing for an eschatological war. The Qumran *War Scroll* (1QM 7:5–6) excludes women and children, as well as those impure for any reason, from the camp "from the time they leave Jerusalem and march out to war until they return." This restriction, however, has a very limited and specific application. There is no reason to think that the community believed itself to be in constant preparation for eschatological warfare. Purity was also required for certain forms of cultic participation. The Mishnah required the high priest to refrain from relations with his wife for a week before Yom Kippur (*m. Yoma* 1:1). There was a widespread Jewish tradition that Moses remained continent from the time the Lord spoke to him.[147] It is not difficult to imagine, then, how the association of sex with impurity might have given rise to an ideal of celibacy.

Elisha Qimron has recently defended the view that the Qumran community was celibate but that it differed in this regard from the rest of the Dead Sea sect.[148] We have already noted that the *Temple Scroll* and the *Damascus Document* forbade sexual relations in the city of the sanctuary (Jerusalem). The *yahad* described in the *Community Rule* was supposed to be "a house of holiness for Israel, an assembly of supreme holiness for Aaron . . . a most holy dwelling for Aaron" (1QS 8). Qimron argues that "the *yahad* was considered by the sectarians as a temporary substitute for Jerusalem. Its members maintained a high degree of purity similar to that which had been maintained in Jerusalem (or perhaps in the Temple). Therefore they kept themselves apart from women."[149] The regulations for married life in the *Damascus Document* do not relate to the *yahad* but to those who live in camps according to the order of the land, while the messianic rule is addressed to the whole congregation of Israel, which joins the *yahad* at the end of days.[150] Without explicit confirmation in the *Community Rule* this explanation remains tentative, but it is at least a plausible explanation of the celibacy of the Essenes.

There is, moreover, an important passage in the *Damascus Document* that indicates that not all members of the sect married. CD 6:11–7:20 specifies the requirement for those who enter the covenant to act according to the exact interpretation of the law. This includes refraining from fornication and avoidance of all uncleanness: "and no man shall defile his holy spirit since God has set them apart." These people, "who walk in these [precepts] in perfect holiness," are promised that "the covenant of God shall be an assurance that they shall live for thousands of generations." This group is then contrasted with others who "live in camps according to the rule of the land, marrying and begetting children." The implication would seem to be that those who walk in perfect holiness do not marry; hence their need for reassurance that they would live for thousands of generations.[151]

The evidence on celibacy at Qumran is not conclusive. What has emerged from the discussion, however, is that there was a strand of Jewish tradition, prominently represented at Qumran, that viewed sexual activity negatively, as a source of impurity, and that required abstinence on certain occasions. It is quite possible, though not certain, that the *yahad* described in the *Community Rule* was celibate. Philo and Josephus tried to explain the celibacy of the Essenes in Hellenistic terms and emphasized the exceptional rather than the typical in their accounts of the Essene lifestyle. Nonetheless, it is unlikely that the notion of a celibate Jewish community was invented out of whole cloth. It should be noted, however, the scrolls provide no theoretical discussion of the relative merits of marriage and celibacy, such as we find in Hellenistic philosophy.[152] The concern of the sectarians was with purity; sexual activity became problematic only when it interfered with that concern.

Celibacy is not necessarily incompatible with the presence of women. Philo says that the major celebration of the Therapeutae was "shared by women also, most of them aged virgins, who have kept their chastity not under compulsion, like some of the Greek priestesses, but of their own free will in their ardent yearning for wisdom" (*De Vita Contemplativa* 68).[153] The young men who served the meal behaved "like sons to their real fathers and mothers" (72). Then they observed a vigil, at first with the men and women forming two choirs, then mingling together in a single choir (85). Baumgarten has suggested that the fragmentary 4Q502 could be related to a similar celebration.[154] This text describes a ritual and regularly pairs male and female, a man and his wife, mature men and women, old men and women. He also notes that virgins who have no protector are listed among those in need of communal support in CD 14:14–16. It is also possible that couples joined the community late in life and lived chastely thereafter.

Both Philo and Josephus find an element of misogyny in the Essene rejection of marriage. Some scholars found the misogyny of the sect confirmed in 4Q184, the document dubbed by J. M. Allegro "The Wiles of the Wicked Woman."[155] Allegro's interpretation has been widely rejected as far-fetched, but the text does portray a female in negative terms, in the tradition of the "strange" or "loose" woman of Proverbs 7: "she is the start of all the ways of wickedness" (4Q184 8) and "her gates are the gates of death" (v. 10). While this text does nothing to promote a positive view of women, it must be seen in perspective. Another composition preserved at Qumran (11QPs^a xxi 11–xxii 1 = Sirach 51) contains a rhapsodic description of the psalmist's search for Lady Wisdom, in erotic terms.[156] Neither of these works is likely to have originated at Qumran.[157]

There is now evidence, moreover, that women enjoyed some rank in the community. Baumgarten cites a passage from 4Q270 (D^e) that refers to the "Mothers" in parallelism to the "Fathers": "One who [mur]murs against the Fathers shall be [sent forth] from the congregation and shall not return. If [he murmurs] against the Mothers he is to be penalized for ten days, for the Mothers do not have authority [?] within the [congregation]."[158] The word translated "authority" (rûqmâ) is elsewhere known only in the sense of ornament, and the translation here is conjectural. It is clear that murmuring against the Mothers was a less serious offense than murmuring against the Fathers, but nonetheless, Mothers were still honored. The analogy with Philo's Therapeutae is appropriate. There is ample evidence in the scrolls to support Josephus's statement in *Bellum Judaicum* that "they guard themselves against the licentious allurements of women." There is no evidence, however, of a systematic distrust of women or that the sectarians were persuaded that not one woman has kept her pledge to one man.

Sex and Procreation

The Dead Sea sect was extreme in its concern for purity and its restriction of sexual activity, but Judaism was distinguished in the ancient world for the strictness of its sexual morality. Josephus declares emphatically that "the Law recognizes no sexual connexions, except the natural union of man and wife, and that only for the procreation of children" (*Ap.* 2.199). We have already seen the emphasis on procreation as the goal of marriage in the prophet Malachi. In the Hellenistic age, this emphasis was reinforced by Stoic philosophy and so had some support in Greek culture.[159] Homosexuality was considered an abomination (Lev. 18:22), in glaring contrast to the sexual ethos of the Greeks.[160] Nudity was abhorred, and the Jews had no counterpart to the public art that suffused the Hellenistic world with sexual imagery.[161] True to Leviticus, Josephus also notes that "even after the legitimate relations of husband and wife ablutions are required." The Song of Songs (Song of Solomon) stands alone in ancient Jewish literature as a rhapsodic affirmation of sexual love.

There is no consensus on the date of the Song of Songs. Opinions range from the time of Solomon to the Hellenistic era.[162] At the very least the work must have been redacted in the second temple period, since it contains numerous Aramaisms and one indisputable Persian loanword, *pardēs* (S. of Sol. 4:13). Recently, Ariel Bloch and Chana Bloch have argued for a Hellenistic date.[163] They point to parallels with the pastoral idylls of Theocritus, who was court poet to Ptolemy Philadelphus in Alexandria in the first half of the third century B.C.E. They write, "The Song is informed by an entirely new sensibility, unique in the Bible,"[164] and the Blochs suggest that the ubiquity of nudity in Greek art may have contributed to this sensibility. The Song also has many parallels, however, with ancient Egyptian love poetry, so its sensibility cannot be entirely ascribed to Hellenistic influence.[165] It may be that the Song was a traditional piece that underwent revision at various times down to the Hellenistic period.

There can be no doubt that the poem is a celebration of sexual love (*dōdîm*) between people who are not married. The woman, called the Shulamite, is not shy about pursuing her lover. She goes out into the city streets at night to search for him (3:1–4; 5:6–7) and refuses to let him go (3:4). Her conduct meets with disapproval: The city watchmen beat her when they find her (5:7). Her brothers are concerned to protect her: "if she is a door, we will enclose her with boards of cedar" (8:9). But the watchmen have no voice in the Song, and the brothers have only a minor one. The major voice is that of a young woman sick with love (5:8), for whom love is as strong as death (8:6).

The fact that the Song was accepted as scripture was probably dependent on an allegorical interpretation, which took the lovers as God and Israel. We learn from the Talmud, however, that some people sang it in banquet halls as a secular air, although the rabbis deemed that such people brought evil on the world.[166] Unfortunately, we know practically nothing about the people who sang in banquet halls or their sexual morality. They were evidently very different from the people who compiled the Bible. With the exception of the Song, the literature that has come down to us is stamped heavily with the view of the sages. It is predominantly androcentric, and it sets strict boundaries for sexual behavior.

This literature is not entirely puritanical. Sex within marriage is affirmed with enthusiasm in Proverbs 5:18–19. ("Rejoice in the wife of your youth, a lovely deer, a graceful doe. May her breasts satisfy you at all times, may you be intoxicated always by her love.") Even that least romantic of authors, Ben Sira, appreciates "the beauty of a good wife in her well-ordered home. Like the lamp burning on the holy lampstand, so is the beauty of a face on a stately figure. As golden pillars on a silver base, so are beautiful legs on firm heels" (Sir. 26:17–18). Very often, however, beauty is perceived as ambivalent in the literature. Proverbs concludes that "charm is deceitful, and beauty is vain, but a woman who fears the LORD is to be praised" (Prov. 31:30). Ben Sira warns that "many have been seduced by a woman's beauty" (Sir. 9:8). One of the more notable descriptions of female beauty in Jewish literature of this period occurs in the *Genesis Apocryphon* from Qumran, apropos of Sarah.[167] It is placed on the lips of Egyptian elders who commend her to Pharaoh, with dangerous implications. Some of the literature urges restraint even within marriage. Philo's statement that "the end we seek in wedlock is not pleasure but the begetting of lawful children" (*De Iosepho* 43) may be attributed to the influence of Stoic philosophy, but even such a traditional Jew as Tobias insists on his wedding night that he is not taking his bride "because of lust" (Tobit 8:7).[168]

The *Sayings of Pseudo-Phocylides*, a Jewish Hellenistic text most probably composed in Egypt around the turn of the era, is representative of much of second temple Judaism on the subject of sex in marriage:

> Remain not unmarried, lest you die nameless.
> Give nature her due, beget in turn as you were begotten. . . .
> Outrage not your wife for shameful ways of intercourse.
> Transgress not for unlawful sex the natural limits of sexuality . . .
> And let not women imitate the sexual role of men.
> Do not deliver yourself wholly unto unbridled sensuality towards your wife.
> For "Eros" is not a god, but a passion destructive to all.[169]

The Adulteress

Much of the discussion of sexuality in second temple Judaism focuses on the figures of the adulteress and the harlot. The sages assumed the availability, and the attraction, of prostitutes. Intercourse with prostitutes entailed no legal penalty for the male, but the sages were at pains to warn of the dangers of the practice. (E.g., Sir. 9:6: "Do not give yourself to prostitutes or you may lose your inheritance.")[170] Adultery was generally perceived as a more serious threat to the fabric of society. Proverbs 6:34 warns about the practical consequences for the adulterer: "For jealousy arouses a husband's fury, and he shows no restraint when he takes revenge." Sirach warns that while an adulterer may escape human detection, "the eyes of the Lord are ten thousand times brighter than the sun" and the sinner will be seized "where he least suspects it" (Sir. 23:16–21). But Proverbs also endows the figure of the loose or strange woman with near mythical proportions: "Her house is the way to Sheol, going down to the chambers of death" (Prov. 7:27; cf. "The Wiles of the Wicked Woman" from Qumran, 4Q184). Much has been written in recent years on the symbolism of this strange woman as a projection of the female as other from the viewpoint of the father-son relationship.[171] In fairness, it is not the feminine as such that is projected as other but the prostitute and the adulteress. The positive figure of Wisdom is also typically portrayed in feminine imagery, as wife and mother. Both figures, admittedly, are viewed entirely from an androcentric point of view in the wisdom literature.

There have been attempts in recent years to demythologize the figure of the adulterous wife and explain her conduct in pragmatic economic terms. In Proverbs 7, the strange woman begins her seduction of the youth by saying, "I had to offer sacrifices, and today I have paid my vows" (7:14, NRSV), or better, "I have to offer sacrifices and today I am to fulfill my vows," taking the verbs in a modal sense.[172] The connection between vows and adultery has intrigued scholars. G. Boström has argued that the vow was "aphroditic," that the woman had pledged to give herself to a stranger as an act of devotion to a goddess.[173] We are reminded of Herodotus's story of the "foul custom" of the Babylonians whereby "every native-born woman must once in her life sit in the temple of Aphrodite and have intercourse with some stranger" (Herodotus 1.199). But such theories are now widely discredited and attributed to the credulity of a Herodotus or to religious polemic (in the case of the Hebrew prophets).[174]

Recently, Karel van der Toorn has offered a different proposal. The propensity of women to make vows throughout the ancient Near East is well attested (cf. Hannah's vow in connection with her prayer for a son in 1 Sam. 1:11). Numbers 30 specifically legislates that fathers and husbands had the authority to nullify the vows of their wives and daughters within a limited period, probably because they were affected by the expense of the vow. The woman in Proverbs 7 goes on to say that her husband has gone on a journey and taken a bag of money (vv. 19–20). Van der Toorn suggests that the wife has to resort to temporary prostitution to pay for her vow, or at least is using an alleged dilemma over the payment of vows as a pretext for the seduction.[175] Deuteronomy 23:18–19 specifically forbids the use of a harlot's hire for the payment of a vow, but the existence of the prohibition shows that the practice was not unknown.

Van der Toorn's theory offers an ingenious explanation of the reference to vows in Proverbs 7, but it remains hypothetical. The text does not say that the woman has any problem about paying for her vows. It may be that she simply wants to have a party in connection with her sacrifices, in her husband's absence. Sexual excess is often associated with religious celebration outside of the actual ritual, from the story of the golden calf in Exodus to the woman taken in adultery at the Festival of Tabernacles in John 8.[176] Financial need was at most incidental to the phenomenon of adultery.

Ben Sira is more prosaic in his condemnation of the adulteress: "First, she disobeyed the law of the Most High, second she committed an offense against her husband, and third, she committed adultery through fornication and produced children by a strange man" (Sir. 23:22–26).[177] Here again, modern scholars have attempted to discover extenuating circumstances. Warren Trenchard concludes that "the woman's primary motivation for her act or acts was the desire to have children of her own. The prospect of an heir was probably her rationalization, since an heir would be an asset to her husband."[178] Claudia Camp envisages a more elaborate scenario, "namely that the wives of poor men engage in sexual activity with wealthy patrons in order to help support their families. The issue here would not be the desire of childless women for heirs but the shameful necessity for a man . . . to accept as legitimate the fruit of his wife's labor for another."[179] I know of no evidence for this scenario in ancient Judaism. It certainly cannot be inferred from Ben Sira's comments. A married woman who had an affair and became pregnant had little alternative but to try to pass off the child as the fruit of her marriage and heir of her husband. The danger of such an eventuality is one of the basic reasons for laws against adultery in the first place.

The circumstances that led to adultery in ancient Judaism were presumably as varied as they have been elsewhere in human history. To judge by the anxiety of the sages, the problem was not uncommon, but there is no way to calculate its frequency. It must suffice to say that the austerity of the laws and sapiential teachings does not necessarily give an accurate picture of the role of sexuality in Jewish society in this period. It should be emphasized, however, that the sages do not envisage the death penalty for adultery, despite Deuteronomic law and despite the use of the death penalty for dramatic effect in the apocryphal story of Susanna.[180]

Parents and Children

Respect for Life

Josephus declares categorically that "the law orders that all offspring be brought up" (*Ap.* 2.202). Hellenistic Jewish writers regularly condemn the Greek and Roman practice of exposing unwanted infants. This practice is not explicitly addressed in the Torah. Both Josephus and Philo base their condemnation on Exodus 21:22–23, which deals with assault on a pregnant woman.[181] The Roman historian Tacitus notes the Jewish position on this issue, which was exceptional in the Roman world (*Hist.* 5.3). Abortion was similarly forbidden in this period.[182] Pseudo-Phocylides expresses the prohibition forcefully: "A woman should not destroy the unborn babe in her belly, nor after its birth throw it before the dogs and the vultures of prey."[183]

Honor of Parents

The obligation of children to honor their father and their mother was already enshrined in the Decalogue and is repeated with emphasis in the wisdom books (e.g., Sir. 3:1–16). In Leviticus 19:3, this commandment follows immediately on the command to be holy, before the injunction to keep the Sabbath. It occupies a similarly prominent place in the moral instructions of Hellenistic Judaism. Pseudo-Phocylides 8 tells the reader to "honor God first and foremost, and thereafter your parents." Josephus, in his summary of the Jewish law in *Ap.* 2.206, likewise links honor of God and parents. The "unwritten laws" of Greek tradition also demand honor first for the gods and then for parents, and this injunction is ubiquitous in Greek gnomic poetry.[184] The priority of father over mother is implicit in most ancient literature. It is made explicit in the Talmud.[185]

Ben Sira follows the Decalogue in suggesting that honoring parents leads to well-being (cf. Ex. 20:12; Deut. 5:16). Children who honor their parents can expect to be honored by their own children in turn. Ben Sira does not rely entirely on the reciprocity of human behavior. He also claims that those who honor their parents atone for sins (Sir. 3:3, 14). There is a tendency in second temple Judaism to associate atonement with good works (cf. Dan. 4:24 [ET 4:27]). Sirach attributes potency to the blessing of a father but also to the curse of a mother (Sir. 3:9); the parallelism of the verse suggests that both blessing and curse are effective on the part of both parents.

Ben Sira accords equal honor to fathers and mothers, although he mentions the father more often. The same equality of honor is found in 4QSapiential Work A from Qumran. The Qumran work also promises length of days to those who honor their parents and exhorts children to honor parents "for the sake of their own honor."[186] Here again, the honor of the parent is linked to the self-interest of the child, since the child's honor, too, is at stake.

Sons and Daughters

Education was primarily the responsibility of the parents, especially of the father (cf. Prov. 4:1–9). The proverbial wisdom of Proverbs and Ben Sira is presumably representative of this instruction. Much of it consists of advice on practical matters, passed down from father to son. The lessons of biblical history might also be included (cf. 4 Macc. 18:10–19). Educational method seems to have relied heavily on corporal punishment: "He who loves his son will whip him often, so that he may rejoice at the way he turns out" (Sir. 30:1). Pseudo-Phocylides, writing in the Diaspora, takes a gentler approach: "Be not harsh with your children but be gentle" (v. 207). The earliest mention of a school (bêt midraš) is found in Sirach 51:23. While the "house of instruction" may be metaphorical in that passage, it is likely that sages such as Ben Sira offered instruction in their private schools. The Jerusalem Talmud attributes the institution of public schools to Simeon ben Shetach in the early first century B.C.E. The Babylonian Talmud attributes this innovation to Joshua ben Gamala in the first century C.E. just before the Jewish

War.[187] The education of girls consisted primarily in preparation for marriage.[188] Women had far less access to formal education than did men.[189]

There is abundant evidence that sons were valued more highly than daughters. Ben Sira stands at or near the negative extreme of his society's attitude toward women, but his pronouncement that "the birth of a daughter is a loss" (Sir. 22:3) cannot be dismissed as his personal eccentricity. Similar sentiments are found in the rabbinic literature: "Without both male and female children the world could not exist, but blessed is he whose children are male, and woe to him whose children are female" (*b. Baba Bathra* 16b).[190] While daughters are not always viewed so negatively, the preference for sons was commonplace in the ancient Near East. Compare *The Story of Ahikar* 1:4–5: "But I ask of thee, O God, that I may have a male child, so that when I shall die, he may cast dust on my eyes" (cf. Tobit 6:15).

Ben Sira perceived daughters as a source of anxiety:

> A daughter is a secret anxiety to her father,
>   and worry over her robs him of sleep;
> when she is young, for fear she may not marry,
>   or if married, for fear she may be repudiated;
> while a virgin, for fear she may be seduced
>   and become pregnant in her father's house;
> or having a husband, for fear she may go astray,
>   or, though married, for fear she may be barren.
> Keep strict watch over a headstrong daughter,
>   or she may make you a laughingstock to your enemies. . . .
> See that there is no lattice in her room,
>   no spot that overlooks the approaches to the house.
> Do not let her parade her beauty before any man
>   or spend her time among married women.
>   (Sir. 42:9–12, NRSV adapted)[191]

Ben Sira's anxiety is extreme and must be seen in the context of the general anxiety about life that pervades his book (cf. Sir. 40:1–2: "A heavy yoke is laid on the children of Adam. . . . Perplexities and fear of heart are theirs, and anxious thought of the day of their death"). Nonetheless, he reflects certain social and economic realities that prevailed throughout the second temple period. Fathers had to provide dowries for their daughters but no longer received any benefit from the *mohar* in this period. If there were no sons and a daughter should inherit, this resulted in the transference of the inheritance from the father's house to that of her husband. If the woman was divorced, the father had to take her in. The economic considerations, however, are minor in Ben Sira's view in comparison to the risk of shame. A headstrong daughter can make her father "a byword in the city and the assembly of the people, and put you to shame in public gatherings" (Sir. 42:11). Hence the preoccupation with virginity before marriage and the demand that daughters be carefully secluded.[192]

Concern for the virginity of unmarried girls is ubiquitous in the ancient world, but especially in Hellenistic Judaism. The draconian laws of the Pentateuch that required the death penalty for a woman who was found not to be a virgin at marriage were not enforced, but a woman who was not a virgin would be difficult to give in marriage. *The Sayings of Pseudo-Phocylides*, 215–16, advises that virgins be locked up and not seen outside the house until their wedding day. Ben Sira warns against a lattice, lest the young woman even be seen. The warning against spending time in the company of married women probably reflects a fear that the virgin may become aware of her sexuality.

But while some of Ben Sira's concerns reflect the society in which he lived, his anxiety is extreme. The economic and social realities of raising a daughter in Ben Sira's time do not seem greatly different from those of earlier centuries. Yet no earlier Jewish writer displays such deep anxiety on the subject. Daughters are never discussed as an isolated topic in the Hebrew Bible. The metaphorical use of *daughter* as a term of endearment for Zion or Israel contrasts sharply with Ben Sira's recommendation "Do not let your face shine upon them" (7:24, author's translation). Ben Sira was scarcely typical of the Hellenistic period either. The roughly contemporary book of Tobit paints a much more affectionate picture of family life. Few parents had as much reason for anxiety as Raguel and Edna, parents of the eventual bride of Tobias, Sarah, whose first seven husbands had died on their wedding night! Yet the concern of the parents is simply that "the Lord of heaven grant you joy in place of your sorrow" (Tobit 7:16).

Attitudes toward Women

Ben Sira has often been accused of misogyny in recent years, and the charge is difficult to refute. His more egregious statements include his reading of Genesis 2—3 (Sir. 25:24: "From a woman sin had its beginning, and because of her we all die") and the conclusion of his discourse

on daughters (42:14: "Better the wickedness of a man than the good-
ness of a woman," author's translation). His gross generalization about
the headstrong daughter in 26:12—"she will sit in front of every tent
peg and open her quiver to every arrow"—verges on pornography. In
the earlier wisdom literature we find occasional negative remarks about
women, but they are mild in comparison. Moreover, Ben Sira sometimes modifies traditional sayings to give them a negative application to
women.[193] Ben Sira is also decidedly more negative in his attitude toward women than are the wisdom texts from Qumran. The most extensive sectarian wisdom text, 4QSapiential Work A, shares Sirach's
emphasis on the authority of the husband over the wife but refrains
from derogatory comments on women in general. The Qumran sage
was mainly concerned that a man entering marriage "take care lest you
be distracted from the mystery that is to come."[194]

It has been suggested that the negative representations of the female,
and specifically the "misogynist expansions of the Eden story" that associate Eve with sin, death, and suffering, resulted from "the superim-
position of Greco-Roman thought and cultural forms on the biblical
world."[195] There is no precedent in Hebrew tradition for the view that
woman is the source of all evil, but there is a clear Greek precedent in
the story of Pandora's box (Hesiod, *Works and Days* 42–105). A tradition of Greek philosophy beginning with Aristotle insisted on the subordination of women in codes of household behavior.[196] Nonetheless,
it is too simple to attribute Ben Sira's misogyny to Hellenistic influence.
On the one hand, there were seeds of misogyny to be found in the Hebrew Bible as well as in Hellenistic culture. The negative use of female
symbolism in the prophets, especially in Ezekiel 16, provides ample illustration of this point. On the other hand, the influence of Hellenism
was multifaceted. Philo's negative symbolism of the female is clearly intertwined with the Platonic dualism of his thought. But Hellenistic influence is equally obvious in some very positive portrayals of women,
such as the enterprising Judith or the daughters of Job in the *Testament
of Job*.

Hellenistic influence did not require a negative view of women on
the part of Ben Sira. The roughly contemporary Pseudo-Phocylides was
more profoundly Hellenized than Ben Sira but is not nearly as negative
on the subject of women. Neither can Ben Sira's misogynistic tenden-
cies be adequately explained by his urban context. Equally negative later
sentiments are later attributed to rabbis in the village culture of Galilee.
The social class of the sages and their high valuation of study over other

forms of work may have contributed to a corresponding devaluation of women and their labor. The individual personality of Ben Sira must also be taken into account.

Ben Sira's view of women is not entirely negative, but the qualities he admires in women are generally passive and inclined to subservience. A good wife, in his view, is marked by silence and modesty (Sir. 26:14–15), female virtues also recommended by Aristotle.[197] He also appreciates her skill (*epistēmē, siklah*, 26:13), but he has nothing to compare to the eulogy of the capable wife in Proverbs 31. He is not one to encourage female independence or, indeed, to do anything that would jeopardize patriarchal authority: "Let neither son nor wife nor kin nor neighbor have power over you while you live. Do not give your goods to another lest you must turn and entreat his favor" (Sir. 33:20, author's translation). A similar emphasis on patriarchal authority can be found in 4QSapiential Work A from Qumran (4Q416–418).

Other Jewish literature of the Hellenistic period, however, contains several descriptions of active and enterprising women. Judith is the most obvious example. Her independence and initiative are all the more noteworthy because she is portrayed as a devout woman, whose reputation is beyond question. In the *Biblical Antiquities* of Pseudo-Philo, several women who are minor figures in the biblical account are developed and given major roles. Deborah becomes a feminine counterpart to Moses. Jephthah's daughter becomes comparable to Isaac.[198] Ben Sira was not alone in his negative view of women, but he did not speak for all of Judaism in the Hellenistic period.

The papyri, limited as they are, provide some remarkable examples of resourceful and enterprising women. Mibtahiah of Elephantine was a woman of substance and a member of a prominent family. Her property rights were legally protected. At the time of her first marriage, her father gave her a building plot. The grant specified, "You have power over it from this day and forever and your children after you. You may give it to whom you wish. . . . This land is yours; build (on it) or give it to whom you wish."[199] In the event of divorce, Mibtahiah was guaranteed half the house, and the whole house would eventually revert to their children. When her second marriage ended in divorce, we find her involved in litigation about "silver, grain, clothing, bronze and iron (vessels): all goods, possessions and the marriage contract."[200] Her ex-husband, an Egyptian, renounced his claim to these items, but only after Mibtahiah swore an oath by Egyptian gods.

For her third marriage, she appears to have provided her own dowry.

The marriage contract provided that if Mibtaḥiah should initiate divorce, she would have to pay seven-and-a-half shekels in divorce money. There is no mention of divorce money if Ashor should divorce Mibtaḥiah, but he would forfeit the *mohar*. Apparently, in this case it was the husband (Ashor) who needed the greater protection. Mibtaḥiah was specifically protected against bigamy, whether from past or from future marriages. While the marriage lasted, Mibtaḥiah "has power over the house of Ashor and his goods and possessions and everything, entirely, which he has upon the face of the earth."[201] The couple had two sons, named after Mibtaḥiah's father and grandfather. Mibtaḥiah outlived Ashor, and her three houses and dowry passed to her sons. The heirs of her first husband, Jezaniah, contested the ownership of the house given to her at the time of her first marriage, on the grounds that property should revert to the husband's family on the death of the wife. (Usually the widow had the use of the property but did not inherit ownership.) But the garrison commander at Elephantine upheld Mibtaḥiah's right to the property, presumably because it was protected in the contract.

Our other archive of an ancient Jewish woman comes from a time more than five hundred years after Mibtaḥiah, but Babatha, too, is a remarkable individual.[202] She came from a town called Maoza, at the southern end of the Dead Sea. Her father gave all his possessions to her mother before his death, and Babatha inherited them.[203] Little is known about Babatha's first husband, who enjoyed the memorable name Yeshua (Jesus) son of Joseph. He apparently died, but he and Babatha had a son, also named Yeshua. Babatha then married one Yehudah Khthusion from En-gedi, who had gone to live in Maoza. This Yehudah had another wife, Miriam, from En-gedi, whose brother was a lieutenant of Bar Kokhba. It was apparently because of this relationship that Babatha's archive ended up in the Cave of the Letters, along with other casualties of Bar Kokhba's campaign and its suppression by the Romans. Yehudah and Miriam had a daughter named Shelamzion, who married another Yehudah, also known as Kimber. On her marriage to Yehuda, Babatha received "a hundred Tyrians" (drachmas), which, according to the Talmud, was the sum paid to a widow or divorcée. The rate was not changed by the fact that Babatha was a relatively prosperous widow.

When Babatha's first husband died, the town council of Petra appointed two men to be guardians of the boy, who had been left a trust fund of four hundred denarii by his father. Almost immediately, Babatha began to complain that the monthly allowance was inadequate.

After she remarried, she summoned the guardians to the governor's court and offered to take full responsibility for her son if the trust funds were put at her disposal. Babatha offered to pay interest on the money and to offer her property as surety. She was apparently unsuccessful, as she was still accepting the original monthly allowance seven years later. Incidentally, this correspondence shows that Babatha was illiterate. Yehuda wrote on her behalf because she did not know how to write.

The incident is instructive in two respects. On the one hand, it shows the dependent position of the woman under the law. She had to accept male guardians of her own son after the death of his father. On the other hand, she was far from being a passive person. She herself had enjoyed the right of inheritance and was a woman of means. She was not hesitant about fighting for her interests in court, even if she was not ultimately successful.

Conclusion

Our survey of marriage and the family in second temple Judaism has shown some widely held notions and some diversity. The narratives of Genesis were widely understood to indicate the goal of marriage. A man and his wife were to become one flesh, and they were to increase and multiply. The later we go in the second temple period, the more influential the text of Genesis becomes. Nonetheless, some obvious implications of the text were not commonly drawn. Only in the Dead Sea Scrolls do we find the inference that polygamy and divorce should be prohibited, but in the same scrolls we find constraints on marriage and hints that some people were exempted from the obligation to increase and multiply, for reasons of holiness. Philo and Josephus, who treat the text of Genesis as fundamental, nonetheless extol the Essenes for their allegedly celibate way of life.

The idea that marriage has as its goal the procreation of children is found already in the prophet Malachi. This teleological view of marriage was strengthened in the Hellenistic period by the influence of Stoic philosophy. It appears in Greco-Jewish authors, such as Pseudo-Phocylides, Philo, and Josephus, but it may also be a factor in the rabbinic construal of Genesis 1:28 ("be fruitful and multiply") as a commandment addressed to all generations. Jewish writers from Ben Sira onward also adopted the common Hellenistic view of the patriarchal household, but in truth, this entailed no great change from the traditional structure of authority in the Israelite home.

Beside the theological understanding of marriage that was grounded in Genesis, however, we find in practice a view of marriage as a contract that was grounded in the legal traditions of the ancient Near East. As witnessed by the surviving documentary evidence, marriage was primarily a legal contract, and concern for property rights and livelihood was of its essence. This practical, pragmatic view of marriage is by no means incompatible with a teleological view that sees the union's goal as the raising of children, but it highlights a different aspect of marriage. This pragmatic aspect was embedded in the legal system and therefore very widespread. In contrast, idealistic preaching such as we find in the prophet Malachi was exceptional in second temple Judaism, as were the restrictive attitude toward sex and obsessive concern with purity that we find in the Dead Sea Scrolls.

In his introduction to the Greek papyri of the Babatha archive, Naphthali Lewis pronounces, "These papyri speak to us of marriage vows and settlements, of money and property and family quarrels over them, of lawsuits real or threatened. Taken at face value they adumbrate a materialistic, litigious coterie, incessantly disputing with one another over shares in the family's wealth."[204] Lewis attempts to mitigate his rather harsh judgment on the materialism of Babatha and her associates by adding:

> But there are also other elements, less immediately apparent, which bespeak a more tightly knit fabric and a more harmonious quality of family life underlying the more visible polarization. Those underlying ties would, as with most families, manifest themselves especially in time of crisis. Thus, for example, the fact the marriage contract and other valuable documents of Shelamzion, her stepdaughter, were found with Babatha's papers must surely mean that those two women lived amicably together and fled from home together to the shelter of the cave. At such times of danger the fact that Shelamzion's mother and Babatha had fought over Judah's household effects faded into insignificance.

Perhaps this is so. Many important issues fade into insignificance in time of war. The link between stepmother and stepdaughter is indeed intriguing. Babatha may have provided Shelamzion's dowry; this would explain why Shelamzion's contract was found in Babatha's archive. It may also be that the impression of litigiousness is due to the kind of documents that were preserved. Where there was no litigation, there was no need to keep documents. There is no reason to think that Jewish families of this period were any less, or more, affectionate than families in other societies.

The pragmatic, contractual character of marriage in second temple Judaism is most evident in the ready availability of divorce. We have no way of calculating the actual frequency of divorce, but both the literary evidence and the papyri accept it as routine. In such a situation, the use of marriage contracts has much to commend it. The contractual view of marriage has the advantage of realism and of avoiding the disillusionment of romantic love. To judge by the evidence of the papyri, the contracts worked well for the protection of women in situations of divorce and widowhood.

But we must also recognize the limitations of our evidence. Especially frustrating is the silence of the marriage contracts on the care of children in the event of divorce. We have very few narratives of family life in this period, apart from Tobit, to illustrate the normal working-out of relationships. It is apparent from the Babatha archive that the contractual view of marriage could degenerate into materialistic litigation. Where polygamy was practiced, it lent itself to contention between the wives, as Ben Sira recognized (Sir. 26:6). The custom whereby a divorced woman returned to her father's house must have produced tensions in the paternal household and may go some way toward explaining the paranoia of Ben Sira on the subject of daughters. Ready divorce may have worked satisfactorily in the case of a woman such as Mibtahiah, who had her own independent means, but must have involved considerable hardship in many cases.

Against this background, we can appreciate the cry of the prophet Malachi, appealing to his contemporaries to be faithful to the wives of their youth and reminding them that what God wants is godly offspring. Jesus of Nazareth, another reformer within the context of second temple Judaism, also took a strict line on divorce: "It was because you were so hard-hearted that Moses allowed you to divorce your wives, but from the beginning it was not so" (Matt. 19:8); "What God has joined together, let no one separate" (Mark 10:9). The protest of the disciples is also intelligible against the background of second temple Judaism: "If such is the case of a man with his wife, it is better not to marry" (Matt. 19:10). Matthew's Jesus responds with a discourse on eunuchs for the kingdom of heaven but grants that "not everyone can accept this teaching, but only those to whom it is given."

Perhaps the same should be said about the teaching on the indissolubility of marriage. Hardness of heart remains a factor in human society that is not inconsiderable. Moses did well to legislate for it. The law cannot be expected to provide the moral ideals of a society, but neither should moral ideals be given the force of law.

NOTES

This chapter is dedicated to the memory of Jonas C. Greenfield, whose premature death in March 1995 deprived the world of a leading expert on marriage in second temple Judaism.

1. See V. Tcherikover, *Hellenistic Civilization and the Jews* (New York: Atheneum Publishers, 1970), 90–116; E. Schuerer, *The History of the Jewish People in the Age of Jesus Christ*, rev. and ed. G. Vermes, F. Millar, and M. Black (Edinburgh: T. & T. Clark, 1979), 2:85–183.

2. See M. Broshi, "La Population de l'ancienne Jérusalem," *RB* 82 (1975): 5–14.

3. See S. Applebaum, "Economic Life in Palestine," in *The Jewish People in the First Century*, ed. S. Safrai and M. Stern (CRINT 1.2; Assen: Van Gorcum, 1976), 632–33. Cf. Josephus: "We the Jews neither inhabit a coastal territory nor welcome the commerce or the association with others which it brings, for our towns are built far from the sea and we cultivate the excellent rural region which we occupy" (*Ap.* 1.60). It is clear nonetheless that Judaea was not isolated from foreign commerce as Josephus claims.

4. Applebaum, "Economic Life," 632. He acknowledges two other Jewish towns "of some importance" in the Hellenistic-Roman periods, Tiberias and Sepphoris, both in Galilee. Only one harbor town, Joppa, may have been predominantly Jewish.

5. Ibid., 663: "A high proportion of city-dwellers cultivated holdings in the immediate vicinity of the town, and the urban upper class's economic basis was almost invariably landed property."

6. Josephus, *Ant.* 12.154–236. See Tcherikover, *Hellenistic Civilization*, 127–42.

7. J. Weinberg, "Das Bêit 'Abōt im 6–4 Jh. v.u.Z.," *VT* 23 (1973):400–414 (="The Bêt 'Abōt of the Sixth to Fourth Centuries BCE," in *The Citizen-Temple Community*, trans. D. L. Smith-Christopher [JSOTSup 151; Sheffield: JSOT Press, 1992], 49–61); D. L. Smith, *The Religion of the Landless* (Oak Park, Ill.: Meyer-Stone Books, 1989), 102–8; J. Blenkinsopp, "Temple and Society in Achaemenid Judah," in *Second Temple Studies*, vol. 1: *Persian Period*, ed. P. R. Davies (JSOTSup 117; Sheffield: JSOT Press, 1991), 47–48.

8. Smith, *Religion of the Landless*, 115.

9. Weinberg, "Bêt 'Abōt," 61.

10. S. Safrai, "Home and Family," in Safrai and Stern, eds., *Jewish People*, 728–92. Safrai's account is based primarily on Mishnaic and Talmudic sources, but it accords well with the archaeological evidence. See Ann Killebrew and Steven Fine, "Qatzrin—Reconstructing Village Life in Talmudic Times," *BAR* 17 (1991):44–56.

11. Family compounds appear to have been larger in the rabbinic period than they were in ancient Israel. During the Byzantine period (fourth to seventh centuries C.E.), houses included as many as fifteen rooms (Killebrew and Fine, "Qatzrin," 46). Safrai comments that "among other factors conducive

to the provision of additional rooms, was the halakic ruling that a woman must remain apart from her husband during the period of her menstrual impurity" ("Home and Family," 732).

12. See O. Eissfeldt, *The Old Testament: An Introduction* (New York: Harper & Row, 1965), 483. E. F. Campbell, *Ruth* (AB 7; New York: Doubleday, 1975), 23–28, argues for a preexilic date.

13. E.g., A. Lacocque, *The Feminine Unconventional: Four Subversive Figures in Israel's Tradition* (Minneapolis: Fortress Press, 1990), 84–116.

14. A. J. Levine, "Ruth," in *The Women's Bible Commentary,* ed. C. A. Newsom and S. H. Ringe (Louisville, Ky.: Westminster/John Knox Press, 1992), 82–83.

15. E. Lipiński, "Marriage and Divorce in the Judaism of the Persian Period," *Transeuphratène* 4 (1991):63–71; B. Porten, "Five Fragmentary Aramaic Marriage Documents: New Collations and Restorations," *Abr-Nahrain* 27 (1989):80–105.

16. The following summaries depend heavily on B. Porten, *Archives from Elephantine* (Berkeley and Los Angeles: University of California Press, 1968), 189–263. C = the edition of A. Cowley, *Aramaic Papyri of the Fifth Century B.C.* (Oxford: Clarendon Press, 1923). K = the edition of E. G. Kraeling, *The Brooklyn Museum Aramaic Papyri* (New Haven, Conn.: Yale University Press, 1953).

17. Lipiński, "Marriage and Divorce," 65–69; R. Yaron, *Introduction to the Law of the Aramaic Papyri* (Oxford: Clarendon Press, 1961), 45–50.

18. L. J. Archer, *Her Price Is Beyond Rubies: The Jewish Woman in Graeco-Roman Palestine* (JSOTSup 60; Sheffield: JSOT Press, 1990), 152–53. The Talmud recommends that men marry by age eighteen or twenty ('Abot 5:21; Qidd. 29b).

19. Porten, *Archives from Elephantine,* 252.

20. Adultery, to be sure, was regarded throughout the ancient Near East as a sin, subject to divine punishment. As such, it was analogous to other offenses proscribed in the Decalogue. But this does not mean that marriage in general had a sacral character, to any greater degree than property transactions. See J. Milgrom, *Cult and Conscience* (Leiden: E. J. Brill, 1976), 131–36.

21. See, for example, the generous dowry provided for Yehoishma, daughter of a slave-woman, by the son of her former master, who was still deemed to have authority over her (Porten, *Archives from Elephantine,* 221).

22. For the older documents, see R. Westbrook, *Old Babylonian Marriage Law* (Archiv für Orientforschung 23; Horn, Austria: Berger, 1988). For the later period, see M. T. Roth, *Babylonian Marriage Agreements: 7th–3rd Centuries B.C.* (AOAT 222; Kevelaer, W. Germany: Butzon & Bercker/ Neukirchen-Vluyn: Neukirchener Verlag, 1989).

23. Yaron, *Introduction,* 49; Archer, *Her Price,* 172.

24. L. M. Epstein, *The Jewish Marriage Contract* (New York: Jewish Theological Seminary of America, 1927), 29; M. Burrows, *The Basis of Israelite Marriage* (New Haven, Conn.: Yale University Press, 1938), 31.

25. M. J. Geller, "The Elephantine Papyri and Hosea 2,3," *Journal for the Study of Judaism* 8 (1977):139–48.

26. Ibid., 140; contra Porten, *Archives from Elephantine,* 247. Geller points to a writ of manumission (K 5), which is an analogous kind of document, and to a deed that seems to be the sequel to a divorce writ, renouncing all claims to the divorced wife's property (C 14).

27. See Lipiński, "Marriage and Divorce," 64.

28. Archer, *Her Price,* 157, 172, dismisses this document as some form of betrothal deed (*shetar*) rather than a marriage contract proper. It is true that no mention is made here of the dowry, which is the central consideration in the marriage contracts from Elephantine, but the most important point is that a document was required.

29. Y. Yadin, J. C. Greenfield, and A. Yardeni, "Babatha's *Ketubba,*" *IEJ* 44 (1994):75–101 (see the text on p. 78, line 5).

30. M. A. Friedman, *Jewish Marriage in Palestine: A Cairo Geniza Study* (New York: Jewish Theological Seminary of America, 1980), 1:162.

31. I am indebted to Professor Jonas Greenfield for his help with this material.

32. The Murabba'at documents were published by J. T. Milik in P. Benoit, J. T. Milik, and R. de Vaux, *Les Grottes de Murabba'at* (DJD 2; Oxford: Clarendon Press, 1961). Text and translation can also be found in Archer, *Her Price,* 291–300.

33. The contracts of Shelamzion and Jesus and Salome are published by N. Lewis in *The Documents from the Bar Kokhba Period in the Cave of Letters* (Jerusalem: Israel Exploration Society, 1989), nos. 18, 37. Babatha's contract (p Yadin 10) has now been published by Yadin, Greenfield, and Yardeni, "Babatha's *Ketubba,*" 75–101.

34. H. Cotton, "A Cancelled Marriage Contract from the Judean Desert (XHev/Se gr 2)," *Journal of Roman Studies* 84 (1994):64–86.

35. Naḥal Ṣe'elim 13, to be published by J. C. Greenfield in the M. Stern memorial volume. A transcription and translation can be found in K. Beyer, *Die aramäischen Texte vom Toten Meer. Ergänzungsband* (Göttingen: Vandenhoeck & Ruprecht, 1994), 191–92. Shelamzion was a common name in this period.

36. Archer, *Her Price,* 176; see the *ketubah* from Maimonides cited on pp. 299–300.

37. See Friedman, *Jewish Marriage in Palestine,* 1:347–56; Yadin, Greenfield, and Yardeni, "Babatha's *Ketubba,*" 93.

38. This Palestinian type of contract is described at length in Friedman, *Jewish Marriage in Palestine.*

39. See Cotton, "Cancelled Marriage Contract." The Jewish character of these contracts is defended in N. Lewis, R. Katzoff, and J. C. Greenfield, "Papyrus Yadin 18," *IEJ* 37 (1987):229–50. A. Wasserstein, "A Marriage Contract from the Province of Arabia Nova: Notes on Papyrus Yadin 18," *JQR* 80 (1989):93–130, insists that the contract "is not a 'Jewish' document (though of course relating to Jews) but a secular document testifying to the

integration of law and custom of Jews . . . with the customary law of their non-Jewish neighbors." See the rejoinder by R. Katzoff, "Papyrus Yadin 18 Again: A Rejoinder," *JQR* 82 (1991):171–76. Cotton's analysis supports the position of Wasserstein.

40. Epstein, *Jewish Marriage Contract*.

41. For a review of scholarship on this verse, see G. P. Hugenberger, *Marriage as Covenant: A Study of Biblical Law and Ethics Governing Marriage Developed from the Perspective of Malachi* (VTSup 52; Leiden: E. J. Brill, 1994), 27–47.

42. See M. Greenberg, *Ezekiel 1–20* (AB 20; Garden City, N.Y.: Doubleday, 1983), 278.

43. See I. M. Gafni, "The Institution of Marriage in Rabbinic Times," in *The Jewish Family*, ed. D. Kraemer (New York: Oxford University Press, 1989), 14: "Marriage, then, was in fact contracted by individuals, and though God's presence—the Shekhinah—may be considered a *sine qua non* for a happy marriage, we do not find the rabbis suggesting—as did the Church—that the institution was, in and of itself, a sacred institution or a sanctifying one."

44. Porten, *Archives from Elephantine*, 208, citing W. Edgerton, *Notes on Egyptian Marriage* (Chicago: University of Chicago Press, 1931), 2.

45. Lewis, *Documents from the Bar Kokhba Period*, 130.

46. See the comments of Cotton, "Cancelled Marriage Contract," and also her comments in "The Archive of Salome Komaise Daughter of Levi: Another Archive from the 'Cave of the Letters,' " *Zeitschrift für Papyrologie und Epigraphik* 105 (1995):171–208. See further T. Ilan, "Premarital Cohabitation in Ancient Judea: The Evidence of the Babatha Archive and the Mishnah (Ketubbot 1.4)," *HTR* 86 (1993):247–64.

47. See the discussion of this passage by Archer, *Her Price*, 155; Epstein, *Jewish Marriage Contract*, 11–12.

48. See further Ilan, "Premarital Cohabitation," 257–58.

49. So especially P. Koschaker, "Eheschliessung und Kauf nach altem Recht, mit besonderer Berücksichtigung der älteren Keilschriftrechte," *ArOr* 18, 3 (1950):210–96. See the criticisms of Westbrook, *Old Babylonian Marriage Law*, 53–60. Westbrook argues that "marriage is not a contract," but his point is that it was not completely negotiable. The status of marriage was regulated by general law, and only the variable features had to be settled in the contract.

50. Westbrook, *Old Babylonian Marriage Law*, 60. For cross-cultural perspectives on bride-price, see J. L. Comaroff, ed., *The Meaning of Marriage Payments* (New York: Academic Press, 1980).

51. Archer, *Her Price*, 160–64; M. J. Geller, "New Sources for the Origins of the Rabbinic Ketubah," *HUCA* 49 (1978):227–45.

52. Geller, "New Sources," 233. This manner of treating the *mohar* is paralleled in Babylonian contracts of the Seleucid period.

53. This reform departed from the Akkadian legal tradition and conforms to demotic marriage deeds from Egypt (Geller, "New Sources," 240–45).

54. Cotton, "Cancelled Marriage Contract."
55. See further Archer, *Her Price,* 166–67.
56. In contrast, only one-third of the neo-Babylonian contracts envisage divorce (Roth, *Babylonian Marriage Agreements,* 12).
57. R. Westbrook, "Adultery in Ancient Near Eastern Law," *RB* 97 (1990): 542–80, argues that the husband had such discretion throughout the ancient Near East. W. C. Trenchard, *Ben Sira's View of Women: A Literary Analysis* (BJS 38; Chico, Calif.: Scholars Press, 1982), 104–6, concludes that the biblical discussions of adultery outside the legal corpora do not support a practice of execution. Ben Sira is ambiguous: the adulteress is "led away to the assembly" (Sir. 23:24).
58. Cf. Porten's restoration of C 18, "Five Fragmentary Aramaic Marriage Documents," 102.
59. H. L. Ginsberg suggested that the divorce money paid by the husband was simply the *mohar,* as in the later rabbinic *ketubah.* This view is defensible in the case of C 15 but not of K 2 and K 7. See Yaron, *Introduction,* 57–58.
60. Yaron, *Introduction,* 59.
61. W. Pestman, *Marriage and Matrimonial Property in Ancient Egypt* (Leiden: E. J. Brill, 1961), 77: "It is quite unknown, however, who, after the dissolution of the marriage by divorce, will take care of the education and the maintenance of the children." Pestman cites a document, however, which states that the wife is contented "on account of the children whom you have borne to me." This might be construed to mean that the wife had custody with the right to support.
62. See Westbrook, *Old Babylonian Marriage Law,* 85.
63. Roth, *Babylonian Marriage Agreements,* 14.
64. The text of this verse is problematic. The usual translation, given here, follows 1 Esd. 9:36. See H. G. M. Williamson, *Ezra, Nehemiah* (WBC 16: Waco, Tex.: Word, 1985), 145.
65. Y. Yadin, *Bar Kokhba* (New York: Random House, 1971), 240–41.
66. S. R. Driver, *Deuteronomy* (ICC; Edinburgh: T. & T. Clark, 1896), 270.
67. Archer, *Her Price,* 219.
68. Contra R. Westbrook, "The Prohibition on Restoration of Marriage in Deuteronomy 24:1–4," in *Studies in Bible,* ed. S. Japhet (ScrHier 31; Jerusalem: Magnes Press, 1986), 399.
69. See J. J. Rabinowitz, "Marriage Contracts in Ancient Egypt in the Light of Jewish Sources," *HTR* 46 (1953):91–97; Yaron, *Introduction,* 55. The verb *hate* is routinely translated as "divorce" in Cowley's edition of the papyri.
70. Westbrook, "Prohibition," 400.
71. Ibid., 402. See also Westbrook's comments on the Akkadian counterpart *zērum* in his *Old Babylonian Marriage Law,* 81.
72. Friedman, *Jewish Marriage in Palestine,* 1:330, 338.
73. Yaron, *Introduction,* 53.
74. E. Lipiński, "The Wife's Right to Divorce in the Light of an Ancient Near Eastern Tradition," *Jewish Law Annual* 4 (1981):9–27. Pestman, *Marriage*

and Matrimonial Property, 65, says that the wife had the right to initiate divorce from about 500 B.C.E.

75. Lipiński, "Wife's Right to Divorce," 15.

76. Cf. Code of Hammurabi 142–43.

77. Westbrook, *Old Babylonian Marriage Law*, 83.

78. Ibid., 84.

79. B. Brooten, "Konnten Frauen im alten Judentum die Scheidung betreiben?" *EvTh* 42 (1982):65–80; E. Schweizer, "Scheidungsrecht der jüdischen Frau? Weibliche Jünger Jesu?" *EvTh* 42 (1982):294–300; H. Weder, "Perspektive der Frauen?" *EvTh* 43 (1983):175–78; B. Brooten, "Zur Debatte über das Scheidungsrecht der jüdischen Frau," *EvTh* 43 (1983):466–78; R. Katzoff in Lewis, Katzoff, and Greenfield, "Papyrus Yadin 18," 243–46.

80. *m. Ketub.* 7:5, 9–10; *m. Ned.* 11:12. For the distinction between power and right, see Katzoff in Lewis, Katzoff, and Greenfield, "Papyrus Yadin 18," 244.

81. D. Daube, *The New Testament and Rabbinic Judaism* (London: Athlone Press, 1956), 371: "Whether he put a formal end to the marriage by giving her a bill of divorce remains uncertain, but no doubt he did." Philo uses the same verb with reference to a woman who was falsely accused by her husband of not having been a virgin at marriage and who was free to "leave," whether he wished it or not (*De Specialibus Legibus* 1.9.105; 3.5.30; 3.14.82).

82. Schweizer, "Scheidungsrecht," 294–95; Daube, *New Testament*, 362–69.

83. K. Beyer, *Die aramäischen Texte vom Toten Meer, Ergänzungsband* (Göttingen: Vandenhoeck & Ruprecht, 1994), 191–92. This text was cited by J. T. Milik in Benoit, Milik, and de Vaux, *Les Grottes de Murabba'at* 108. See the discussion by T. Ilan, "On a Newly Published Divorce Bill from the Judaean Desert," *HTR* 89 (1996):195–202.

84. So J. C. Greenfield, in his forthcoming edition in the DJD series.

85. Schweizer, "Scheidungsrecht," 296, argues that the Nahal Hever evidence is representative of only a very limited area around the Dead Sea, but it is unlikely that a very small area could diverge from the rest of Judaism in a matter such as this. The Palestinian Talmud reports a local custom of allowing for divorce by the woman in marriage contracts, but the temporal and spatial extension of this custom is uncertain (*p. Ketub.* 30b; *p. Baba Bathra* 16c). See Friedman, *Jewish Marriage in Palestine*, 1:312–46. Friedman concludes, "Jewish law certainly never empowered a wife to issue a bill of divorce unilaterally and thus dissolve her marriage. However, it was stipulated in *ketubbot*, which, from Talmudic times, followed the Palestinian tradition, and the rabbis eventually recognized this as binding law that through the wife's initiative, if she found life with her husband unbearable, the court would take action to terminate the marriage, even against the husband's will" (346).

86. Cf. Brooten, "Konnten Frauen," 79, who concludes that there were two traditions on this matter in Palestine in the pre-rabbinic period.

87. See Safrai, "Home and Family," 749–50.

88. S. Lowy, "The Extent of Jewish Polygamy in Tannaitic Times," *JJS* 9 (1958):115–38. He cites several examples of polygamous marriages from talmudic literature but concludes that there was no widespread practice.

89. Lewis, *Documents from the Bar Kokhba Period*, 22–26.

90. Williamson, *Ezra, Nehemiah*, 161.

91. Cn: Hebrew, "and a remnant of spirit was his."

92. Hebrew, "he."

93. Some scholars, notably C. C. Torrey, "The Prophecy of 'Malachi,' " *JBL* 17 (1898):1–15, have pronounced crucial verses "hopelessly corrupt."

94. So Torrey, "Prophecy of 'Malachi,' " 4–5; F. F. Hvidberg, *Weeping and Laughter in the Old Testament* (Leiden: E. J. Brill, 1962), 120–21; A. Isaksson, *Marriage and Ministry in the New Temple* (Lund: C. W. K. Gleerup, 1965), 31; J. M. O'Brien, *Priest and Levite in Malachi* (SBLDS 121; Atlanta: Scholars Press, 1990), 68. D. L. Petersen specifies the goddess by emending the phrase, *'aser 'āhāb*, "which he loves," to *'ăšerāh 'āhāb*, "he loves Asherah" (*Zechariah 9—14 and Malachi: A Commentary* [OTL; Louisville, Ky.: Westminster John Knox Press, 1995]).

95. B. Glazier-McDonald, "Intermarriage, Divorce, and the Bat-'Ēl Nēkar," *JBL* 106 (1987):604, points out that by this reasoning "the children of YHWH" would be gods.

96. So, e.g., J. M. P. Smith, *Malachi* (ICC; Edinburgh: T. & T. Clark, 1912), 52–53; A. von Bulmerincq, *Der Prophet Maleachi* (Tartu, Est.: Kruger, 1926–32), 2:259; Hugenberger, *Marriage as Covenant*, 36.

97. Glazier-McDonald, "Intermarriage," 610; idem, *Malachi: The Divine Messenger* (SBLDS 98; Atlanta: Scholars Press, 1987), 119–20.

98. Hvidberg, *Weeping and Laughter,* 123.

99. Isaksson, *Marriage and Ministry*, 33. Petersen, *Zechariah 9—14 and Malachi*, takes a similar position.

100. Glazier-McDonald, "Intermarriage," 611.

101. It is similarly unsatisfactory to identify the wife of the covenant as the covenant itself, as does B. Vawter, "The Biblical Theology of Divorce," *Proceedings of the Catholic Theological Society of America* 22 (1967):223–43, following Torrey, "Prophecy of 'Malachi,'" 1–15.

102. So Smith, *Malachi*, 52.

103. Hugenberger, *Marriage as Covenant,* 99–100.

104. So W. Rudolph, "Zu Malachi 2. 10–15," *ZAW* 93 (1981):90.

105. Petersen, *Zechariah 9—14 and Malachi.*

106. So Hugenberger, *Marriage as Covenant,* 70.

107. R. Fuller, "Text-Critical Problems in Malachi 2:10–16," *JBL* 110 (1991):47–57.

108. Hugenberger, *Marriage as Covenant,* 57–58.

109. S. Schreiner, "Mischehen-Ehebruch-Ehescheidung. Betrachtungen zu Mal. 2.10–16," *ZAW* 91 (1979):207–28, argues that the passage sanctions divorce (of foreign wives) but only as the lesser evil, so that it still

constitutes violence. See the critique of this position by Hugenberger, *Marriage as Covenant*, 60–62.

110. Westbrook, "Prohibition," 403. Hugenberger takes the initial particle in a conditional rather than a causative sense: "If one hates and divorces . . . he covers his garment with violence" (*Marriage as Covenant*, 76).

111. Westbrook, "Prohibition," 403. He points to a similar asyndetic use of "hate . . . divorce" in a neo-Assyrian marriage contract.

112. Hugenberger, *Marriage as Covenant*, 83.

113. So Petersen, *Zechariah 9—14 and Malachi* (pp. 204–206), regards v. 16 as the addition of some "scholiast" or "epigone."

114. Glazier-McDonald, *Malachi*, 109: "And not one does it (intermarries) and has a remnant of spirit (reproductive potential)." But the intelligibility of this rendering depends on supplying a reference to intermarriage and taking "spirit" in an unusual sense.

115. See Hugenberger, *Marriage as Covenant*, 132–33.

116. This was first proposed by A. van Hoonacker, *Les douze petits prophètes* (Paris: J. Gabalda, 1908), 726, 728. For further references, see Hugenberger, *Marriage as Covenant*, 132. See also M. Gilbert, "Une seule chaire (*Gn* 2,24)." *Nouvelle Revue Theologique* 100 (1978):79. Hugenberger retains the MT pointing ("Did He not make one, with a remnant of spirit belonging to it?"), but "a remnant of spirit" is scarcely intelligible.

117. The expression "godly seed" may mean simply "progeny." See the discussion in Hugenberger, *Marriage as Covenant*, 140–41, who favors the view that the phrase means "children pleasing to God."

118. It is not clear how Malachi would regard divorce on the grounds of infertility.

119. *m. Yebam.* 6:6. The school of Shammai required two sons, the school of Hillel a son and a daughter.

120. 4Q416 2 iii 21–iv 1. See D. J. Harrington, "Wisdom at Qumran, " in *The Community of the New Covenant*, ed. E. Ulrich and J. VanderKam (Notre Dame, Ind.: University of Notre Dame Press, 1994), 148.

121. P. Grelot, *Man and Wife in Scriptures* (New York: Herder & Herder, 1964), 72.

122. G. Anderson, "Celibacy or Consummation in the Garden? Reflections on Early Jewish and Christian Interpretations of the Garden of Eden," *HTR* 82 (1989):121–48.

123. L. Ginzberg, *Legends of the Jews*, 7 vols. (Philadelphia: Jewish Publication Society, 1908–38), 5:134, although some of his examples are problematic.

124. Unfortunately, this passage is not preserved in the fragments of *Jubilees* found at Qumran.

125. Compare J. M. Baumgarten, "Purification after Childbirth and the Sacred Garden in 4Q265 and Jubilees," in *New Qumran Texts and Studies*, ed. G. J. Brook, with F. García Martínez (Leiden: E. J. Brill, 1994), 3–10, who concludes, "In sum, both 4Q265 and *Jubilees* view the purifications

required of a parturient after the birth of a male or female child before being allowed access to the Temple as patterned after the respective preparatory periods of Adam and Eve before their entrance into the garden of Eden" (9–10).

126. P. Winter, "Sadoqite Fragments IV 20, 21 and the Exegesis of Genesis 1:27 in late Judaism," *ZAW* 68 (1956):74–77; G. Vermes, "Sectarian Matrimonial Halakah in the Damascus Rule," *JJS* 25 (1974):197–202.

127. So Vermes, "Sectarian Matrimonial Halakah," 200–201.

128. The pronominal suffix, "their," is masculine. If this is taken to apply only to the men, it would seem to exclude a second marriage under any circumstances. So J. Murphy-O'Connor, "An Essene Missionary Document? CD II, 14–VI, 1," *RB* 77 (1970):220. Some scholars emend the suffix to the feminine form or take the masculine suffix as inclusive. On this interpretation, divorce would be permitted, but not remarriage while the first wife was alive. See Vermes, "Sectarian Matrimonial Halakah," 199–202.

129. This parallel was adduced by Y. Yadin, "L'Attitude essénienne envers la polygamie et le divorce," *RB* 79 (1972):98–99.

130. See J. A. Fitzmyer, "Divorce among First-Century Palestinian Jews," *Eretz Israel* 14 (1978):103–10* (please note: asterisk refers to the English language sections).

131. J. Baumgarten, "Qumran-Essene Restraints on Marriage," in *Archaeology and History in the Dead Sea Scrolls*, ed. L. H. Schiffman (Sheffield: JSOT Press, 1990),14–15; he claims that the fragmentary beginning of 11QTemple 64 cites the provisions in Deut. 21:15 concerning a man who has two wives.

132. M. O. Wise, *A Critical Study of the Temple Scroll from Qumran Cave 11* (Chicago: Oriental Institute Press, 1990), 139–47, argues that the laws of CD are prior to the *Temple Scroll*. CD 4–5, however, belongs to a different, allegedly later section of the document. B. Z. Wacholder, *The Dawn of Qumran* (Cincinnati: Hebrew Union College Press, 1983), 126, argues that CD depends on 11QTemple.

133. Fitzmyer, "Divorce," 109*. Against Vermes, he shows that CD 13:17 is not legislation for divorce. L. H. Schiffman, "Laws Pertaining to Women," in *The Dead Sea Scrolls: Forty Years of Research*, ed. D. Dimant and U. Rappaport (Leiden: E. J. Brill, 1992), 217, thinks it probable that CD allowed divorce, but perhaps only in cases of adultery.

134. *b. Qidd.* 29b; Baumgarten, "Qumran-Essene Restraints," 14.

135. 11QTemple 45:11; CD 12:1–2. The *Temple Scroll* forbids access to the city for thirty days after intercourse. L. Ginzberg, *An Unknown Jewish Sect,* 2d ed. (New York: Jewish Theological Seminary of America, 1970), 76, suggests that the law in CD applied only to pilgrims, but that restriction is not explicit in the texts. See Wise, *A Critical Study,* 144–47.

136. J. Baumgarten, "The Laws of the Damascus Document in Current Research," in *The Damascus Document Reconsidered*, ed. M. Broshi (Jerusalem: Israel Exploration Society, 1992), 53.

137. J. M. Baumgarten, "The Cave Four Versions of the Qumran Penal Code," *JJS* 43 (1992):270.
138. For the identification with the Essenes, see John J. Collins, "Essenes," *ABD* 2 (1992):620–26. The most complete history of the debate, culminating in a revised but vigorous Essene hypothesis, can be found in H. Stegemann, "The Qumran Essenes—Local Members of the Main Jewish Union in Late Second Temple Times," in *The Madrid Qumran Congress*, ed. J. Trebolle Barrera and L. Vegas Montaner (Leiden: E. J. Brill, 1992), 1:83–175.
139. Compare the simple statement in *Ant.* 18.1.5 (§21) that the Essenes do not take wives. See the commentary on the passage in *BJ* by T. S. Beall, *Josephus' Description of the Essenes Illustrated by the Dead Sea Scrolls* (SNTSMS 58; Cambridge: Cambridge University Press, 1988), 38–42.
140. See Stegemann, "Qumran Essenes," 127. R. Bergmeier, *Die Essener-Berichte des Flavius Josephus. Quellenstudien zu den Essenertexten im Werk des jüdischen Historiographen* (Kampen, Neth.: Kok Pharos, 1993), 167–78, distinguishes a Jewish Hellenistic source and a "Pythagoreanizing" source that assimilated the Essenes to the Greek philosophers.
141. Stegemann, "Qumran Essenes," 126–34.
142. H. Hübner, "Zölibat in Qumran?" *NTS* 17 (1971):153–67; E. Schuller, "Women in the Dead Sea Scrolls," in *Methods of Investigation of the Dead Sea Scrolls and the Khirbet Qumran Site*, ed. M. O. Wise, N. Golb, J. J. Collins, and D. Pardee (New York: New York Academy of Sciences, 1994), 115–32.
143. R. de Vaux, *Archaeology and the Dead Sea Scrolls* (Oxford: Oxford University Press, 1973), 47.
144. J. Coppens, "Le Célibat Essénien," in *Qumrân: Sa piété, sa théologie et son milieu*, ed. M. Delcor (Louvain: Leuven University Press, 1978), 297, claims that the passage in the *Hôdāyôt* refers to all believers, not specifically members of the community. This position cannot be defended in the case of the *Pesher on Psalm 37*.
145. E.g., Stegemann, "Qumran Essenes," 131: "The concept of a Jewish celibate brotherhood would be a contradiction in terms."
146. A. Guillaumont, "A propos du célibat des Esséniens," in *Hommages à André Dupont-Sommer*, ed. A. Caquot and M. Philonenko (Paris: Maisonneuve Press, 1971), 395–404.
147. Guillaumont, "A propos du célibat," 396–400. The tradition is found in *Midrash Exodus Rabbah, Targum Onqelos, b. Yebam.* 62a, and Philo, *De Vita Mosis* 2.68–69.
148. E. Qimron, "Celibacy in the Dead Sea Scrolls," in Barrera and Montaner, eds., *The Madrid Qumran Congress*, 1:287–94.
149. Ibid., 288.
150. Against J. Baumgarten, Qimron insists that 4Q502 does not refer to marriage within the *yahad*. The phrase *simhat yahad* has been restored at several points in this document, but in this phrase, *yahad* means "together" rather than "community."

151. Baumgarten, "Qumran-Essene Restraints," 18. He notes that Pliny says the Essenes had lasted "for thousands of generations" despite a celibate life. See also Qimron, "Celibacy," 290.

152. See Will Deming, *Paul on Marriage and Celibacy* (Tübingen: J. C. B. Mohr (Paul Siebeck), 1995), chap. 3.

153. See R. S. Kraemer, "Monastic Jewish Women in Greco-Roman Egypt: Philo Judaeus on the Therapeutrides," *Signs* 14 (1989):342–70.

154. J. Baumgarten, "4Q502, Marriage or Golden Age Ritual," *JJS* 34 (1983): 131.

155. J. M. Allegro, *Qumran Cave 4 I (4Q158–4Q186)* (DJD 4; Oxford: Clarendon Press, 1968), 82. J. Strugnell, "Notes en marge du volume V des 'Discoveries in the Judaean Desert,' " *Revue de Qumran* 7 (1970):264, points out that the restoration *hazōnāh*, "the prostitute," in the first line is hardly possible.

156. J. A. Sanders, *The Psalms Scroll of Qumran Cave 11* (DJD 4; Oxford: Clarendon Press, 1965), 84.

157. See the comments of Schuller, "Women in the Dead Sea Scrolls," 126.

158 Baumgarten, "The Cave 4 Versions," 270.

159. See D. Biale, *Eros and the Jews* (New York: Basic Books, 1992), 37–38.

160. T. Frymer-Kensky, "Sex and Sexuality," *ABD* 5 (1992): 1145. The condemnations focus on male homosexuality. Lesbianism is not discussed in the biblical laws or in the sapiential writings.

161. See S. B. Pomeroy, *Goddesses, Whores, Wives and Slaves: Women in Classical Antiquity* (New York: Schocken Books, 1975), 142–48, on the representation of sexuality in Hellenistic art.

162. M. H. Pope, *Song of Songs* (AB 7C; Garden City, N.Y.: Doubleday, 1977), 22–33. Pope concludes that equally good arguments can be given for an early date or for a late date.

163. A. Bloch and C. Bloch, *The Song of Songs* (New York: Random House, 1995), 25–27.

164. Ibid., 26.

165. M. V. Fox, *The Song of Songs and the Ancient Egyptian Love Songs* (Madison: University of Wisconsin Press, 1985).

166. *b. Sanh.* 101a. See R. Murphy, *The Song of Songs* (Hermeneia; Minneapolis: Fortress Press, 1990), 13.

167. See Max Küchler, *Schweigen, Schmuck und Schleier* (Göttingen: Vandenhoeck & Ruprecht, 1986), 131–35.

168. C. Camp, "Understanding a Patriarchy: Women in Second Century Jerusalem through the Eyes of Ben Sira," in *"Women like This": New Perspectives on Jewish Women in the Greco-Roman World,* ed. A. J. Levine (Atlanta: Scholars Press, 1991), 20–21, offers a novel translation of Sir. 9:1, usually rendered "Do not be jealous of the wife of your bosom." Camp takes the verbs *qānē', zēloō,* as "be zealous, passionate for." On this interpretation, Ben Sira would be urging sexual restraint even within marriage.

169. P. W. Van Der Horst, *The Sentences of Pseudo-Phocylides* (Leiden: E. J. Brill, 1978), 100–101.

170. Trenchard, *Ben Sira's View of Women,* 120–21.
171. See especially C. A. Newsom, "Woman and the Discourse of Patriarchal Wisdom: A Study of Proverbs 1–9," in *Gender and Difference in Ancient Israel,* ed. P. L. Day (Minneapolis: Fortress Press, 1989), 243–60; C. V. Camp, "What's So Strange about the Strange Woman," in *The Bible and the Politics of Exegesis,* ed. D. Jobling, P. L. Day, and G. T. Sheppard (Cleveland: Pilgrim Press, 1991), 17–31.
172. W. McKane, *Proverbs: A New Approach* (London: SCM Press, 1970), 221.
173. G. Boström, *Proverbiastudien: Die Weisheit und das fremde Weib in Spr. 1–9* (Lund: C. W. K. Gleerup, 1935), 103–34.
174. P. Bird, "'To Play the Harlot': An Inquiry into an Old Testament Metaphor," in Day, ed., *Gender and Difference,* 87–88; R. Oden, "Religious Identity and the Sacred Prostitution Accusation," in idem, *The Bible without Theology* (San Francisco: HarperCollins, 1987), 131–53; K. van der Toorn, "Prostitution (Cultic)," *ABD* 5 (1992):510–13.
175. K. van der Toorn, "Female Prostitution in Payment of Vows in Ancient Israel," *JBL* 108 (1989):193–205.
176. Ibid., 202–3.
177. He offers a more picturesque sketch of the adulteress in 26:9: "A wife's fornication occurs by the lifting up of her eyes, and by her eyelids she will be known" (author's translation).
178. Trenchard, *Ben Sira's View of Women,* 100.
179. Camp, "Understanding a Patriarchy," 28.
180. On the view of sexuality in the story of Susanna, see M. Bal, "The Elders and Susanna," *Biblical Interpretation* 1 (1993):1–19.
181. Philo, *De Specialibus Legibus,* 3.110–16; cf. *De Vita Mosis* 1.11, on the horror of having to expose the infant Moses. See also *Sib. Or.* 3:765–66.
182. Later Jewish tradition is not uniform on this issue. See R. Biale, *Women and Jewish Law* (New York: Schocken Books, 1984), 219–38.
183. Pseudo Phocylides, *Sayings,* 184–85. Compare Josephus, *Ap.* 2.202.
184. See R. Bohlen, *Die Ehrung der Eltern bei Ben Sira* (Trier: Paulinus, 1991), 82–117.
185. *Qidd.* 31a; Archer, *Her Price,* 45.
186. Harrington, "Wisdom at Qumran," 148.
187. *b. Baba Bathra* 21a; Archer, *Her Price,* 80.
188. R. Kraemer, "Jewish Mothers and Daughters in the Greco-Roman World," in *The Jewish Family in Antiquity,* ed. S. J. D. Cohen (BJS 289; Atlanta: Scholars Press, 1992), 93.
189. See Archer, *Her Price,* 97–99, on the case of Beruriah, wife of Rabbi Meir.
190. See further Archer, *Her Price,* 17–27.
191. Cf. Sir. 7:24–25; 26:10–12.
192. On the importance of honor and shame in Ben Sira, see Camp, "Understanding a Patriarchy," 35–37, who sees the sage as typical of Mediterranean anthropology in this respect.
193. See Trenchard, *Ben Sira's View of Women,* 155, who argues the composition

of 42:9–15: "Ben Sira has appended to a traditional parenetic statement about a father watching his daughter three lines that suggest negative consequences. . . . The opening traditional parenesis may be viewed as neutral, even positive. However, in the company of Ben Sira's statements of consequence it is made to reflect negatively upon the daughter."

194. See Harrington, "Wisdom at Qumran," 148–49.

195. C. Myers, *Discovering Eve: Ancient Israelite Women in Context* (New York: Oxford University Press, 1988), 196.

196. See D. Balch, *Let Wives Be Submissive* (SBLMS 26; Chico, Calif.: Scholars Press, 1981).

197. Ibid., 35.

198. See Cheryl Anne Brown, *No Longer Be Silent* (Louisville, Ky.: Westminster/John Knox Press, 1992). Brown contrasts Pseudo-Philo's positive portrayal of women with the more negative account of the contemporary Josephus. Also B. Halpern-Amaru, "Portraits of Women in Pseudo-Philo's Biblical Antiquities," in Levine, ed., *"Women like This,"* 83–106.

199. Cowley, *Aramaic Papyri*, 23 (papyrus C 8). See Porten, *Archives from Elephantine*, 240–45.

200. C 14. Porten, *Archives from Elephantine*, 247.

201. C 15. Porten, *Archives from Elephantine*, 253.

202. See Yadin, *Bar Kokhba*, 222–53.

203. On the laws of inheritance, see H. M. Cotton and J. C. Greenfield, "Babatha's Property and the Law of Succession in the Babatha Archive," *Zeitschrift für Papyrologie und Epigraphik* 104 (1994):211–24.

204. Lewis, *Documents from the Bar Kokhba Period*, 26.

4

The Israelite and Early Jewish Family: Summary and Conclusions

LEO G. PERDUE

Israelite and early Jewish life did not take place within a social and cultural vacuum.[1] In its interaction with other cultures, Israel was influenced to a degree by the social, political, and religious characteristics of institutions—including the family—in Egypt, Mesopotamia, Canaan, and the Hellenistic world.[2] There is a wealth of epigraphic and literary data on families in these surrounding cultures that often provides a more complete picture of the household than the one we have from sources of ancient Israel and early Judaism. The nature and practice of families in other cultures may have impacted on the Israelite family, at least indirectly, though this effect is extremely difficult to pinpoint with precision. Even so, the household in Israel and early Judaism did not simply appropriate characteristics of family life from other cultures through a kind of cultural transfusion; rather, these properties would have been adapted, transformed, and at times rejected.

There is another way that the wealth of data on families in the ancient world may be used to understand the family in ancient Israel and early Judaism. These data may assist us in ascertaining both the general similarities with and the distinctive features of the family in ancient Israel and early Judaism.[3] On the whole, then, our knowledge of the families of the ancient Near East and the Hellenistic world may assist us in understanding the household in Israel and early Judaism, though the rather different social, economic, and religious realities of these cultures significantly limit their relevance and import.

Sources and the
Limits of the Evidence

Archaeological
and Epigraphic Data

There are significant archaeological and written materials available
for the reconstruction of family life and practice in ancient Israel and
early Judaism. The previous chapters have drawn on these data for the
reconstruction of the household in this society. Even so, material, non-
literary culture, while of immense importance in pointing to the social
and economic realities of the ancient family, cannot uncover in a direct
manner the values, beliefs, and laws that were shaped by and that in
turn shaped this institution over the centuries. This is why it is important, especially when the written data are limited or have experienced
significant transformation in their formulation and transmission, to
construct social models that suggest how the family operated as a social
and economic system within a larger cultural world and what values
and practices would correspond to this reality.[4]

Epigraphic and literary texts produced in Israelite and early Jewish
society, outside of the Bible, are important witnesses to the nature and
practice of the family. However, these materials are limited, scattered,
and often rather sketchy. Even the large written repositories from Qumran and Elephantine do not cover significant areas of family life and do
not allow a complete look at the household in the periods and regions
represented by these "libraries."

Biblical Resources

The Bible does contain a significant amount of material that directly or
indirectly relates to family life in ancient Israel and early Judaism. At the
same time, it is important to recognize the limitations of these resources.
The development of biblical texts over many generations was a complex
process, involving the transmission and eventual writing down of an oral
tradition, the formation and weaving together of socially and religiously
diverse traditions, the editing of materials into narratives and collections
of poetry, and the final canonizing of biblical books by the early Jewish
community. Consequently, the oral and literary histories of these canonical books are very difficult to unravel. It is not always clear when a book
or one of its earlier stages may have been written, who wrote it, and for
what reason. In addition, it is often a formidable challenge to decide

whether texts describe the actual social life of ancient Israelites and Jews or are ideological prescriptions by particular groups bent on reshaping this social life in another direction. For example, are the sapiential instructions concerning women in Sirach the common views of the larger Jewish society in the second century B.C.E., those of aristocratic men seeking to control and dominate women and young girls, or those of an individual who harbored sexist views that he wished to impose on others? Thus a "hermeneutics of suspicion" needs to be at work when the interpreter seeks to represent the nature and character of the family in biblical texts and in early Israelite and Jewish society.

The Changing Character
of the Family

There is another challenge to face in the effort to assess ancient materials in order to reconstruct the family in ancient Israel and early Judaism, namely, the fact that this institution reflects considerable change and diversity over a twelve-hundred-year period. As Carol L. Meyers notes, the term *family* is a "deceptively simple English word" that "masks a unit of social connection and interaction that is incredibly complex and varied."[5] The family is complex and diverse even within the same culture, and it is significantly influenced by the changes occurring within its larger sociopolitical and religious world. No social institution, even one as basic as the family, is static and thus insulated against change. Yet, in spite of the complex, diverse, and dynamic character of the family, it provides the key institution for understanding the nature and character of human society and social interaction.[6]

These general observations are equally true of the family in ancient Israel and early Judaism. The changes and developments in Israelite and Jewish society and religion over a twelve-hundred-year period—from the beginning of the settlement in Canaan in 1200 B.C.E. to the beginning of the common era (C.E.)—affected, to a degree, the form and character of the family. And there is evidence of some diversity of the family's expression even during the same periods. However, the family in this culture continued in largely the same form and with some of the same character for twelve centuries.

The Rural Family

Preindustrial societies are largely rural, meaning that approximately 90 percent of people live in rural settings,[7] and this was true as well of ancient Israel and early Judaism. Indeed, much of what we know of the family in ancient Israel and early Judaism concerns the rural, agrarian family, although the literary tradition itself was largely produced by the literati of urban culture, particularly of Jerusalem (rulers, priests, royal and priestly scribes, and urban prophets). What may have been characteristic of urban families, in contrast to rural ones, cannot be easily ascertained from this literature.

The Household:
Three Major Features

The three preceding chapters on the family in ancient Israel and early Judaism point to both continuity and change within this institution during a twelve-hundred-year period. These diachronic studies delineate several defining features of the family in this culture.

The Household as the Form of the Family

The major feature of the Israelite family was the form of the household, which operated within the larger social structures of the clan and the tribe. The kinship structure, extending both authentically and fictionally into the larger social units of the clan and tribe, integrated other primary characteristics of the family.[8] Households in ancient Israel were multigenerational and consisted of two or three families, related by kinship and marriage, who lived in a residential complex of two or three houses connected together. Families were patrilineal (i.e., descent was reckoned through the male line), patrilocal (i.e., the wife joined the household of her husband), and at least became largely patriarchal.[9]

The Economic Character of the Household

A second major feature of the family was its significantly economic character. The household, involving members within the kinship structure as well as others who were integrated into its social fabric, consisted of roles that, taken together, provided the labor necessary for the survival of the whole. The traditions of the household, including its stories, customs, laws, and rituals, often exhibit an economic interest. While the family in early Israel may have been more egalitarian than its later expressions, its largely patriarchal nature in subsequent periods is indicated by the authority of the male head of the household, as well as by its patrilineality, patrilocality, and patrimony. This patriarchal complexion emerged, in part, as a means to ensure the household's economic viability in the present and into the future.

The Ethics of Household Solidarity

Central to family values was the emphasis placed on solidarity, grounded in the interdependence of the members that was necessary for survival and continuity. While encompassing a familial hierarchy based on gender, role, and age, this moral understanding pointed to the responsibilities of members of the household for the care and well-being of the collective whole. The needs of the household took precedence over those of individual members who formed its constituency. While the economic interests of the individual household provided the central core of identity and responsibility, the ethics of solidarity shaped a network of understanding and care that moved beyond the immediate compound family to include clans, tribes, and the totality of the "children of Israel." Even the development of the concept of individual responsibility, occasioned by the undermining of family traditions by the monarchy and by the disruptions of conquest, exile, and return, did not suppress this prevailing sense of community.

The Religion
of the Household

These three major characteristics of the household formed the social basis of Israelite and early Jewish religion. The formative tradition of the households pointed to God's election of the founding ancestors, whose compound families issued forth in larger clans and tribes. God shaped their past, sustained their present, and promised their future. God provided descendants through whom the chosen families could survive into the future. Court historians, prophets, and priests took this household tradition and integrated it with the larger national epic, which included the exodus out of Egypt, the wilderness wandering, the law of Sinai, and the gift of the land of Canaan. The household tradition also came to be grounded in the cosmological and anthropological theologies of creation faith.

Divine legitimation was given to the laws and customs that protected and sustained the households and that ensured their viability. The divine imperative to care for the poor was carried out largely through the networks of families and clans, who provided for their kinsmen and kinswomen and who, in keeping with the fictional ideal of the consanguinity of the tribes of Israel, offered charity to the destitute even outside their immediate kinship structure. The household's worship gave expression to its sacred memory through story and rite, celebrated the deity who chose and protected its members, established the legitimacy of its law and customs, and nurtured the solidarity of the kinship group that would sustain it into the future.

With the emergence of the royal state, monarchs began to implement social, political, and religious policies that sought to undermine the importance of the family household and to shift its allegiance to the ruling house. The end of the royal state, occasioned by the Assyrian and then the Babylonian conquests and exiles, ended this serious threat to the viability of the household. During the second temple period, the family household regained its prominent place as the center of Jewish social life.

The Functions of the Family

The three previous chapters have provided a diachronic study of the developing and changing form of the family in ancient Israel and early Judaism, and they have underlined both the family's continuity and its diversity during this period of about twelve centuries. The present chapter presents a synoptic overview of the family in ancient Israel and early Judaism that attempts to focus on its major features. We begin with the general functions of the family in this culture and then move into more specific areas: the household as a normative form of the family, gender roles, marriage and divorce, the roles of children, the family and the clan as a network of care, and the household as the formal model for defining relationships between family, state, and religion.

Economics:
Production and Consumption

Throughout Israelite and early Jewish history, a defining function of the family involved production and consumption. The family unit was a pragmatic necessity for human survival in what was largely a village, agrarian society.[10] Intense labor and extensive social cooperation were required for the family and the larger society to subsist, especially in the central highlands, where Israelite village life began and, in large part, continued.[11] While the land of Israel has great diversity of soils, climates, and elevations, the highlands are not conducive to high crop yields. This land lacks valuable minerals, forests of large trees, and extensive, grain-producing fields. The growing and harvesting of crops and fruits were staggered during the agricultural year to provide the food necessary for households. Small numbers of sheep, goats, and cattle supplemented the households' diet and provided raw materials for the manufacturing of textiles.[12]

Extended families comprised the clans that inhabited farming villages, whose small fields, orchards, vineyards, animals, and grazing lands provided the fundamental economic resources for the households' subsistence. Farming in this rugged terrain was labor intensive, requiring the participation not only of adults, both male and female, but also of older children in well-defined socioeconomic roles. While adult males, including older boys, were engaged in clearing fields, planting and harvesting, hewing cisterns, building houses, and constructing and maintaining terraces, women, including older girls, cared for small children, tended gardens, produced textiles, and prepared and preserved food.[13]

Familial land ownership resided at the economic base of Israelite and early Jewish households.[14] Traditions of land distribution (Joshua 13—22) and laws protecting land ownership (e.g., the law of redemption, Lev. 25:24–55; the law of jubilee, Lev. 25:10–12, 28; and the law of levirate marriage, Deut. 25:5–10; Ruth 4:10) point to the inherent economic value of this commodity necessary to sustain households. Land was to be transferred from generation to generation within the family household, normally through inheritance of the patrimony (naḥălāh) at the father's death, with the eldest son receiving the largest portion.[15] The household's land was not a commodity to be bought and sold. This was due not to some romantic notion of "blood and soil" but rather to the necessity of land ownership for the viability of the family household. Without land, it was impossible for the family as a social entity to exist, and the loss of land made it impossible for most households to survive intact. Insolvency, resulting eventually in the selling of land, usually led to the dissolution of the household. Without land, families fragmented and members dispersed, seeking to survive by joining related households as family members, by becoming marginal members of other households to work as debt servants and day laborers, or by joining the underclass of the poor who lived off the charity of Israelite households (Ex. 21:2–11; Lev. 25:35–55; 2 Kings 4:1; and Neh. 5:1–5).

Social cooperation among families in the clan (mišpāḥāh) was necessary for building and maintaining terraces to conserve the soil and reduce water runoff, for sharing a common water source (wells or streams), for constructing cisterns that retained water from the rainy season, for establishing and supporting the boundaries of fields, for harvesting of crops, for judicial settlements, and for a common defense. A network of mutual care was necessary for households to survive crop failures and food shortages caused by drought, blight, and disease. This network of care extended beyond individual clans to the tribes and to the "sons of Israel," whose marginal "poor" included Levites, widows, fatherless children, resident aliens, debt servants, slaves, and sojourners.

The family had to be largely self-sufficient in the cultivation and preservation of foodstuffs, mostly consumed by the household itself; in the production of the raw materials of wool and skins; in weaving and sewing materials into clothing and other textiles; and in building and preserving houses and other structures. The manufacture of cloth and pottery required specialized, skilled labor, which led to what might be called village "cottage industries" that existed through barter. The activities of labor and other elements of family life were located in the surrounding fields and in the household itself.[16]

The social identity and network of support extended beyond the clan village to include other clans and large tribes, bound together by trade, defense, religious practice, language, custom, bloodlines, and marriage. Trading networks among villages and non-Israelite cultures allowed for the barter and exchange of goods such as excess foodstuffs, pottery, and textiles.[17]

Reproduction

Reproduction was another major function of the family (Gen. 1:28; 9:1). The woman's most important role was the bearing of numerous children (Gen. 24:60), while the man hoped to produce many progeny who would contribute needed labor and continue the household into the future (Gen. 15:4–6). While children were a necessary economic commodity, for they eventually became laborers within the family whose productivity contributed to the survival of the whole, they were also the means by which the household hoped to claim its future. For the most part, male children became the heirs to the family's resources, especially the land that was to remain within the domain of the household's ownership. They continued the ancestral name and defining traditions of the household, which provided identity and meaning. In a figurative sense, the dead survived through both the ongoing existence of the household and the maintenance of family tombs located on the household's land.

The primary purpose of marriage was reproduction, although the responsible provision of protection and care and the presence of love between spouses are duly noted in texts. As an institution, marriage was placed under the purview of the households of the man and the woman. In essence, marriage was an economic arrangement between two households, normally within the same kinship structure, to ensure their viability and to strengthen their solidarity and sense of cooperation. While monogamy was the standard practice, concubinage and polygamy were practiced on occasion to ensure a household's producing of needed progeny. Divorce was allowed to permit the remarriage of both exhusbands and ex-wives, in order that other household arrangements could be made to strengthen the chances for the households and their members to endure and produce offspring.

Nurture

It is clear that children were valued beyond their economic worth to their families. The announcement of pregnancy was a time of great rejoicing, and the day of birth was the occasion for celebration among family members. Tenderness, love, and affection for children are often expressed in the Hebrew Bible, as is the sustaining care provided to children. The child was raised under the care of his or her mother and nursed for a customary period of three years. One of the harsh realities of family life was that child mortality was high, often due to childhood illnesses.

Villages, consisting usually of related family households, provided the network of care for their children. Yet the nurturing responsibility of the household extended beyond small children to other members of the family. Care was extended to aged and sick parents and grandparents and to widows and divorced women who returned to the houses of their fathers, with or without offspring. The next of kin served as the "redeemer" (go'ēl) of the extended household and larger clan, with the responsibility to avenge the murder of a kinsperson, maintain the family's ownership of its patrimony, and secure a kinsperson's release from debt service. The practice of levirate marriage, in which the next of kin, generally the brother, married the widow in order to raise legal descendants to inherit the estate of her childless dead husband, also served to keep the household intact. The sabbatical year resulted in the forgiveness of debt, while the jubilee year (fiftieth year) required the restoration of the patrimony redeemed by the go'ēl to the original household.

Beyond the immediate kinship structure, the households also could include debt servants, slaves, concubines, widows and fatherless children, resident aliens, temporary sojourners, and, on occasion, Levites. These marginal members contributed to the tasks of the household in return for socially and even legally defined support, for both themselves and their families. Through marriage and perhaps adoption, it was possible for these individuals to merge into the household's kinship structure. Otherwise, they remained marginals living within the household and enjoying its protection while outside its kinship structure.

Beyond the household, there existed an underclass of day laborers, widows, orphans (specifically, the fatherless), beggars, and Levites unattached to families and sanctuaries. Without the protection of their own household, the existence of these poor was precarious. Gleanings were left in the fields and fruit on the trees and vines to be gathered by the poor; day laborers were to be paid the evening of the same day they worked; and the tithe every third year was designated for the poor. The term *neighbor* came to include not only a "brother" or kinsman but also a fellow Israelite and even a resident foreigner, who was to be loved as oneself and thus provided with the support necessary for survival.

Education

Most education[18] occurred within the household through the oral transmission of knowledge and skills relating to household tasks, social customs, and religious tradition.[19] Small children and girls were taught by the mother (Prov. 1:8; 6:20), while the father assumed responsibility for teaching boys—especially at the time of transition to manhood—and young men (Ex. 10:2; 12:26; 13:8; Deut. 4:9; 6:7, 20–25; 32:7, 46; Prov. 1:8; 6:20; and Sir. 30:1–13).

In the household, boys and young men were taught the body of knowledge and skills required for farming, while girls and young women received instruction in parenting, food preparation and preservation, tending gardens, and producing textiles. Yet education went beyond the pragmatic necessities of labor to include social customs, moral values, and religious beliefs and rituals.[20] The titles for the student ("son") and the teacher ("father" or "mother") in wisdom literature may reflect this household ethos of parents instructing children (Prov. 1:8, 10, 15; 2:1; 3:1, 11, 21; Sir. 2:1 and 3:1). It was not only the father who taught the law (Deut. 6:7; 11:19; 32:46–47), traditions of morality and religion, the knowledge and skills associated with economic roles, and social customs (Ex. 12:26–27; 13:14–16; Deut. 4:9; 6:7, 20–25; Josh. 4:6–7, 21–23); it was also the mother (Prov. 1:8; 6:20; 30:17; 31:1–9). Proverbs frequently mentions the authority and instruction of both the father and the mother within the same saying (Prov. 10:1; 15:20; 20:20; 23:22, 25; 28:24; 30:11, 17) and points to the firm discipline of parents (13:24; 19:18; 23:13–14; 29:15, 17).[21] Family traditions would have included the stories, laws, and customs concerning the household's patrimony and relationships with other families, clans, and tribes. These stories and instructions also transmitted the household's religious knowledge, which undergirded and legitimated family life.[22]

Literacy is another matter. It is highly probable that the members of farming households in the Israelite countryside were, in large measure, illiterate throughout this entire period.[23] The evidence for a social context of teaching reading and writing is quite limited. During the early period, prior to state formation, there appears to have been some literacy in the Israelite towns (Judg. 8:14). Later, during the period of the first temple, Isaiah of Jerusalem, living in a place where literacy flourished—at least among scribes and officials in the court and the temple—referred to some who could read but others who could not (Isa. 29:12).[24] It is logical to assume that most instruction in the scribal arts of reading and writing developed during the monarchy (2 Sam. 8:17) and would have occurred within the contexts of court and temple schools in Jerusalem and Samaria, and perhaps in local schools in the towns throughout Israel. However, explicit archaeological and literary evidence for schools not only in the capitals Jerusalem and Samaria but also in local towns is extremely sparse.[25]

While there is limited epigraphic evidence for the geographic expansion of literacy throughout Israel during the first temple period,[26] it is probable that most households would have been without any members who were capable of reading and writing, even at a very basic level.[27] Perhaps there were scribal households, located presumably in the large royal cities, where the literary arts were transmitted in the manner of guilds, but this would not have been true of ordinary village households, largely engaged in agricultural work (Sir. 38:25–26).

Military

Prior to state formation, Israelite households within their larger clans established a protective agency of defense against military invaders who threatened them.[28] Judges 5 reflects a larger military coalition of various tribes and clans banding together to fight the Canaanites in the Valley of Jezreel (see Gideon in Judg. 6:33–35). Men from the associations of families in the clans formed a nonprofessional militia led by the charismatic warrior who was believed to have been imbued with the spirit of God and called by a messenger or prophet of Yahweh (Judg. 6:7–24). He was chosen from one of the clans and served during the duration of the conflict. After the crisis was averted, he returned to his household, to dwell there the rest of his life (Judg. 8:23, 29–32). This understanding of clan and tribal warfare developed its own rituals and tradition, commonly called "holy war" by biblical scholars. This was largely understood as a war that was declared by God in defense of clan and tribal domains and households.

Judiciary

Within the household, the male head of the household was responsible for maintaining order and adjudicating disputes, arranging marriages, assigning household tasks, maintaining the economic and social support for daughters whose husbands died or divorced them, and settling matters of inheritance.[29] The authority of the senior male in the household was significant, though not absolute. The developing corpus of family law and legal precedent in ancient Israel and early Judaism continued to place limitations on the authority of the head of the household (cf., e.g., the release of Hebrew debt servants and slaves, Ex. 21:2–11 and Deut. 15:12–18). Clan elders served as judges to resolve disputes between households and to make the decisions of life or death for unruly adult children who were charged by both parents (Deut. 21:18–21).[30] Tribal elders adjudicated conflict between tribes.[31]

The Question of a Normative Form of the Family

The three primary units of social organization shaped by kinship structures are the "tribe" (šēbeṭ/maṭṭeh), the "clan" (mišpāḥāh), and the "family household" (bêt 'āb) (see Josh. 7:16–18; cf. Judg. 6:15; 1 Sam. 9:21; 10:20–21).[32] The form of the family household provided the major, continuous feature of the family throughout the twelve-hundred-year history of ancient Israel and early Judaism.

Bêt 'āb

The primary terms for the family household are bayit and bêt 'āb,[33] translated respectively and literally as "house" and "house of the father."[34] In view of the literary and archaeological evidence, these terms are best rendered "family household" and "extended" or "compound family." Family households did not consist of nuclear families in the modern understanding of a married couple and their children but rather were multigenerational (up to four generations) and included the social arrangement of several families, related by blood and marriage, who lived in two or three houses architecturally connected. Israelite and early Jewish families were patrilineal (i.e., descent was reckoned through the male line) and patrilocal (i.e., the wife joined the *bêt 'āb* of her husband).

Those who belong to the family household are mentioned a number of times in the Hebrew Bible (Gen. 7:1, 7; 36:6; 45:10; cf. Gen. 46:26; Ex. 20:8–10, 17; Deut. 5:12–15, 21; Josh. 7:16–18; Judg. 6:11, 27, 30; 8:20). These texts indicate that the family household was primarily a kinship system that included lineal descent and lateral extension: grandparents, adult male children and their wives and children, unmarried children, and widowed and divorced adult daughters who may have had children.[35] Marginal members of households outside of this immediate kinship structure could include debt servants, slaves, concubines, resident aliens, sojourners, day laborers, orphans, and Levites, together with any family they may have had (Ex. 20:8–10; Deut. 5:12–15; 16:11, 14). In Judges 17—18, Micah lived with his widowed mother, his sons, perhaps their families, and a Levite who tended the family shrine. Micah's Levite had his own house (Judg. 18:15), and there were other dependents living in houses within the same compound (18:14–22). Together these formed a family household (*bayit*, 18:25; cf. v. 29). Marginals could be included within the kinship structure through marriage and possibly adoption, though evidence for the latter practice is limited. Of course, only very large families would have had members representing each of these social categories.

In addition to people, the household or compound family included the estate (Gen. 36:6; Ex. 20:17; Deut. 5:21).[36] The family residence consisted usually of two or three houses that were architecturally connected by the sharing of several walls and perhaps a common courtyard.[37] The estate of the household also included its fields, orchards, vineyards, pastures, livestock, and the tools and implements for living and working.

The household was comprised of living members but also of the ancestors, who were remembered through story and ritual and, in some sense, continued to live through their descendants. In ancient Israel, two separate views of life after death developed that were in tension with each other. One tradition speaks of the afterlife in Sheol, the abode of the dead, while the other tells of the dead continuing to live in the tomb of interment. Family tombs were located on the household's land, in part so that the ancestors could maintain a presence as members of the family. At death, a family member was "gathered to the ancestors" (Judg. 2:10) or gathered to his or her kin by being interred in the family tomb or cemetery (Gen. 25:8, 17; 49:29–33). A good burial was highly desired and was considered to be the reward for a good life (1 Kings 14:13; 2 Kings 22:20). To remain unburied was a terrible fate (1 Kings 13:22; 14:11; 16:4; 21:24; 2 Kings 9:10; Jer. 7:33; 8:1–2; 9:21; 14:16; 22:19; 25:33). One of the most important ways that children honored their parents was to provide them with a suitable burial.[38]

Archaeological excavations indicate that offerings were made to the dead (mentioned in Deut. 26:14; Ps. 106:28), and these gifts were not directly prohibited by law. In popular religion, worship of the dead appears to have been practiced, although it was opposed by orthodox Yahwism.[39] There is some suggestion of an ancestral cult in popular religion, designed to worship the dead as divine powers ('ĕlohîm; cf. 1 Sam. 28:13; 2 Sam. 14:16; Isa. 8:19–20), though the details are not known.[40] In any case, it was through memory and honor, along with interment in the family tomb, that the ancestors continued to be members of their households.

Unborn progeny, comprising the future generations of the household, were also considered in a way to be members of the family; at least, future generations were often in mind in the stories and teachings of the Hebrew Bible and in the literature of early Judaism. In Genesis, the ancestors of Israel are promised that they will become the fathers of a "great nation" (e.g., Gen. 12:2) and that their numerous descendants will inherit the land of Canaan as their household patrimony (e.g., Gen. 13:14–17). In Deuteronomy, faithfulness to the tradition of story and law (torah) would enable future generations to be born and to be blessed by Yahweh. The future of Job's household, as set forth in the story of his redemption (Job 42:7–17), was secured in the birth of another seven sons and three daughters, to replace those who had died earlier. Through his children, Job's household and name would continue beyond his own time.

Household members comprised, then, the dead ancestors of the past, those living in the present, and those yet to be born. The solidarity of the Israelite and early Jewish family was strengthened and made more comprehensive by its inclusion of members from the wide sweep of the generations of its existence.

However, the diversity of family arrangements cautions against making a hasty assumption that this form is normative, either in its biblical setting or for the modern context. Perhaps it is best to say that the household in ancient Israel and early Judaism was both a pragmatic necessity and a traditional form that still allowed for some variation. As the previous three chapters have noted, the diversity and continuing developments of this social institution are reflected in laws, customs, and practices. For instance, while monogamy seemed to be the preferred and normal arrangement for marriage and sexual activity, there are instances of polygamy and even—rarely—celibacy.

Mišpāḥāh

The term *mišpāḥāh*[41] has a variety of meanings in the Hebrew Bible and early Jewish literature, including "family," though its most specific meaning is "a residential kinship group of several families" or, more commonly, a "clan." The *mišpāḥāh* often pointed to a village consisting of several farm households related by kinship and marriage.[42] Households inhabited their own settled space; worked their own fields, orchards, and vineyards; and tended their own animals and pastures (see the clan of David, Ephrathah, which lived in Bethlehem; Micah 5:2). Pastures were probably shared. Most villages were quite small, occupying from less than an acre to several acres.[43] Carol L. Meyers has estimated that most early Israelite villages consisted of less than one hundred members and this would also have been true of later Israel, even though Israelite occupation of towns and cities emerged during state formation, leading to increasing urbanization.[44]

In addition to bonds of kinship and marriage, clans were held together by language, economic cooperation, shared traditions of law and custom, ancestral stories, and a common religion. Joseph Blenkinsopp has pointed to an ancestral clan gathering each year, religious in content, that through story and rite would forge and sustain the solidarity of the group.[45] Clan elders comprised a judicial council for addressing disputes between families over such matters as boundaries and marriage contracts and for judging the case of a disorderly son brought to them by his parents. They may also have participated in decisions that involved the levies expected of households to provide protection against military threats, though the mustering of troops seems to have depended on the voluntary decision of the local households to join in the effort.

Šēbeṭ/Maṭṭeh

The "tribe" refers to a larger social unit that provided the major geographical and kinship organization (real and fictional) for ancient Israel.[46] Broadly speaking, Israel was comprised of twelve tribes named after one household—the sons of Israel (Jacob), which included two grandsons, Ephraim and Manasseh (Joseph's two sons). The tribe combined real and fictional kinship structures for clans and households, provided a judicial council for settling disputes between clans, spoke the same language, shared traditions and practices of law and custom, practiced a common religion, and offered the means for mustering a citizen militia for protection.

Israel/House of Israel

The community of the tribes formed the people, or nation, of Israel (Josh. 24:1, 31). Prior to state formation, the tribes may have participated in a federation for common defense.[47] It is important to note that even this larger federation understood itself as the extended, multigenerational household of Israel (Jacob). This self-understanding, largely fictional, provided the ethos of solidarity and the corporate identity for the entire nation. Israel was both a people and a community whose ethic of solidarity provided the social basis for various forms and measures of cooperation in the areas of defense, religion, and law. Holy war seems to have been a system of protection that included more than one tribe, while a council of tribal elders may have convened to solve disputes between tribes. There also may have been shrines for the religious gatherings of several tribes during the prestate period.[48]

The Household as a Cosmos for Human Dwelling

Households were more than socioeconomic units that were defined by kinship structures based on blood and marriage and augmented by marginal members enjoying protection and contributing to the labor force. They also were a social world constructed by tradition, ethos, law, customs, and religion. They projected a reality of time, space, values, action, and people bound together in solidarity by the common effort to promote the well-being of the whole. The household was grounded in the order of creation (Gen. 1:26–28; 2:21–24). It established a spatial context for human dwelling through residence and patrimony; defined social and economic roles for human interaction, with the common goal of group survival and continuation; received religious legitimation through divine actions in history, rehearsed in story and ritual; and responded to divine imperatives that shaped socioreligious life and moral behavior.

The ancient ancestor founded the primordial household, from which all others issued (Genesis 12—50). The liberation of his household from Egyptian bondage, narrated and confessed in story and ritual (Deut. 26:5–9), constituted the historical epic for the gift of the land to the households of Israel and the tradition that shaped their religious self-understanding and moral ethos. The exodus, the wilderness wandering, and the conquest reached their culmination in the Israelite families' inheritance, through gift and domination, of the land of Canaan, where they became households with patrimonies that especially included the land. Exile meant the disintegration of the households, but the return offered the chance for the continuity of older households and the formation of new ones. Throughout Israelite and early Jewish history, then, the household was the primary and essential cosmos for human dwelling.

Gender and Gender Roles in the Family

Social roles in the household were defined primarily on the bases of kinship structure, arranged marriages, age, and gender. Most human activities in ancient Israel and early Judaism took place within the household. It served as a workforce and as a workplace, where gender played a major role in defining and carrying out the various responsibilities of labor, reproduction, nurture, education, informal judicial decisions, and protection.[49] The close confinement of family members and the significant interdependence of males and females in forming and running the household led to the defining of specific social and economic roles for both genders. In addition, the household's kinship structure included a hierarchy of authority and responsibility for those related by blood and by marriage, while its social arrangements placed marginal members outside the immediate kinship structure, in subservient roles.

Males

The familial roles of males in the household's kinship structure included those of lineal descent and marriage—grandfather, father, son, and husband[50]—and those lateral relationships—brother, uncle, nephew, and cousin. The primary responsibility of the latter group in the household was to perform the role of the *go'ēl* (redeemer), which is discussed below. Functional roles for males within the household included procreation, agricultural labor, education, judicial decisions, religious instruction and practice, and protective associations.

The primary designation of the household, *bêt 'āb,* translates literally as "house of the father," indicating that much of the authority within the extended family was vested in the "father," or head, of the household (*'āb*), who usually was the grandfather or father (*rō'š* = "head"; Num. 25:15; 1 Chron. 24:31).[51] The designation "house of the father" also expresses the fact that the extended family was patrilineal (father-son descent in inheritance and authority) and patrilocal (wives left their households to join the *bêt 'āb* of their husbands). In the Hebrew Bible, the ancestral fathers (i.e., the patriarchs in Genesis 12—50) are portrayed as the founders of eponymous households that expanded into clans and tribes over the generations, through descent and the incorporation of new members. In the folklore of the household, the ancestral fathers embodied in their lives and experiences the traditions and customs of the family.

In the household, the authority of the senior male in all areas of family life was considerable, ranging from assigning economic roles to family members, deciding on the male heir who would assume his role and own much of the family's patrimony, and judging family disputes to arranging marriages with other households, handling the sale of children when the household was not economically viable, and having, at least for a time, the power of life and death over children and other household members judged in violation of certain laws (Gen. 19:8; 38:24; Ex. 21:7–11; Judg. 11:29–40; 19).[52] Married sons and their families remained under the authority of the head of the household until he died or became incapacitated.[53]

Females

In biblical and early Jewish literature, women's lineal kinship and marriage roles in the household were those of grandmother, mother, daughter, and wife,[54] while lateral ones were sister, aunt, niece, and cousin.

Throughout their lives, women were legally subordinate to men, primarily as daughters and wives. When their husbands and fathers were deceased, women existed as members of the household of either their *go'ēl* (next of kin) or their master whom they served as slaves or concubines.[55] This means that women's roles were legally defined and determined by men, though there are numerous instances in the literature that point to women's subversion of male power and informal wielding of authority and influence within the household.[56]

Daughters were raised to leave their own households and join those of their husbands, to have children, to participate in the economic tasks of the family, and to educate small children and girls in the ethos and work roles of the household. However, they were still to some extent outsiders in their husbands' households. Normally, women were exchanged between the households that made the marriage arrangements and were required to marry within their own kinship group (Num. 36:6–9).

Counted among a man's assets was his wife (*'iššâ* Ex. 20:17; contrast Deut. 5:21), and while she called her husband "master" (*ba'al*) or "lord" (*'ādôn*), it is doubtful she was viewed as property. Normally, women did not inherit the property of their husbands or fathers. (Numbers 27:1–11 is an exception.) Men (a father or husband) are presented as having to consent to women's vows for them to be legal (Num. 30:3–17), and men are most often depicted as those who offer sacrifices (as priests, fathers, or husbands). The birth narrative of Samuel, however, tells of his mother, Hannah, vowing a vow with no obvious male consent, making her own petition to Yahweh, and, after the birth and weaning of her son, bringing offerings to the temple at Shiloh (1 Samuel 1).

Wives did possess certain rights. They could not be sold. Divorce was predicated on the husband's finding some "indecency" in his wife; a bill of divorce granted the woman freedom to remarry, and she was dismissed by her husband with the economic protection of a marriage fee and perhaps a dowry (see below). Women are depicted in biblical and early Jewish literature as wielding significant influence over males in their household, though largely in informal or subversive ways (Sarah, Genesis 12—23; Rebekah, Genesis 24—27; Samson' wife, Judg. 14:17; Bathsheba, 1 Kings 1:15–21; and the "capable wife" of Prov. 31:10–31).

Women served in the roles of prophet, sage, medium, and midwife, though apparently not as priests in the Yahwistic religion. However, parallel to the case of men as "fathers," the woman's primary social role was that of "mother" (*'ēm*) in the household.[57] A woman married shortly after puberty and left her own family to live with her husband's household. While divorce appears to have been practiced, the lack of laws governing divorce makes it difficult to know the exact circumstances and reasons involved for its implementation. It appears the husband could divorce the wife, though it is not clear whether the wife was extended the same privilege.[58] Having many children, especially sons, was highly valued (Gen. 30:1; 1 Sam. 2:5; Ps. 127:3–5; 128:3–4), and they provided their households, including their mothers, both economic security and social status (Gen. 16:5; 30:1). Barrenness was considered a disgrace and evidence of divine disfavor (Gen. 30:23; 2 Sam. 6:20–23). In addition, the desire to have many children may reflect the extremely high infant mortality in this culture. Divorce and widowhood before any children were born were especially threatening to women, if they did not later remarry. Sons in particular could take care of their mothers, especially in their old age. Pragmatically speaking, the mother produced the children who would provide the labor and the heirs for the household's (and her) survival.

The mother's own economic tasks, beyond providing care, were necessary for family survival. She managed the household and loved and cared for her husband and children (Prov. 31:10–31). She taught her children during their early childhood, and then her older daughters. She taught the knowledge and skills of household tasks, as well as the customs and traditions of the family. The mother was closely bonded to her children (2 Sam. 21:8–14; Isa. 49:15; Jer. 31:15–22),[59] and her compassion for them is compared to God's compassion for Israel (Isa. 66:13). Within the household her authority and influence, both formal and informal, were second only to those of the father or senior male. Sarah tells Abraham to cast out Hagar (Gen. 21:10), while Rebekah helps Jacob steal the birthright from Esau (Gen. 27:11–17). The mother, along with the father, was to be honored and respected (Ex. 20:12 = Deut. 5:16; Prov. 1:8; 6:20; 10:1; 15:20; Ezek. 22:7).[60] Tradition (Prov. 19:26; 20:20; 23:22; 30:17; Sir. 3:1–16) and legislation required that she be respected and obeyed (Ex. 20:12; Lev. 19:3). Disrespect and disobedience were prohibited (Ex. 21:15, 17; Lev. 20:9; Deut. 21:18; 27:16), and rebellious children could be executed (Deut. 21:18–21).

Marriage and Divorce

Marriage

The Hebrew Bible has no word or laws for marriage. And one does not find an indisputable reference to marriage contracts (Mal. 2:14; cf. Prov. 2:17; Ezek. 16:8) until Elephantine and Tobit 7:13–15. However, the institution was critically important to social and religious life in ancient Israel and early Judaism.[61]

Households normally looked within the boundaries of the kinship structure—that is, clan and tribe—to find suitable partners for their children, though incest restrictions in Leviticus 18 and 20 prohibited most sexual relations and marriages among members of the individual household, save for the levirate marriage.[62] Marriages were arranged by the parents of the two households, and the son and daughter were not always consulted (Gen. 21:21; 34:4–6; 38:6; Josh. 15:16; 1 Sam. 18:17–27; 25:44).[63] While love between husband and wife is mentioned (Gen. 34:3–4; 1 Sam. 18:20), what appears most important in the literature is the securing of the household's economic interests and property rights. This appearance may in part be due to the legal character of many of the texts that refer to marriage, but even in poems and narratives, economic considerations often play a role. The concern to maintain a household's patrimony through its daughters, who were allowed to inherit the family estate only when there were no sons, led to the law requiring them to marry within the father's kinship group (Num. 36:5–9). Marriages to foreigners were normally forbidden, though this prohibition was often ignored. Marriages to foreign women were prohibited, ostensibly for religious reasons: the foreign wife would maintain her own alien culture, especially her pagan religion (Ex. 34:11–16; Num. 25:1–2; Deut. 7:3–4; Judg. 3:5–6; Neh. 13:23–27), which would lead the household and, by extension, Israel to adopt the ways of foreign cultures and their gods. However, other reasons seem just as plausible. The potential loss of the patrimony of the household to foreigners may have been a strong incentive to avoid these mixed marriages. In addition, foreigners would not as easily adapt to the social customs, work patterns, and religion of the household.[64]

The rights and authority of the husband dominate the marriage relationship as portrayed in the literature. Once betrothed, the woman was considered legally married, and her sexuality was protected on pain of death (Deut. 22:23–29).[65] The husband "took" a wife (Gen. 4:19; 11:29) and "ruled" (*māšal*) over her (Gen. 3:16).[66] To "take a wife" (*bāʿal*) means "to become master" (Deut. 21:13; 24:1). The noun for husband is either *baʿal* ("master," Gen. 20:3; Ex. 21:3, 22; Deut. 24:4; 2 Sam. 11:26; Prov. 12:4; 31:11, 23, 28; Hos. 2:18 [ET 2:16]) or *ʾādôn* ("lord," Gen. 18:12), while the wife is the *bĕʿulat baʿal*, the "property of the master" (Gen. 20:3). In the Decalogue in Exodus 20:2–17, the wife is listed among the household's assets that are not to be coveted (v. 17), though this contrasts with the older formulation of the Decalogue in Deuteronomy 5:6–21, which does not list her as a household asset (v. 21).

In addition to the exchange of marriage gifts between families to strengthen their bonds, the husband's household was responsible for paying the *mohar* (Deut. 22:29), the marriage fee, to the betrothed's father (Gen. 34:12; Ex. 22:16–17; 1 Sam. 18:25). The amount varies (Gen. 34:12; 1 Sam. 18:25), depending on the social status of the husband's family and the price set by the woman's father.[67] Since households were patrilocal, wives joined their husband's families (Gen. 24:5–8, 58–59; Deut. 20:7). Rather than signifying a purchase, the *mohar* probably compensated the woman's household for the loss of her labor, signaled the transfer of responsibility from her family to the husband's (although see the complaint of Rachel and Leah, Gen. 31:15), and provided her economic security in case of divorce or widowhood.[68] The marriage fee does suggest that the unmarried daughter was an economic asset of her household. This is also clear from the legal text in Exodus 22:16–17, which indicates that the man who seduces or rapes a young woman not engaged to be married is obligated to pay the marriage fee to her father and then to make her his wife. He must pay an amount equal to the marriage fee if her father refuses to give her in marriage. In reshaping this law, Deuteronomy 22:28–29 does not allow the father to reject the seducer or rapist as a son-in-law. However, in becoming her husband, the man who violated her could not divorce her.

While it is not clear that in ancient Israel the marriage arrangement included a dowry (Gen. 24:59–61; 29:24, 29; Josh. 15:18–19), the archives at Elephantine point to the existence of the practice, at least in this locale. Here certain assets are taken by the woman to her new family household. These assets would be hers in case of the later dissolution of marriage through either divorce or the death of her husband.

Also protected by marriage laws and customs was the husband's sole right to his wife's sexuality. Before marriage, the woman's virginity was to be guarded and assured by her father (Gen. 34:5–7; Deut. 22:13–21, 28–29). The husband controlled her sexuality after marriage (Num. 5:11–31; see Ex. 20:17). In the legal tradition, adultery by either the husband or the wife was to be punished by death (Lev. 20:10; Deut. 22:22, including both male and female offenders), though it is clear that prostitution was widespread (e.g., Genesis 38), adultery frequent, and thus the laws were often ignored or not enforced. In Proverbs, the "strange woman" (not necessarily a foreigner but anyone who lives outside the bounds of social convention), portrayed largely as a prostitute and an adulterer, was to be avoided at the cost of one's life.[69]

Monogamy and Polygamy

Monogamy was the preferred marriage arrangement in ancient Israel and early Judaism (see Gen. 2:24; Hos. 2:3–15 [ET 2:1–13]; Mal. 2:14–16), though there are notable exceptions.

Polygamy, which included concubinage, allowed a household to increase its labor force and its chances to provide a living male heir to inherit the estate (Genesis 12—22). This arrangement also provided a support system for women who would not have otherwise married, widows, divorcées, and any children of the last two groups, as well as for aged parents. However, there is no explicit evidence for how the management of a household would have been carried out by two or more wives. Perhaps the favorite wife enjoyed a special status (Gen. 29:30–31; Ex. 21:10; Deut. 21:15–17; 1 Sam. 1:6), though presumably each wife had responsibility for her own children.

Deuteronomy 21:15–17 not only presupposes the existence of polygamy (at least bigamy) but also legislates against the husband's being partisan to the younger son of the more favored wife in the distribution of the household's patrimony. In actual practice, however, polygamy seems to have been limited to the very wealthy, including especially the patriarchs (Gen. 29:15–30; 30:1–9; 36:1–5), judges (Gideon: Judg. 8:30–31), and royalty (e.g., 2 Sam. 3:2–5; 5:13; 15:16; 16:21–22; 1 Kings 11:3). Save for Samuel's father (1 Sam. 1:5–6), no commoner in the entire Deuteronomic History (Samuel–Kings) had more than one wife.[70] Toward the end of the period before the common era, the Dead Sea community came to prohibit the practice of polygamy.

Divorce

In the Hebrew Bible, it may be that only the husband could initiate divorce, though this is not clear. The difficulty that confronts us is that there is no specific law of divorce. While Deuteronomy 24:1–4 serves primarily to place restrictions on the remarriage of a former husband and wife, the passage points to elements involved in divorce as practiced at the time. According to this text, the husband could divorce his wife if she "finds no favor [ḥēn] in his eyes because he has found some indecency ['erwat dābār] in her." The nature of the "indecency" that would provide the grounds for divorce is not clearly specified, and whether it is limited to sexual indiscretions is not obvious. However, the meaning of this expression was later debated by the school of Shammai, which interpreted it as referring to sexual misbehavior, and the school of Hillel, which broadly extended the meaning to include many other things (e.g., childlessness, failure to perform household tasks, etc.).[71] In other contexts, the expression points to the shame of "nakedness," which is to be covered (Ex. 28:42); to sexual intercourse (Ezek. 16:8); and to disgraceful activity, especially involving illicit sexual relations: homosexuality, adultery, prostitution, and incest (Gen. 9:20–27; Lev. 18:6–30.; 20:17; Deut. 23:14; Lam. 1:8; Ezek. 16:36–37; 23:10, 29; Hos. 2:11 [ET 2:13]).[72] Elsewhere, it is also apparent that the husband may have had the option of forgiving his faithless wife, especially if she returned to him (see Hosea 1—3).

In any case, Deuteronomy 24:1–4 indicates that the husband is to give his wife a written document, a "bill of divorce" (sēper kĕrîtût), and that he is then to send her from his household (cf. Isa. 50:1; Jer. 3:8). The divorced woman becomes the "dismissed one" (gĕrûšâ), who is sent away (Lev. 21:7, 14; 22:13; Ezek. 44:22). This written document was perhaps accompanied by the legally binding statement (presumably uttered before witnesses) "You are not my wife, and I am not your husband" (Hos. 2:2 [ET 2:4]). With the written document and the public attestation, she was free to return to her own household and to remarry.

Deuteronomy 22:13–21 also speaks to the issue of divorce. The husband could divorce his wife by bringing against her a legal accusation of premarital promiscuity, but her parents were offered the opportunity to produce evidence that she was a virgin in the form of bloodstains from her first experience of marital intercourse. If the case was decided in her favor, then the slanderer was beaten and made to pay a fine to her father for trying to shame her and her paternal household. In addition, the husband could not then entertain the possibility of divorce. If the husband's charges proved true, the spurned woman was stoned in front of her paternal household (Deut. 22:20–21). A man who seduced or raped an unmarried woman had to marry her and could not divorce her later (Deut. 22:28–29), and a husband could neither dismiss a Hebrew slave whom he married nor reduce her support if he took an additional wife (Ex. 21:10). Indeed, if he did so, the married slave could leave him without the economic liability that otherwise would have been assumed by her paternal household's go'ēl.

Deuteronomy 7:3–4 prohibits mixed marriages with foreigners. During the second temple period, Nehemiah and Ezra enforced the practice of endogamy, in which marriage was to be restricted to Jews only (Neh. 10:27–29 [ET 10:28–30]; 13:3, 23–30), and Ezra issued a proclamation that Jewish husbands were to put away their foreign wives and their children (Ezra 9—10). The reason given for prohibiting and dissolving marriages to foreign women is that these women practiced pagan worship and thus caused the holy nation to become impure. These texts argue that faithlessness to Yahweh, in part caused by marriages to foreigners, was the reason for the devastation of the exile. However, the prophet Malachi, in condemning the frequent occurrence of divorce, may be reacting against this endogamous decree. He makes a theological argument that marriage is a covenant grounded in the providential design of creation and the covenant with Yahweh (Mal. 2:10–16).[73]

In ancient Israel, laws governing divorce were designed primarily to protect the economic interests and rights of both the households that had arranged the marriage and the divorced couple themselves. These laws were to safeguard the interests of the husband's household in matters of progeny, paternity, and inheritance and to preserve his name and that of the ancestral house. Yet the wife's interests and rights, along with those of her household, were also guarded. She was protected against slander, which would shame her and her household. She also was provided the legal writ that allowed her to return to her paternal household after her divorce and then to remarry, while her husband's *mohar* and perhaps her family's bridal dowry provided her some economic support. The economic interests of a woman's household were secured not only by the *mohar* but also by requiring one who violated a daughter to pay her father the marriage price. The father also had the right to determine whether to force the violator to marry his daughter (Ex. 22:16–17). Later legislation (Deut. 22:18–19) mandated that the violator would pay a fine to her father and then be compelled to marry this daughter, whom he could never divorce.

In the Elephantine colony the wife was allowed to divorce her husband, though whoever initiated the divorce, wife or husband, had to pay the other or at least had to forfeit the *mohar*. Divorce came to be prohibited at Qumran.[74]

Levirate Marriage

A particular type of marriage arrangement responded to the case of the husband who died before producing offspring.[75] Levirate marriage sets forth the responsibility of the next of kin (*go'ēl*) to marry the wife of his dead, childless relative. The practice is reflected in the cases of

Tamar in Genesis 38 and of Ruth. In the former case, Tamar's husband died, leaving her childless. Judah, her father-in-law, required his son Onan to marry Tamar. But Onan spilled his semen on the ground, thus refusing to raise up children to his dead brother. Divine punishment for this action brought about his death. Fearing another son would die, Judah procrastinated in giving Tamar to the next brother, Shelah, and returned her to her paternal household until he grew up. Tamar later disguised herself as a prostitute, seduced her father-in-law, conceived, and gave birth to twin sons. She escaped execution for her prostitution when Judah, identified as the father of the twin sons, acknowledged that he had not fulfilled his responsibility by giving her Shelah to be her husband.

In the case of Ruth, her dead husband's first next of kin refused to marry her and to redeem the property her mother-in-law, Naomi, had sold because of debt. The unnamed next of kin refused because he realized that any children born to Ruth by him would continue the dead husband's name and eventually would inherit his land (Ruth 4:4–6). After this next of kin legally renounced his responsibility, Boaz, as the kinsman next in line, purchased the land and married Ruth (4:9–10).[76]

Deuteronomy 25:5–10 sets forth legislation designed to deal specifically with the case of a deceased, childless husband who had lived in the same household with his brother. The brother of the deceased husband was to marry his dead brother's widow, in order to produce for the deceased a son who, along with his progeny, would carry on his father's name, thus allowing the dead man a postmortem existence within the continuing household. This would also keep the widow from marrying outside the household's kinship structure and would ensure that the deceased would have a legal heir to his property. The brother who refused to perform this duty of the *levir* had to endure a legal process designed to shame him and his household (cf. Genesis 38 and Ruth 4).[77] But in refusing to perform the duty of the *levir*, a man might hope to inherit his dead brother's property (Num. 27:9). According to Numbers 27: 8–11, the property rights to the estate of a man who died without a son belonged first to his daughters, then to his brothers, then to his paternal uncles, and then to his nearest of kin. In this passage, widows had no right to inherit their husband's property (though contrast Ruth 4:3, 9; 2 Kings 8:1–6; and Judith 8:7).[78]

Concubinage

Concubinage (concubine = *pilegeš*) involved a female slave, either foreign or Hebrew, who was owned by a household and bore for it children to add to the labor pool (Gen. 22:20–24; 25:6; 36:11–12; Judg. 8:31; 19). She was something of a second-class wife of one of the males in the family. She was especially valued if she produced sons (Gen. 35:25–26). One of her sons could become an heir, especially if the wife had no children (Gen. 21:10). A concubine could assume the role of a surrogate mother for the childless wife (Genesis 16 and 21; 30:3, 9–13). She was to be supported by the household and was even allowed to rest on the Sabbath (Ex. 20:8–11 = Deut. 5:12–15). The wealthy, especially kings, might have many concubines (1 Kings 11:3).

In the event that a Hebrew daughter was sold to another household, she enjoyed certain legal rights: She could not be sold to foreigners, she could be redeemed by her kinsman if she did not please her owner, she was to be treated as a daughter if her owner gave her to his son, and her support was to continue even if the owner or his son took another wife (Ex. 21:7–11).

Celibacy

Celibacy appears to have been rare in ancient Israel and early Judaism. Jeremiah, due to the crisis of his time, was told by Yahweh not to marry and have children (Jer. 16:2). The community at Qumran may have practiced celibacy.[79]

The Roles of Children

Children

The Hebrew Bible often refers to the desire of households to have many children (yeled = child; Gen. 15:5; 22:7; 24:60; 26:4; Ruth 4:11–12). Barrenness and childlessness were at times viewed as either a test or a punishment by God and even as a cause for disgrace (Gen. 16:2; 30:2; 1 Sam. 1:3–11). The household's concern for children was based not only in the fact that they were future contributors to its labor force but also in that they provided the lineage for preserving the patrimony and perpetuating the ancestral name. In addition, they provided the care network for sustaining older parents. These factors may explain in part why there is no reference in scripture to intentional abortion[80] or infanticide.

Children, including adult children who married, were required to honor and, at least while they lived within their birth household, to obey both parents (Ex. 20:12; Deut. 5:16; Prov. 19:26; 30:11; Sir. 3:1–16). To honor the parents meant not only to obey them but also to care for them in their old age and to provide them a proper burial. In the Covenant Code, the penalty for cursing or striking one's mother or father is death (Ex. 21:15, 17). When a woman joined her husband's household, obedience to her birth parents was transferred to the husband's head of the household.

A child's name was given at birth, usually chosen by the mother (Gen. 29:31–30:24; 35:18), sometimes by the father (Gen. 16:15). According to 2 Maccabees 7:27, the child was weaned at the age of three (cf. 1 Sam. 1:20–23). Work probably began as early as age seven or eight and increased with adolescence and adulthood. Infants and small children were dependent on parents and other adult members of the household, but the household also depended on children as soon as they began to be involved in the labor tasks of the family. If a man had no children, then his property was distributed according to a defined succession of male heirs within his household and larger kinship structure (cf. Lot, e.g., who, as Abraham's nephew, was the probable heir to his uncle in Gen. 11:27–32, though they later separated in Genesis 13). An heir could be produced by a surrogate childbearer (Gen. 16:1–4). If adoption was practiced, an adopted son may have been allowed to inherit a childless father's patrimony (cf. Gen. 15:1–3).[81] Parents were responsible for the religious (Deut. 6:7; 11:19) and moral (Prov. 1:8) instruction of their children, nurtured and sustained them (Deut. 1:31; Hos. 11:1–3), and loved and showed them compassion (2 Sam. 18:33; Ps. 103:13).

Most laws and admonitions dealing with children are concerned with young adults who are members of the household and still under the authority of the senior parents, who, as noted earlier, had great, though not absolute, authority. Children could be sold into debt service or slavery, though this likely occurred only in extreme cases of household hardship. This extreme act may have been necessitated by household indebtedness and the threat of insolvency (Neh. 5:1–5; cf. 2 Kings 4:1–7). Parents could present an ungovernable son to the elders of a clan to be executed for disrupting the order of the household (Deut. 21:18–21), but this court alone had the right to determine guilt and carry out the sentence. Child sacrifice is mentioned at times (Genesis 22; Judges 11; 2 Kings 16:3; 17:17; 21:6; Ezek. 20:25–26), but traditional Yahwistic religion came to regard the practice as abhorrent and forbidden (Lev. 20:2–5). Exodus 13:11–15; 22:28 (ET 22:29); and 34:20 provided for the redemption of the firstborn son through sacrifice (cf. Genesis 22); the Levites eventually came to substitute for this sacrifice (Num. 3:12–13; 8:14–19).

Sons

A household preferred to produce sons (*bēn* = son), in part because they did not eventually leave their paternal family to join other households, as did daughters. In addition, descent and inheritance came primarily through sons. A son was circumcised on the eighth day after his birth (Gen. 17:12; Lev. 12:3). At the death of the father, his property was normally transferred to his sons, with the oldest son usually receiving the double portion and assuming the role of the father (Deut. 21:15–17). While primogeniture was not always followed, it seems to have been practiced in most cases.[82] According to Deuteronomy 21:15–17, a father could not show preference to a younger son simply because he was the offspring of his favorite wife. How inheritance was worked out practically is not clear, though it seems probable that the eldest son would have received the house and field while any others would have inherited the household's movable property.

Daughters

Daughters (*bat* = daughter) were also valued by households and contributed as young girls to the labor force. When a daughter left to marry and join another household, her father and his household were compensated for the loss by the *mohar*. A daughter could inherit the father's estate if he had no sons and if she married within the paternal clan (Num. 27:1–11; 36:1–12). As noted earlier, this legislation was designed to preserve the patrimony within the kinship group.

A daughter remained under the authority of her father until her arranged marriage. She then came under the authority of her husband and the senior male in his household. If her father died before her marriage, then she was under the protection of a close male relative who served as the household's senior male. As a prospective bride, her virginity was highly valued. A daughter's virginity was both a matter of honor—her own and that of her paternal household—and a matter of economics, since this allowed her to marry and produce children (Deut. 22:13–29). A male's leaving of father and mother to take up residence with his wife does not mean he joined her household but rather that they set up a common home either within or outside his larger household compound (Gen. 2:24).

The Household as a Provider
of Care for Members and Marginals

The household in ancient Israel and early Judaism provided the primary system of care for its members, both for those who belonged to the kinship and marriage structure and for the resident marginals. This system of care was augmented by household acts of charity on behalf of the poor who did not enjoy the nurture and support of their own households. Israel was largely a village society that protected and cared for its poor. In addition, the monarchy during the first temple period had some responsibility for the poor, as did the temple and other sanctuaries through cultic legislation and the distribution of some of the offerings.

The Redeemer

Central to the household system of care for family members was the institution of the go'ēl (redeemer), who was the next of kin responsible for the justice and well-being of the family. Norman Gottwald succinctly summarizes the four major functions of the go'ēl:[83] "(1) to raise up a male heir for a deceased family head; (2) to buy up or buy back property so that it remains in or returns to the social group; (3) to purchase the release of a group member who has fallen into debt slavery, or to pay off his debt so that he does not fall into debt slavery; (4) to avenge the death of a member of the group."[84] The line of responsibility to serve as the household's or clan's go'ēl began with the brother, then the uncle, then the cousin, and, finally, any close relative (Lev. 25:47–49). The go'ēl's responsibility was to the household and at times even to the larger clan, depending on the line of succession.

In addition to assuming the role of the levir (see discussion of marriage, above), the go'ēl was expected either to purchase or to buy back the destitute kinsman's property, in order to keep it within the household or larger clan (Lev. 25:23–28; Jeremiah 32). The go'ēl also was to redeem his kinsperson and his or her family from debt-induced servitude (Lev. 25:25–55). Furthermore, the go'ēl was to sustain in his own household his impoverished kinsman (and his family, if he had one), who was to enjoy the same protection and care offered a resident alien, a hired laborer, or a sojourner. The kinsman could not be placed in debt servitude or enslaved. No interest was to be charged to the kinsman, and food was to be provided him at no profit. At the time of jubilee, the go'ēl was to allow the kinsman and his family to return to their own household and was to return their patrimony (Leviticus 25). According to Deuteronomy 25:5–10, the person who rejected his responsibility of serving as a go'ēl was shamed in public (cf. Naomi's kinsman who refused to serve as go'ēl in Ruth 4).

Children

As noted above, sons, daughters, and grandchildren were nurtured by members of the household. From birth, infants and the very young received the care of their parents and other household members, until they began to contribute to the labor tasks of the family.

The Fatherless

It is not clear whether orphans are those without any parents or children without fathers,[85] though the latter seems more likely. The household offered care for the "fatherless" (yātôm), that is, children who were from broken families that no longer provided nurture and protection.[86] Frequently the fatherless are placed alongside widows in scriptural texts, suggesting not only two classes of poor people but also that impoverished widows often had children to support (Job 22:9; 24:3; 29:12–13; Ps. 68:6; Isa. 1:17, 23). Within the kinship structure of the household, clan, and tribe, and perhaps through adoption, the fatherless could be incorporated within a new household (Job 31:18; Esth. 2:7, 15).

The fatherless enjoyed the protection of the law (Deut. 27:19). Their rights were not to be subverted, and their just cause was not to be turned away at court (Ex. 22:21–25; Deut. 24:17; 27:19; Prov. 23:10). In addition, the fatherless were to be the recipients of the support of households outside the kinship structure, to sustain their lives. Households were to leave gleanings in the fields and fruit on the vine during harvests to support the poor, who included the fatherless (Deut. 24:19–21). They were among those who received tithes gathered from households after their harvests every third year (Deut. 14:28–29; 26:12). The fatherless were to share in the festivities of households during the harvest festivals, when food was plentiful (Deut. 16:9–11, 13–14).

That the fatherless and other poor were often victims of oppression, whose rights were subverted and needs ignored, is indicated by the prophets and sages. Prophets often spoke out in support of justice and urged acts of kindness for the fatherless, while condemning those who afflicted them (Isa. 1:17, 23; 9:17; 10:1–2; Jer. 5:28; 22:3; Zech. 7:10;

Mal. 3:5). Sages also supported the just cause and needs of the poor, including the fatherless (Job 29:12; 31:17–18, 21; Prov. 23:10). That the
laws of protection and the teachings of the sages were at times ignored
is demonstrated by Job's indictment of the wicked who oppress orphans, remove the landmarks of their fields, seize their property, demand they be used as payment for debt, and take in pledge the infants
of the poor, while God pays no mind to their plight (Job 24:2–12).

Fatherless children could remain in their deceased father's household with their widowed mothers and continue to be nurtured within
this setting while eventually contributing to the household tasks. If the
widow married again and joined a new household, her fatherless children accompanied her. She also could return to the care and protection
of her own paternal household or that of the *go'ēl* and take her fatherless children with her. The widowed mother served as a trustee for her
children's inheritance from the dead father until they reached the age of
adulthood. Without other resources, widows might be forced to sell
their children to pay the dead husband's debt (2 Kings 4:1). However,
without the protection and nurture of these households, the fatherless
and the widowed mother joined the ranks of the destitute, who required charity to survive.

Widows

A widow (*'almānāh*) who was childless could remain a member of
her husband's family if, under levirate law, a kinsman took her as wife.[87]
If the kinsman lived in her dead husband's household, she would remain with him. If he resided elsewhere, she would join his house. A son
produced by this union continued the name of the dead husband and
inherited his property. Without a *go'ēl* the widow could return, along
with any children, to her father's household (Gen. 38:11; Lev. 22:13;
Ruth 1:8). She was then allowed to remarry and join another household
(Ruth 1:9).

The frequent references to widows and their children (fatherless) often point to their extreme poverty, though Judith, as a wealthy widow,
proves an exception. Widows with children were destitute if they had
no household to provide them support and nurture (1 Kings 17:8–15;
2 Kings 4:1–7). Widows, along with the fatherless and Levites, enjoyed
the protection of charity laws when they had no household to care for
them (Deut. 10:18; 24:17–21; 26:12–13; 27:19; cf. Job 29:13; Isa. 1:23;
Jer. 7:6; 22:3). Deuteronomy 27:19 issues a curse against those who

subvert the justice due to widows. When approached by widows seeking to borrow property (e.g., utensils and implements), households were not to require them to leave their garments in pledge (Deut. 24:17; Job 24:3; cf. Ex. 22:22–26; Amos 2:8). Households were enjoined to include widows in the festivals that followed the harvests (Deut. 16:9–15). Their rights to economic justice were supported by the prophets (Mal. 3:5).

Divorced Women

Unless she was a convicted adulteress placed under the threat of execution, a divorced woman (gĕrûšâ) could return to her father's household (Lev. 22:13), with the mohar kept by her family to support her. Her husband's household may have been required to return any dowry to her paternal household.

It may have been that husbands could forgive even faithless wives and not divorce them. Hosea, for instance, does not divorce Gomer, his wife, for her adultery but redeems her, presumably from the sexual bondage into which she had sold herself (Hosea 1—3). However, divorced women who had no paternal household to which to return or whose household would not take them back because of shame had little recourse but to sell themselves into bondage as slaves or concubines or to become prostitutes.

The Sick and the Aged

Healthcare was largely given to the sick and infirm by members of their household (2 Samuel 13; 1 Kings 17:17). Grown children cared for aged and infirm parents and provided for them a proper burial. Parents were also protected against abuse by their children (Ex. 21:15), including their destructive curses (21:17).

Debt Servants and Slaves

Debt servitude ('ebed = servant, slave) was perhaps the last option for an Israelite facing destitution who had neither a household for nurture and protection nor possessions to sell nor a go'ēl to be a redeemer (Ex. 21:1–11; Lev. 25:39; 2 Kings 4:1).[88] That Israelite sold himself into debt servitude and, in effect, exchanged his labor for the nurture and support of a family household in which he became a marginalized family member.[89] Fathers also were permitted to sell their children into temporary debt servitude and slavery (Ex. 21:7–11), and widows sometimes sold their children to pay off their deceased husband's debt (2 Kings 4:1). While this legal right of parents was more than likely subject to abuse, its practice resulted from poverty and debt that threatened the survival of the household. Thus the selling of children was one means of payment of debt by an impoverished household, at the same time providing a new household for the poor offspring.

In the household, debt servants were under the authority of the senior male (and possibly his wife), who bought and sold them, arranged their marriages, and determined their tasks of labor. However, debt servitude for a Hebrew male was not necessarily lifelong slavery, and laws of release continued to be issued, eventually leading to the abolishment of the enslavement of Israelites. According to the Covenant Code (Ex. 21:2–11), the Hebrew male debt servant could go free after six years, with no price to pay for his release. If he entered the household married, then he could leave with his wife; if single, then he was to leave single. However, if he had a wife given him by his master and they had children, the family would remain while he was set free. If the debt servant loved his master and family, he could refuse his freedom and become a slave for life. (It is important to note at this point that the household owned any children born to the debt servant (or slave) during his servitude.)

Hebrew daughters sold into concubinage by their fathers did not enjoy the same opportunity for release that their male counterparts had in the Covenant Code. While these women likely performed household tasks, their major role was concubinage and the producing of children. A female Hebrew slave was not offered release after six years. However, there was some legal protection to ensure her well-being. If her master, who bought her for himself to be a concubine, was not pleased with her, he could not sell her to a foreigner; rather he had to allow her *go'ēl* to redeem her. This restriction was the result of the owner's having been faithless to her, that is, he had not lived up to the agreement made with her household, that she would be his concubine. In addition, if the buyer purchased the woman to be a concubine for his son, then she was to be treated as a daughter. And if the buyer took another woman for his wife, he could not reduce his concubine's conjugal rights, food, or clothing.

In the later Deuteronomic reformulation of this law on debt servitude and slavery (Deut. 15:12–18), Hebrew debt servants, male or female, again are to be freed after six years of service.[90] Yet their release is to be accompanied by the household's provision of goods (animals, grain, and other produce), and there is no indication that the family is to remain behind (or, for that matter, that it is to be released). If a debt servant does not wish to go free because he or she "loves you" and "is well off with you," then the servant shall be a slave forever. This law ensured that slaves who were unable to establish economically viable households on their own could remain with their owners.

The enslavement of Hebrews was finally prohibited. In Jeremiah 34, a text that gives evidence of Deuteronomic redaction, King Zedekiah made a covenant during the Babylonian siege of Jerusalem with the city's people and proclaimed the manumission of their Hebrew debt servants and slaves (male and female). When the siege was lifted, however, the covenant was ignored and owners took back their debt servants and slaves. Eventually the enslavement of fellow Israelites and Jews came to be abolished, according to a second temple text, Leviticus 25:39–46 (cf. 2 Chron. 28:8–15). Here, if an impoverished Israelite sells himself to another household, he is to serve not as a slave but rather as a hired servant and sojourner. He is to be released from debt service at any time if he has acquired the means or has a go'ēl to redeem him. And in the jubilee year, the Hebrew in debt servitude, along with his family, would be released to return to his own household.

In addition to the law of release, Hebrew slaves enjoyed other limited rights protected by laws. They were, at least until later in the second temple period, regarded as the property of the household (see Ex. 21:32), and they could be bought and sold (though not to a foreigner). However, a harsh beating could result in the slave's release (Ex. 21:26–27), and an owner who beat his slave was to be punished if the slave died soon thereafter (Ex. 21:20). If the beaten slave survived a day or two, his master was not to be punished, "for the slave is the owner's property" (Ex. 21:20–21). If a slave obtained the means or had a redeemer, he might be freed (Lev. 25:47–54). Deuteronomy 23:15–16 does not allow an escaped slave to be returned to his master.

Debt servants and slaves also participated in the religious rites and observances of their households. These debt servants and slaves were permitted to worship in the family cult, to participate in Sabbath rest (Ex. 20:10; 23:12), and to partake in the variety of sacrificial feasts and religious festivals (Ex. 12:44; Deut. 16:11, 14). By the second temple period, male debt servants and slaves were circumcised (Gen. 17: 12–13), thus signifying their admission to the community of Israel. They might even have been allowed to share in the household's inheritance (Prov. 17:2), and possibly they could have inherited the entire patrimony if there were no heirs (Gen. 15:3).

Israelites bought and sold foreign slaves and children of resident aliens with far fewer legal restrictions than applied to Hebrew slaves and debt servants (Lev. 25:44–45; cf. Ex. 12:44; Lev. 22:11; Eccl. 2:7). Foreign slaves were often captives taken in war. A foreign slave-woman who was taken by an Israelite as a wife could be divorced but not sold (Deut. 21:10–14; cf. Num. 31:26–47). The children of foreign slaves belonged to the household, and the owner could bequeath the slave family as property to his heirs (Lev. 25:45–46).

Resident Aliens

The "resident alien" (gēr) was the foreign immigrant who did not own land.[91] The gēr wished not only to enjoy the law of hospitality operative in the household but also to gain its protection. While the role of the gēr as a marginal member of the household is not exactly clear, it appears this person served the household as a hired laborer (Deut. 24:14–15).

Certain laws offered the gēr protection as a marginalized household member. Perhaps the most comprehensive and inclusive statement is found in Leviticus 19:33–34, which not only proscribes the mistreatment of the resident alien but also instructs that this marginalized member of the household be treated as a native Israelite and "loved as oneself." The resident alien was to partake in the household's Sabbath rest (Ex. 20:8–10; 23:12; Deut. 5:13–14) and worship (Lev. 16:29; 17:8; 22:18; Num. 15:11–16; Deut. 16:11, 14; 26:11). The resident alien also was expected to follow certain commandments (Ex. 12:19, 48–49; Lev. 18:26; 20:2) and was guaranteed justice and particular rights under the law (Deut. 1:16). The gēr could even be admitted to the congregation's covenant of faith (Deut. 29:10–15; 31:12).

After the return from exile in Babylonia, the resident alien was integrated into the community of the Jewish people. If circumcised, he became a member of the people through the covenant of Abraham (Genesis 17). In the reallocation of land, Ezekiel 47:21–23 instructs that it shall be an inheritance (naḥălâh) for both native members of the tribes of Israel and the "aliens who reside among you and have begotten children among you." Resident aliens, then, in this portrayal of the return, were to be like "citizens of Israel," and those with families could possess land. Thus they were to establish their own households.

That resident aliens were often destitute and without household protection is also indicated in biblical literature. The oppression of the resident alien was prohibited in Israelite and Jewish law (Ex. 22:21; 23:9; Lev. 19:33–34; Deut. 24:14–15, 17–18; 27:19), and the prophets warned against their mistreatment (Jer. 7:6; 22:3; Zech. 7:10). In Deuteronomy 14:29 the resident alien, along with the Levite, the widow, and the fatherless, is to receive the tithe of produce given for distribution to the poor every three years. Like the other poor, resident aliens also shared the right to gleanings left in the field and fruit remaining on the vine (Lev. 19:10; 23:22; Deut. 24:19–21). According to Deuteronomy 10:18, resident aliens enjoy the love of God, who provides them with food and clothing.

Sojourners

The household offered temporary hospitality (shelter and food) to the sojourner (*tôšāb*), who could be either a foreigner or a native Israelite (Gen. 18:1–8; 23:4; 24:28–32; Ex. 12:45; Lev. 22:10–11; 25:6–7, 23, 45, 47; Num. 35:15; Judg. 19:16–26; Ps. 39:12). The *tôšāb* was not a permanent member of the household but was to be provided temporary shelter, food, and protection while residing there.

Hired Laborers

Those without their own kinship households formed an underclass of poor people. Among these were hired laborers (*śākîr*), either Israelites or resident aliens, who sold their services to households in return for payment. This group would have grown in numbers during the monarchy as many family households began to disintegrate and their land was incorporated into the large estates of wealthy families.

At times, hired laborers lived within the household as marginal members (Lev. 25:6, 53). While their condition is described as a pitiful one (Job 7:1–4), for they lived from hand to mouth (Job 14:6), hired laborers received the protection of the law, including the requirement that their payment be given to them on the same day they had worked (Lev. 19:13; Deut. 24:14–15). They also were to share in the produce from the sabbatical year (Lev. 25:6). Malachi condemned those who cheated the hired laborers of their wages (Mal. 3:5).

Levites

Households also could include as marginal members Levites (*lēvî*), who served household members as priests, officiating during family rituals

(Judges 18).[92] Priestly Levites appear to have owned no land (Num. 18:20; 26:62; Deut. 10:9), though they could marry and establish households that had other assets if not land (Joshua 13—19). Their support came from tithes and offerings (Num. 18:1–24; Deut. 18:1–5; Josh. 13:14) to the sanctuaries they served.

As a result of the Deuteronomic reform during the seventh century B.C.E. that attempted to centralize the cult in Jerusalem, eliminate household cultic activities, and close clan sanctuaries where country Levites would have served, the destitution of these priests became acute. Although country Levites were invited to join the temple cult in Jerusalem and serve as priests (Deut. 18:6–8), it is highly doubtful that this opportunity, even if implemented, was sufficient to support the large numbers of Levites throughout the countryside. This is why Deuteronomic law mentions them as residing within the towns and villages of Israel, perhaps indicating that they were marginal members of households (see the household list in Deut. 12:18–19; 26:11). Deuteronomy also lists the Levites among the classes of the poor who were to receive various kinds of charity, including the third-year tithe of the produce of households (Deut. 14:28–29; 26:12–13), and to partake in the harvest festivals and their bounty (Deut. 16:9–15).

Josiah's reform, along with the Assyrian and Babylonian conquests, imposed great hardships on the Levites. The second temple program for the revitalization of Judah, after the return from the exile, may have led to the establishment of Levitical towns and pasturelands (Num. 35:1–8; Josh. 14:1–4; 21:1–42; 1 Chron. 6:54–81) to provide these priests with a means to exist, which would have been supplemented by the meager earnings they would have received from their staggered courses of cultic service in the Jerusalem temple. These towns, along with their houses and pasturelands, could be redeemed at any time and were to be returned to the Levites in the year of the jubilee (Lev. 25:32–34). The establishment of Levitical towns with pasturelands may have been a measure designed to deal with the acute problem of Levitical poverty, worsened by the closure of family, clan, and tribal sanctuaries.

Care for the Poor
outside the Household

The household provided the essential network for the care and nurture of both members who were related by blood and marriage (grandparents, parents, children, uncles, aunts, nephews, nieces, cousins, widows, and the fatherless) and its marginal members, some permanent and some temporary (household debt servants and slaves, resident aliens, widows, the fatherless, day laborers, sojourners, and Levites). This network of protection and sustenance also extended outward to provide some care for the larger associations of clans knit together by kinship and marriage (e.g., Ruth). This social system provided the means by which care could be provided for clan households in distress or that had fragmented, their members dispersed.

But what of the large numbers of the poor who faced the enormous challenges of trying to survive as marginals outside the protective care of household and clan? Once again, the household bore the major responsibility for providing care, in this case through a system of charity. This charity came to be expressed in the foundational imperative of the Holiness Code (Leviticus 19—26): "You shall love your neighbor [rēa'] as yourself" (Lev. 19:18). Responsibility to love another as oneself moved beyond the kinship structure (brother = 'āḥ; neighbor = rēa') to include even the resident alien who was in need of life's basic necessities (Lev. 19:34).

References to the poor are found in many types of biblical texts: legal codes, prophetic oracles, narratives, and wisdom instructions and sayings.[93] The poor in the Hebrew Bible are those who are in need even of the minimal necessities to exist: food, clothing, and shelter. Among the terms for the poor in the Hebrew Bible, three are especially important: 'ebyôn (essentially those who are destitute and without the means to survive apart from charity; Ps. 35:10; 72:12; 109:16, 22), dal (primarily those who have lost their social status and prosperity; Ex. 23:3; 30:15; Lev. 14:21), and 'ānî (those who are victims of oppression; Ps. 10:2; Isa. 3:14; Ezek. 18:14–18; Amos 2:7).[94]

Charity to the poor is encoded in Israelite and Jewish law. Justice for the poor, including the responsibility to defend their legal rights and to support their existence, was safeguarded by a legal code that was to be administered by righteous judges (Ex. 23:3; Deut. 16:19; Ps. 82:3). Laws of charity included the giving of alms to the poor (Deut. 15:7–11), the return of property the poor left in pledge when borrowing tools and implements from their more affluent neighbors (Ex. 22:26–27; Deut. 24:10–13), and the prohibition against charging the poor interest (Ex. 22:25; Lev. 25:36; Deut. 23:20).[95] The poor were allowed to eat grain or fruit from their neighbor's fields and vineyards before the harvest (Deut. 23:24–25) and, after the harvest, to gather the gleanings and fruit that were left in the fields and on the vines (Lev. 19:9–10; 23:22; Deut.

24:19–21; and Ruth). The tithe of the third year was collected to benefit the destitute (Deut. 14:28–29; 26:13). In desperate circumstances,
the poor could sell their children to other households, though not to
foreigners (Ex. 21:7–11; Neh. 5:5), or they could even sell themselves
(Lev. 25:39–42).

Several laws had far greater scope and perhaps were intended to
eliminate poverty in Israel, though their actual implementation is ques-
tionable. The sabbatical year required that the seventh-year harvest be
left for the poor and wild animals (Ex. 23:11; Lev. 25:6), debts be rescinded (Deut. 15:1, 4), and debt servants and slaves be offered their
freedom (Ex. 21:2–6; Deut. 15:12–18), while the year of the jubilee (the
fiftieth year in a cycle of seven times seven years) required the returning of ancestral land to the original household owners (Lev. 25:10).

These laws designed to protect and care for the poor undoubtedly
arose to deal with the challenges of poverty that increased not only during natural and military disasters (e.g., drought and conquest) but especially as a result of the appearance of the monarchy. The first temple
period witnessed the rise of large estates, owned by the nobility and
wealthy merchants, at the expense of small households. But even after
the institution of poverty laws, the legal responsibility to defend the
rights and support the needs of the poor was at times ignored and even
directly violated. The prophets frequently proclaimed God's favor for
the poor and pronounced oracles of warning and judgment to those
who ignored the needs of the poor and subverted their rights to protection under the law (Isa. 14:30; 25:4; Jer. 2:34–35; 5:28; 20:13; Amos
2:6; 4:1; 5:12; 8:4, 6). The prophets also condemned those in positions
of power and wealth who victimized the helpless poor (Isa. 3:14–15;
32:7; 58:7; Ezek. 16:17).

The sages were ambiguous in their treatment of the topic of rich and
poor.[96] On the one hand, wealth was valued highly for its many bene-
fits (Prov. 10:15; 13:8; 14:20; 18:16, 23; 19:4, 6–7) and was perceived
to come from wise and righteous living, while poverty was generally regarded negatively (Prov. 14:20; 18:23; 22:7) and at times was assumed
to result from lack of discipline or from foolish and wicked behavior
(Prov. 6:6–11; 10:4–5; 12:3; 13:25; 24:30–34; 26:13–16). On the other
hand, sages acknowledged that the wicked at times achieved positions
of wealth and power through acts of iniquity and oppression (Job
24:2–12; Prov. 11:16; 28:15–16; 30:14), and that righteous and God-
fearing poor, who often were their victims, were those deserving of ap-
probation (Prov. 15:16–17; 16:8, 16, 19; 17:1; 28:6). Sages did see a

future in which wicked oppressors would come to ruin and the righteous poor would be redeemed (Prov. 21:13; 22:16; 28:20).[97] Whatever the causes of the poverty, the sages taught that they and their audiences had an unqualified responsibility to sustain the poor (Prov. 14:31; 17:5; 22:2, 22–23; 29:13).

Religion, the Household, and the Royal State

Religion and the Household

The social world of the Israelite and early Jewish household was shaped, legitimated, and given authority by its religious traditions and practices. These also aided in the socialization of family members—that is, those born within the household, women who joined their husbands' families, and marginals, including debt servants, slaves, resident aliens, widows, the fatherless, sojourners, and Levites. As would be expected, these rites and beliefs shaped and reflected the social fabric of the household over the generations.

Simply put, households practiced family religion.[98] But what were the defining features of household religion? Much of this remains hidden behind the more explicit descriptions of official Yahwistic religion in the biblical literature. But there are several major features that appear to be typical.

Household Gods

Households worshiped the ancestral deity, the "god of my/our ancestor," who, according to the founding myth of the household and its related clans, chose the original head of the household and provided protection and blessing to his family throughout the generations. In return, the household offered to this deity, among the many gods, its worship and gifts of adoration. This is not to say that families in ancient Israel did not worship pagan gods, either in rejecting the original ancestral deity for another (i.e., Baal for Yahweh) or in offering their devotion to these deities at the same time. Polytheism is evident in several biblical texts that refer to the worship of "household gods" (těrāpîm; Gen. 31:19, 34–35; cf. 1 Sam. 19:11–17), in inscriptions that mention Yahweh and "his Asherah,"[99] in the frequent legal and prophetic texts directed against worshiping deities other than Yahweh (e.g., Jer. 44:15–28), and perhaps in the archaeological discoveries of numerous female figurines in Israelite houses.[100]

Household religion appears to have included at times the adoration of a mother goddess (e.g., Asherah, Deut. 16:21; Jer. 44:15–19), especially popular with women, who offered them fertility, children, and nurture. Official religion (priests and prophets) tried to compensate for the lack of a female partner for Yahweh by such strategies as the assignment of feminine functions to Yahweh, the personification of feminine metaphors for divine attributes (e.g., Wisdom = ḥokmâ), and the depiction of Israel/Jerusalem/Zion as the bride of Yahweh.[101]

Household Holdings

In addition to the election of the ancestor by the ancestral deity, a major feature of family religion emphasized the divine gift of the household estate.[102] For the agricultural families of ancient Israel and early Judaism, the land was central to this estate. The household deity gave the family its ancestral land and made it fertile. This naḥălâh (inheritance) was not to be sold but was to be kept within the household throughout its generations, for it was the deity's gift. Yahweh came to legitimate a legal tradition that served to maintain the household's ownership of its patrimony (e.g., boundary stones were not to be moved, Deut. 19:14; 27:17; Job 24:2; Prov. 23:10; Hos. 5:10). In addition, Israelites believed God provided the family with fruitful harvests and fertile flocks, protected against its natural (drought, disease, famine) and historical enemies, and provided offspring to become laborers and heirs.

Another understanding of the land occurred in the development of Yahwistic religion. Yahweh became the landlord and head of the household, who, in effect, leased the land to the twelve tribes (Lev. 25:23). This divine ownership of the land provided the theological basis for offering firstfruits, tithing, and the observing of the sabbatical and jubilee years (Lev. 25:2–24). In addition, Israelites believed faithlessness to Yahweh could result in natural disasters that brought famine (Amos 4:7–9) and even in Israel's loss of the land through conquest (Jer. 7:12–15). The two understandings of household and divine ownership of the land continued throughout the history of the family in Israel and early Judaism.

Household and Clan Shrines

Family worship occurred in household shrines, as well as in sanctuaries and high places located in villages inhabited by clans. Tribal gatherings at major sanctuaries (e.g., Shiloh, Shechem, and Gilgal) took place after seasonal harvests. These agricultural, pilgrimage festivals to major shrines included the Feasts of Tabernacles, Weeks, and Unleavened Bread, the last of which was eventually connected to the Passover (Ex. 23:14–17; 34:18–24). Passover originally was a household celebration (Ex. 12:1–13, 43–49) and continued to be until the time of Josiah's reform, when it became, for a time, a pilgrimage festival (Deut. 16:2, 5–7).

Joseph Blenkinsopp argues that the most important festival was the annual clan ritual and ceremony associated with the kinship structure of the *mišpāḥāh* (clan), wherein solidarity among the living and dead members of clan households was celebrated and strengthened. In his view, this clan festival would have served to legitimate and sustain the social order of the household: patrilineal descent, clan membership, and hierarchical status in the group (see 1 Sam. 20:5–6, 28–29).[103]

Household Priests

Male heads of households, at least early on, were the priests who led the family worship, offered sacrifice, and performed other family rituals.[104] Even with the establishment of male priesthoods, the role of the head of the household in religious observance undoubtedly continued. In the Passover as a household celebration, the role of the father is outlined (cf. Exodus 12; Deuteronomy 16). In addition, even in early Israel, prior to state formation, at least substantial households are portrayed as having or seeking to have a Levite serve in the role of household priest, to attend the family shrine and offer sacrifices (e.g., Judges 18).

Women were excluded from the official priesthood, and perhaps from performing the role of priest in the household.[105] Yet it is clear that they had public roles in corporate religion and were involved in informal and active ways in the religious life of the family. The formal religious roles of women included composing psalms of worship (e.g., Ex. 15:20; Judges 5), singing and playing instruments during festivals and other worship services (Ex. 15:20; 1 Sam. 18:6), participation in the mourning rites associated with funerals (Jer. 9:17–22), and offering prayers (1 Samuel 1—2). The roles of women in popular religion and in the household may have included participation in festive meals, magic and divination, and the ancestral cult wherein mothers were the living link between the generations.[106]

Household and Clan Festivals

Harvest festivals celebrated in clan and tribal shrines, probably until the Deuteronomic reform, followed the agricultural calendar: barley in the spring (the Feast of Unleavened Bread), wheat in the early summer (Sukkot, or the Feast of Weeks), and fruit from orchards and vineyards in the fall (the Feast of the Tabernacles).

The origins of the Sabbath are not clear, but the Decalogue's two biblical formulations point to the sabbatical regulations as being directed to the members of the household, who are to "remember" or "observe" this day (Ex. 20:8–11; Deut. 5:12–15). In Exodus 20, the theological basis for remembering the Sabbath is God's resting on the seventh day after the act of creation (Gen. 2:1–3), while in Deuteronomy 5, the reason for observing the Sabbath is to remind households that their ancestors were once slaves in Egypt and enjoyed no respite from labor or liberation from enslavement.

Veneration of Ancestors

It is clear from grave offerings and several texts mentioning this practice that household worship included the veneration of its ancestors, who, at death, entered into the world of the *rĕpā'îm* (shades)[107] and were, in some sense, divine powers (*'ĕlohîm*).[108] If possible, ancestors were buried in the family tomb on the household's land. Funeral rituals included the singing of lamentations for the dead, lacerations, the shaving of the mourner's hair, the wearing of sackcloth, and the placement of ashes on the forehead. In the funeral ceremony, the memory of the deceased was recalled and grief expressed at his or her passing (2 Sam. 1:17–27; 3:33–34). Mourning the deceased lasted normally seven days (Gen. 50:10; 1 Sam. 31:13; 1 Chron. 10:12). There may also have been a wake that included a feast; at least, this is suggested by the "house of mourning" and the "house of feasting" (Jer. 16:5–9).[109]

Offerings were given to the deceased, whose souls (*nepeš* = soul) were thought to remain in the tomb. Death did not totally separate the living from the dead; rather, the dead continued as members of the household. Their *nĕpāšôt* continued to dwell in the family tomb and their memories were recalled. In a way, perhaps, the dead continued to live through the generations of the household.

Oral Tradition

The oral tradition of the household would have included narratives involving the ancestral founding of the family; the original gift of the family's land; the history of the family; the kinship relationships of the family to clan, tribe, and greater Israel; and the religion, mores, wisdom, and laws of the family passed down through time.

Thus, household religion legitimated the family's social customs and laws, which defined the relationship of people to one another and to the ancestral deity. Family religion focused not on individual piety but rather on the household's communal relationship to other households and the ancestral deity. The social reality of Israel as a cluster of families held together by kinship, tradition, custom, law, and religion was never abandoned, even when one household, that of David, established a royal state that competed with and attempted to restrict a society and religion based on the family household.

Religion and the Royal State

The rise of the Israelite monarchy through the military exploits first of Saul and then of David led to the establishment of a royal state in Israel that, during the time of the "United Kingdom" (1000–922 B.C.E.), reshaped the sociopolitical organization of the tribes and clans of Israel and centralized considerable power in the hands of the "house of David."[110] It was this household that was able to maintain rule over the other households of Israel for some eighty years and over Judah for approximately four centuries. The compound family in the farming villages of Israel and Judah continued to survive during the time of the royal state, though the monarchy instituted measures to undermine the rural household's social integrity.

The social cooperation among households, clans, and tribes included voluntary protective associations to defend against military invasion.[111] Saul rose to power in the role of a tribal military chieftain (nāgîd) and then became king (1 Samuel 8—31). Later, David became the nāgîd of Judah and eventually the ruler of a united Israel and Judah (2 Samuel 1—1 Kings 2). His military defeat of the Philistines catapulted him into the role of a king (melek) who expanded Israelite and Judahite territory east into the Transjordan and north into Syria. David's taking of Jerusalem made this former Jebusite city the political and religious capital of his new empire. At the same time, Jerusalem remained the estate of David's household.

Solomonic Measures

Solomon, who succeeded his father David to the throne, consolidated David's military successes and completed the reorganization of the nation into a kingdom that increased dramatically Israel's economic wealth and military power in the ancient Near East.[112] The initiatives involved in this process, when formulated into policy, placed enormous burdens on the farming households in Israel and Judah and threatened their viability as the core social institution of the nation. Indeed, many households could not sustain themselves or their patrimonies during this often oppressive dynastic rule, which endured—at least in Judah—for four centuries.[113]

Solomon appointed governors to operate a new system of twelve royal administrative districts that contravened tribal boundaries and thereby restricted traditional solidarity (1 Kings 4:7–19, 27–28). A population census (see 2 Samuel 24) allowed for the raising of royal taxes on the produce and flocks of households to fuel the state's economic expansion. A state monopoly of exports and imports traded agricultural products for needed raw materials and luxury items; underwrote the costs of ambitious building projects; supported the extravagant lifestyle of the court and of a growing, privileged upper class; and raised revenues for other things, including, eventually, tribute to foreign rulers. This system also imposed military conscription on the tribes, to provide troops for a standing army, and established compulsory tribal quotas to provide corvée labor for construction projects, including a temple and palace in Jerusalem and military fortresses throughout the kingdom.[114] Royal courts were set up to enforce the new legal agenda, which challenged the legitimacy of local household, clan, and tribal judiciaries.[115]

Solomon's ambition eventually outstripped his resources, leading to his trading of twenty cities for gold and timber. Toward the end of his reign, one of his royal administrators, Jeroboam, began to plot a revolution that led, after the king's death, to the partitioning of the empire into the two separate kingdoms of Israel and Judah (1 Kings 1—11). After this partition, the house of David enjoyed lordship only over Judah.

Royal Religion

To legitimate the new institution of dynastic rule, major innovations in Israelite religion occurred.[116] Two related traditions attempted to authenticate the monarchy and its control: the promise to David (2 Samuel 7 and Psalm 89) and Yahweh's residence on Zion (Jerusalem). The divine promise to David, issued within the context of a covenant between his house and Yahweh, sought to establish a perpetual rule of his house (a dynasty) over Israel, though later Deuteronomic redaction added that the ruling king must be subject to the Mosaic covenant and would be punished for disobedience. Furthermore, the king was the son of Yahweh (Psalm 2), anointed by his prophet (1 Sam. 16:6; 2 Sam.

1:14), and appointed by God to rule as his vassal.[117] However, there are only slight traces of a possible tradition of divine kingship in ancient Israel (2 Sam. 7:14; Ps. 45:6).

To signify Yahweh's residence on Zion, David drew on two ancient, premonarchical symbols of early Israelite religion: the ark and the tent. The ark, likely a portable throne, symbolized Yahweh's presence among his people (Num. 10:35–36; 2 Sam. 6:2–3), while the tent, also portable, pointed to periodic theophany, divine encounter, and oracular revelation (Ex. 33:7–11; Num. 11:16–17, 24–26; 12:5, 10; Deut. 31:14–15). When David brought the ark to Jerusalem and placed it in a tent (2 Samuel 6), he revived these ancient symbols and their traditions to provide divine legitimation for his rule and to signal Yahweh's presence and revelation in Jerusalem. Jerusalem, the estate of David's house, became not only the new capital of the empire but also the center of royal religion.

Solomon reinforced this religious innovation in a powerful way when he replaced the tent with a Canaanite-style temple (1 Kings 5—8). Now the monarchy had the visible symbol of divine approval of the new dynasty and the empire that Yahweh would rule and defend through his son, the ruling Davidic king (Psalms 2, 46, 48, 76).[118] National pilgrimage festivals to the temple in Jerusalem rivaled and sought to replace local clan harvest celebrations. Josiah even succeeded in making the Passover a pilgrimage festival, thus circumventing its role in the local households of reminding them of their ancestors' liberation from oppressive kings. The king acted as priest during occasions of great national moment (e.g., David's transfer of the ark to Jerusalem, 2 Samuel 6; Solomon's dedication of the temple, 1 Kings 8:22–53; and Hezekiah's prayer during the Assyrian crisis, 2 Kings 19:14–19). The king also had authority over both the Jerusalem temple, which largely served as the royal cult to legitimate his household's dynastic rule, and its priests, who were royal officials (2 Sam. 20:23–26; 1 Kings 2:26–27). There may have been a New Year's festival celebrating the kingship of Yahweh (Psalms 47, 93, 95—98) and the enthronement and reign of his surrogate ruler over Israel (Psalms 2, 110). In addition, the economic and judicial roles of the royal temple should be underscored: It served as a national bank or treasury for the royal state and as a type of state court for the adjudication of legal cases.[119]

Royal Destabilization of the Household

Royal exploitation of farm families led to the steady decline of the traditional household and undercut its system of economics, education,

care, law, and protection, as well as the religious rituals and traditions
that strengthened and legitimated its identity and solidarity (see the
warning in 1 Sam. 8:10–18). A royal treasury, supported by military
booty, taxation, and offerings to the temple, and royal control of mar-
kets were strategic elements of a new economic system that provided
the monarchy with enormous wealth and power. Royal "wisdom
schools" undoubtedly emerged to educate scribes who could administer the kingdom, assume posts in the royal bureaucracy, and create new
traditions that would authenticate religiously the ruler's authority and
power.[120] The royal distribution of charity was designed to transfer the
loyalty of the underclass and perpetual poor to kings and away from the
households. The monarch as supreme judge and national benefactor established courts to administer the king's justice in the royal state (2 Sam.
12:1–6; 1 Kings 3:16–28; Psalm 72), thus rivaling the system of justice
carried out by households, clans, and tribes.[121] Royal courts to enforce
and carry out the new governmental system led to the increasing confiscation of household estates and the ignoring of the rights of the poor
(Isa. 10:1–4; cf. 5:8; Micah 2:2). Blood vengeance was circumscribed
by more formal means of justice in royal and temple courts.

With the appearance of the monarchy, citizen militias comprised of
men from the households and their charismatic warriors were replaced
by a professional army under the command of the king and his designated military commander. A system of conscription was levied on the
clan through the governors of royal districts of the kingdom, to raise
troops to supplement the forces of the professional army. Warfare
changed from holy war, a protective agency for households, clans, and
tribes, to religious wars that, while drawing on divine legitimation,
served as the instrument of Israelite and Judahite kings to conduct and
enforce policies in the royal interest.

Significant tensions between the older tribal system of a volunteer
army from the households and a professional army of the king developed and continued (2 Samuel 24) until the demise of the monarchy.
Only with the Maccabees in the second century B.C.E. does a sustained
war of liberation from Seleucid rule, supported by many Jewish households in the countryside, reemerge as an important activity for families.

Most ominously, as debts to the monarchy and to wealthy landowners increased, households sold members and assets, including land, to
survive, resulting in the expanding wealth of the royal house and the
elite upper class (1 Chron. 27:25–31; 2 Chron. 26:9–10; 32:27–29) and
the steady impoverishment of farm families (Ezek. 45:8).[122] Prophetic

condemnation of the wrongful confiscation of household estates by the wealthy and the royal house underscores the threat to the existence of many farm families (Isa. 3:13–15; 5:8–10; Micah 2:1–5).[123] Paradigmatic is the story of Naboth's vineyard, which tells of the head of a household who is executed on false charges because he refused to sell his household land to the king (1 Kings 21).

As Joseph Blenkinsopp's important observations make so very clear,[124] the religious traditions and practices that strengthened families were restricted and at times even prohibited by royal design. During Josiah's reform (2 Kings 22—23), the centralization of worship in Jerusalem sought to strengthen royal control of religion and thereby concentrate greater power in the hands of the king by eliminating not just pagan cults but also the local sanctuaries and priesthoods (country Levites) that were integrated into the social fabric of the households and clans. Transforming Passover from a household sacrificial meal to a national pilgrimage festival held at Jerusalem was designed to centralize religious control of the royal sanctuary and to negate the major cultic celebration that strengthened family identity and solidarity. The proscription of the veneration of dead ancestors sought to break the link between the living members of the household and their ancestors, who were thought to continue as members of the family throughout the generations.[125] The attempts to replace the belief in the continuance of life after death with the view of the oblivion of death and to prohibit ancestor veneration also sought to destroy the family's linkage with its past.[126] The subverting of the material means by which families continued to exist cost them their future; prohibiting the veneration at the ancestral burial site on the family estate helped negate the sense of the importance of the household's land tenure and cost families their past.

With the rise of the royal state, then, significant conflict emerged between the different social systems of loosely knit tribes, clans, and households on the one hand and the royal state and the rule of one household on the other hand. This adversarial relationship is attested frequently by the prophets, who decry the devaluation of human life in the monarchical state, the subverting of care for the weak and the poor, the growing debts of farm families, and the confiscation of their land. The overall design of the monarchy was to shift citizens' allegiance and resources away from kinship structures and responsibilities, especially represented in the households and clans, to the king's household in particular and the royal state in general. Indeed, before the fall of Jerusalem in 586 B.C.E., families and villages had largely come under the expanding and controlling orbit of towns, cities, royal districts, the kingdom, and ultimately the king himself. Without the abrupt end of the monarchy in the Babylonian conquest, the family household in its described form likely would not have survived.

NOTES

1. For earlier studies of the family in Israel and early Judaism, see Hector Avalos, "Legal and Social Institutions in Canaan and Ancient Israel," *Civilizations of the Ancient Near East* 1 (1995):624–27; J. R. Porter, *The Extended Family in the Old Testament* (London: Edutext Publications, 1967); C. S. Rodd, "The Family in the Old Testament," *BT* 18 (1967):19–26; S. Safrai, "Home and Family," in *The Jewish People in the First Century* (Assen: Van Gorcum/Philadelphia: Fortress Press, 1976), 2:728–92; Lawrence Stager, "The Archaeology of the Family in Ancient Israel," *BASOR* 260 (1985): 1–36; Roland de Vaux, *Ancient Israel: Its Life and Institutions* vol. 1 (New York: McGraw-Hill Book Co., 1961); and C. J. H. Wright, "Family," *ABD* 2 (1992):761–69.

2. For an overview, see I. Mendelsohn, "The Family in the Ancient Near East," *BA* 11 (1948):24–40.

3. For the family in ancient Egypt, see Geraldine Pinch, "Private Life in Ancient Egypt," *Civilizations of the Ancient Near East* 1 (1995):363–81 (and bibliography); for Mesopotamia, see Marten Stohl, "Private Life in Ancient Mesopotamia," *Civilizations of the Ancient Near East* 1 (1992):485–501 (and bibliography).

4. Carol L. Meyers's chapter in this volume, "The Family in Early Israel," provides an important paradigm for using archaeological data within a social model to reconstruct family life in a period that has only very limited written materials.

5. See pp. 173–74.

6. For the history of the family in human cultures, see P. Laslett and R. Wall, eds., *Household and Family in Past Time* (Cambridge: Cambridge University Press, 1972); R. Netting, R. R. Wilk, and E. J. Arnould, eds., *Households: Comparative and Historic Studies of the Domestic Group* (Berkeley: University of California Press, 1984); E. A. Wrigley, "Reflections on the History of the Family," *Daedalus* 106 (1977):71–85; and S. J. Yanagisako, "Family and Household: The Analysis of Domestic Groups," *Annual Review of Anthropology* 8 (1979):161–205.

7. G. Lenski and J. Lenski, *Human Societies*, 5th ed. (New York: McGraw-Hill Book Co., 1987).

8. See F. I. Andersen, "Israelite Kinship Terminology and Social Structure," *BT* 20 (1979):29–39.

9. Carol L. Meyers, in chapter 1 of this volume, prefers to speak of the Is-

raelite family's *androcentrism*, instead of *patriarchy*, indicating her opinion that the family was centered more on the males and their interests than on women (see pp. 34–35). Meyers may be correct, but her argument seems to lessen the domination and control men are portrayed as having in the Israelite family. It may be that this portrayal of male domination and power in biblical texts is more ideological than it is reflective of the actual social reality of the household. Even so, I am convinced that *patriarchy* is an appropriate term for speaking of the character and practice of the Israelite household—a patriarchy that brings into question the value of biblical discourse about this topic for contemporary family life.

10. See David Hopkins, "The Dynamics of Agriculture in Monarchic Israel," *SBLSP* 1983:177–202; and Oded Borowski, *Agriculture in Iron Age Israel* (Winona Lake, Ind.: Eisenbrauns, 1987).

11. David Hopkins. *The Highlands of Canaan: Agricultural Life in the Early Iron Age* (Sheffield: Almond Press, 1985).

12. See Meyers in chapter 1, pp. 22–32.

13. Ibid.

14. See Z. Ben Barak, "Meribaal and the System of Land Grants in Ancient Israel," *Bib* 62 (1981):73–91; and Christopher J. H. Wright, *God's People in God's Land: Family, Land, and Property in the Old Testament* (Grand Rapids: Wm. B. Eerdmans Publishing Co., 1990).

15. "This term designates a portion of land as an inalienable, continually owned piece of earth that one has acquired through inheritance, allotment, or allocation" (Horst Dietrich Preuss, *Old Testament Theology* [Louisville, Ky.: Westminster John Knox Press, 1995], 1:123). See 1 Chron. 16:15–18; Ps. 105:8–11; and Ezek. 47:14, which speak of the *nuḥălâh* in the context of the promise to the fathers. While the term is used mainly for the land of a clan or tribe (Gen. 31:14; Num. 32:18–19) and the territory of Israel as a whole (Deut. 4:21, 38; 12:9–12; 15:4; 19:3, 10, 14), the word also designates an individual's or household's portion (Num. 27:7; Deut. 21:16; Josh. 19:49b, 50; 24:30; Judg. 2:9, 21:23–24; Ruth 4:5–6, 10; 1 Kings 21:3–4).

16. See Meyers in chapter 1, pp. 22–32.

17. Ibid.

18. See James L. Crenshaw, "Education in Ancient Israel," *JBL* 104 (1985): 601–15 (and bibliography).

19. In addition to Meyers's chapter in this volume, see especially Carole R. Fontaine, "The Sage in Family and Tribe," in *The Sage in Israel and the Ancient Near East*, ed. John G. Gammie and Leo G. Perdue (Winona Lake, Ind.: Eisenbrauns, 1990), 155–81.

20. Fontaine, "Sage in Family and Tribe," 158–63. See Crenshaw, "Education in Ancient Israel."

21. Robert Gordis, "The Social Background of Wisdom Literature," *HUCA* 18 (1944):77–118.

22. The priestly education of children is noted in the cases of Samuel (1 Sam.

2:21, 26) and Jehoash (2 Kings 12:2). There is no direct evidence for a formal school until Ben Sira's *bêt midraš* (Sir. 51:23). Some older boys and young men took up residence in schools, probably associated with the court during the time of the monarchy and with the temple during the second temple period. Young people trained to become scribes and bureaucrats who would be employed in the larger economic and social institutions of Israelite and early Jewish society. Perhaps some of these older boys and young men came from the villages and towns, but most were probably urban children and were either the offspring of scribal families, educated as apprentices by their fathers, or the children of aristocratic families that sought advanced education for their offspring. Priests also provided religious instruction, for the most part during local festivals and national pilgrimages to local and central shrines.

23. Isaiah is presented as having the ability to write (Isa. 8:2), but the traditions of Jeremiah present the prophet as requiring a scribe, Baruch, to write down his oracles (Jeremiah 36). When he performed the duty of the *go'ēl* and purchased the farm in Anathoth (chap. 32), Jeremiah, though he signed the deed, appears to have used Baruch as his lawyer to preserve the deed and a copy, and perhaps even to have drawn up its terms. Deuteronomy 6:9 and 24:1 suggest the audience has the ability to write, though even if the book is addressed to a general audience, not merely a literate one, these references may mean no more than that scribal services were available for the purposes of writing religious instructions and legal documents.

24. The mention in Judges 8 of Gideon's capture of a young man of Succoth who wrote down the names of the officials and elders of Succoth, even if a historical incident, hardly suggests a random capture that would support the existence of either widespread literacy or public education in reading and writing during the prestate period.

25. M. Haran, "On the Diffusion of Literacy and Schools in Ancient Israel," in *Congress Volume: Jerusalem 1986*, ed. J. A. Emerton (VTSup 40; Leiden: E. J. Brill, 1988), 81–95; André Lemaire, *Les Écoles et la formation de la Bible dans l'ancien Israël* (OBO 39; Göttingen: Vandenhoeck & Ruprecht, 1981); idem, "Sagesse et écoles," *VT* 34 (1984):270–81; idem, "The Sage in School and Temple," in Gammie and Perdue, eds., *Sage in Israel*, 165–81; and Bernhard Lang, "Schule und Unterricht im alten Israel," in *La Sagesse de l'Ancien Testament*, ed. M. Gilbert (BETL 51; Gembloux, Belgium: Duculot, 1979), 186–201.

26. Lemaire, *Les Écoles*.

27. The biblical evidence for literacy outside the social group of scribes is sparse: Judg. 8:13–17; Job 31:35–37; Isa. 8:16; and Hab. 2:2. See Crenshaw, "Education in Ancient Israel," 604. Friedemann Golka argues that literacy was transmitted through the private instruction of families, not by a wisdom school associated with the court or temple ("Die israelitische Weisheitsschule oder 'des Kaisers neue Kleider,'" *VT* 33 [1983]:257–70;

and idem, *The Leopard's Spots: Biblical and African Wisdom in Proverbs* [Edinburgh: T. & T. Clark, 1993]). In 63 B.C.E. the high priest Joshua ben Gamla issued the decree that every village and town would have a school that children, beginning at the age of six or seven, would attend (de Vaux, *Ancient Israel*, 1:50). Qumran points to a scribal community, but it is difficult to derive from this indication evidence for widespread literacy throughout the farming villages of Palestine.

28. A. van der Lingen, *Les Guerres de Yahve* (LD 139; Paris: Editions du Cerf 1990); S.-M. Kang, *Divine War in the Old Testament and in the Ancient Near East* (BZAW 117; Berlin and New York: Walter de Gruyter, 1987); Gerhard von Rad, *Der Heilige Krieg im Alten Israel*, 3d ed. (Göttingen: Vandenhoeck & Ruprecht, 1958); and Rudolf Smend, *Yahweh War and Tribal Confederation* (Nashville: Abingdon Press, 1970). Norman K. Gottwald argued this military function of the clans was designated by the term *'eleph* (*The Tribes of Yahweh: A Sociology of the Religion of Liberated Israel, 1250–1050 B.C.E.* [Maryknoll, N.Y.: Orbis Books, 1979], 270–76).

29. Joseph Blenkinsopp, *Wisdom and Law in the Old Testament*, 2d ed. (Oxford: Oxford University Press, 1995); Hans Jochen Boecker, *Law and the Administration of Justice in the Old Testament and the Ancient Near East* (Minneapolis: Augsburg Publishing House, 1980); Calum Carmichael, *Law and Narrative in the Bible: The Evidence of the Deuteronomic Laws and the Decalogue* (Ithaca, N.Y.: Cornell University Press, 1985); Samuel Greengus, "Law," *ABD* 4 (1992):242–52; Dale Patrick, *Old Testament Law* (Atlanta: John Knox Press, 1985); A. Phillips, "Some Aspects of Family Law in Preexilic Israel," *VT* 23 (1973):349–61; Raymond Westbrook, *Studies in Biblical and Cuneiform Law* (CahRB 26; Paris: J. Gabalda, 1988); idem, *Property and the Family in Biblical Law* (Sheffield: JSOT Press, 1991); and Wright, "Family," 764.

30. E. Bellefontaine, "Deuteronomy 21:18–21: Reviewing the Case of the Rebellious Son," *JSOT* 13 (1979):13–31.

31. For a discussion of elders, see J. L. McKenzie, "The Elders in the Old Testament," *Bib* 40 (1959):522–40.

32. For an overview of social organization in early Israel, see Gottwald, *Tribes of Yahweh*, 236–341.

33. Gottwald, *Tribes of Yahweh*, 285–92.

34. However, one also occasionally finds the expression *bêt 'ēm*, "mother's household," indicating that the formal character of the household was not exclusively patriarchal (Gen. 24:28; Ruth 1:8; S. of Sol. 3:4; 8:2; cf. Prov. 9:1–6; 14:1; 31:10–31). See Carol Meyers, "'To Her Mother's House': Considering a Counterpart to the Israelite *Bêt 'āb*," in *The Bible and the Politics of Exegesis: Essays in Honor of Norman K. Gottwald on His Sixty-Fifth Birthday*, ed. David Jobling, Peggy L. Day, Gerald T. Shepherd (Cleveland: Pilgrim Press, 1991), 39–51, 304–7.

35. Hans Walter Wolff, *Anthropology of the Old Testament* (Philadelphia: Fortress Press, 1974), 214.

36. Westbrook, *Property and the Family*.

37. Yigal Shiloh, "The Casemate Wall, the Four Room House, and Early Planning in the Israelite City," *BASOR* 268 (1987):3–15; and Stager, "Archaeology of the Family."

38. See Nicholas Tromp, *Primitive Conceptions of Death and the Netherworld in the Old Testament* (BO 21; Rome: Pontifical Biblical Institute, 1969); Karel van der Toorn, "Funerary Rituals and Beatific Afterlife in Ugaritic Texts and in the Bible," *BO* 48 (1991):40–66; Paolo Xella, "Death and the Afterlife in Canaanite and Hebrew Thought," *Civilizations of the Ancient Near East* 3 (1995):2059–70.

39. Xella, "Death and the Afterlife," 2069.

40. See Joseph Blenkinsopp's chapter in this book, "The Family in First Temple Israel," chapter 2, pp. 81–82.

41. See Gottwald, *Tribes of Yahweh*, 257–84; C. U. Wolff, "Some Remarks on the Tribes and Clans in Israel," *JQR* 36 (1946):287–95.

42. Gottwald defines the *mišpāḥāh* as a "protective association of extended families" (*Tribes of Yahweh*, 257). See J. Liver, "The Israelite Tribes," in *The World History of the Jewish People*, ed. B. Mazar (New Brunswick, N.J.: Rutgers University Press, 1971), 3:183–211.

43. David Hopkins, "Life in Ancient Palestine," *New Interpreters Bible* 1 (1994): 213–27.

44. See Meyers in chapter 1, p. 12.

45. See Blenkinsopp in chapter 2, pp. 78–81.

46. See Gottwald, *Tribes of Yahweh*, 245–56; and C. U. Wolff, "Terminology of Israel's Tribal Organization," *JBL* 65 (1946):45–49.

47. For a discussion of the tribal federation, or amphictyony, see J. D. Martin, "Israel as a Tribal Society," in *The World of Ancient Israel*, ed. R. E. Clements (Cambridge: Cambridge University Press, 1989), 95–117.

48. See the classic study of Martin Noth, *Das System der zwölf Stämme Israels* (BWANT 4; Darmstadt: Wissenschaftliche Buchgesellschaft, 1930). For a critique of the concept of the tribal federation (amphictyony), see O. Bächli, *Amphiktyonie im Alten Testament: Forschungsgeschichtliche Studie zur Hypothese von Martin Noth* (Basel: Friedrich Reinhardt, 1977).

49. See Meyers in chapter 1, pp. 22–32.

50. For the roles of son, husband, and brother, see the discussions below.

51. See P. A. H. de Boer, *Fatherhood and Motherhood in Israelite and Judaean Piety* (Leiden: E. J. Brill, 1974).

52. In regard to the last point, Deut. 21:18–21 attempted to circumscribe this paternal authority by requiring both parents to present a case against an unruly offspring to the elders of the clan or town who would judge the matter.

53. Stager, "Archaeology of the Family." He notes that after state formation and the increasing density of the population, young males who were not the firstborn and could not establish their own families within the household sometimes left to become soldiers and priests.

54. Phyllis Bird, "Women (OT)," *ABD* 6 (1992):951–56; A. Brenner, *The Israelite Woman: Social Role and Literary Type in Biblical Narrative* (Sheffield: JSOT Press, 1985); P. L. Day, ed., *Gender and Difference in Ancient Israel* (Minneapolis: Fortress Press, 1989); G. I. Emmerson, "Women in Ancient Israel," in Clements, ed., *World of Ancient Israel*, 371–94; B. S. Lesko, ed., *Women's Earliest Records: From Ancient Egypt and Western Asia* (BJS 166; Atlanta: Scholars Press, 1989); Carol L. Meyers, *Discovering Eve: Ancient Israelite Women in Context* (Oxford: Oxford University Press, 1988); idem, "Everyday Life of Women in the Period of the Hebrew Bible," in *The Women's Bible Commentary*, ed. C. A. Newsom and Sharon H. Ringe (Louisville, Ky.: Westminster John Knox, 1992), 244–51.

55. Bird, "Women (OT)," 956.

56. Cheryl Exum and Johanna Bos, eds., *Reasoning with the Foxes: Female Wit in a World of Male Power, Semeia* 42 (1988).

57. De Boer, *Fatherhood and Motherhood.*

58. Women at Elephantine were clearly allowed to divorce their husbands; see John J. Collins's chapter in this volume, "Marriage, Divorce, and Family in Second Temple Judaism," chapter 3, pp. 104–62.

59. Phyllis Trible notes that the Hebrew word for "womb" (*reḥem*) in the singular becomes "compassion" (*raḥămîm*) in the plural (*God and the Rhetoric of Sexuality* [Philadelphia: Fortress Press, 1977], 31–59).

60. Rainer Albertz, "Hintergrund und Bedeutung des Elterngebots im Dekalog," *ZAW* 90 (1978):348–74.

61. Millar Burrows, *The Basis of Israelite Marriage* (AOS 15; New Haven, Conn.: American Oriental Society, 1938); P. Grelot, "The Institution of Marriage: Its Evolution in the Old Testament," in *The Future of Marriage as Institution,* ed. Franz Bockle (Concilium 55; New York: Herder & Herder, 1970); D. R. Mace, *Hebrew Marriage: A Sociological Study* (New York: Philosophical Library, 1953); E. Neufeld, *Ancient Hebrew Marriage Laws* (London: Longmans, Green, & Co., 1944).

62. Forbidden in Leviticus 18 are sexual relations (including marriage) with one's father's wife and with one's mother, sister (full or half), granddaughter, aunt by blood or marriage, daughter-in-law, sister-in-law, as well as those with a woman and her daughter or her son's or daughter's daughter and with both of two sisters. Certain of these restricted marriages did occur earlier (Gen. 20:12; 29:1–30; Ex. 6:20; Num. 26:59; 2 Sam. 13:13). See Joshua R. Porter, *The Extended Family in the Old Testament* (London: Edutext Publications, 1967).

63. However, in Genesis 24, Rebekah is asked if she will go with Abraham's servant and marry Isaac, and Samson asks his parents to arrange for a Philistine woman to be his wife (Judg. 14:2–3). After his rape of Dinah, Shechem asks his father to arrange a marriage with her (Genesis 34).

64. See Meyers in chapter 1, p. 36. Marriage to foreigners is prohibited in scripture (Ex. 34:15–16; cf. Gen. 24:3; 27:46), though such did occur (Esau married two Hittite women, Gen. 26:34; Joseph married an Egyptian,

Gen. 41:45; Moses married a Midianite, Ex. 2:21; Naomi had two Moabite daughters-in-law, Ruth 1:4; David married the daughter of the king of Geshur, 2 Sam. 3:3; Bathsheba married Uriah the Hittite, 2 Sam. 11:3; Solomon "loved many foreign women," 1 Kings 11:1; 14:21; and Ahab married the daughter of the king of Sidon, 1 Kings 16:31). Kings presumably married foreigners for the purpose of treaty arrangements with foreign nations. Foreign women taken in war could be married by Israelites (Deut. 21:10–14). However, 1 Kings 11:4 notes that foreign wives led Solomon to worship other gods. Ezra instructed Jewish men who had married foreign women to send them away with their children (Ezra 9–10; Neh. 10:30), and Nehemiah punished those who married foreign women and made them swear not to perpetuate the practice of marriages to foreigners (Neh. 13:23–27). The divorce of foreign wives is countered by Malachi, who emphasized faithfulness in marriage (2:10–16).

65. This concern with sexuality reflected the desire to ensure knowledge of paternity. The standard length of the engagement cannot be ascertained (1 Sam. 18:17–19, 26–27). Jacob labored for seven years to marry Leah and another seven for Rachel, though this length of time was the service he offered to Laban as the *mohar,* or marriage price, which he presumably could not pay from his resources or those of his household (Genesis 29). A man who was engaged was not required to go to war but rather was allowed to remain with his household (Deut. 20:7). This practice maintained the marriage arrangement between the two households.

66. Meyers argues that the husband's "rule" pertained to the woman's sexuality and the need for children, which prevailed over her reluctance to have more pregnancies (*Discovering Eve,* 115–17).

67. The marriage fee could be paid in service (Jacob: Gen. 29:15–30; David: 1 Sam. 18:25–29; and Othniel: Josh. 15:16; Judg. 1:12).

68. Wright, "Family," 766, and de Vaux, *Ancient Israel,* 1:26–27, argue that the *mohar* does not suggest that brides were purchased.

69. G. A. Yee, "'I Have Perfumed My Bed with Myrrh': The Foreign Woman ('iššâ zārâ) in Proverbs 1–9," *JSOT* 43 (1989):53–68.

70. For the royal harem, including wives and concubines, see de Vaux, *Ancient Israel,* 1:115–17. The discord that existed in polygamous households is often noted (Gen. 16:4–5; 29:30–31; 30:1; 1 Sam. 1:6).

71. See W. Plautz, "Die Form der Eheschliessung im Alten Testament," *ZAW* 23 (1973):349–61; Robert W. Wall, "Divorce," *ABD* 2 (1992):218; and Gordon J. Wenham, "Marriage and Divorce in the Old Testament," *Didaskalia* 1 (1989):6–17.

72. P. C. Craigie suggests that the "indecency" is not adultery but perhaps a "physical deficiency such as the inability to bear children" (*The Book of Deuteronomy* [NICOT; Grand Rapids: Wm. B. Eerdmans Publishing Co., 1976], 305).

73. See Collins in chapter 3, pp. 123–27.

74. Ibid., pp. 115–21.

75. E. W. Davies, "Inheritance Rights and the Hebrew Levirate Marriage," *VT* 31 (1981):138–44, 257–68; and D. A. Leggett, *The Levirate and Goel Institutions in the Old Testament, with Special Attention to the Book of Ruth* (Cherry Hill, N.J.: Mack Publishing Co., 1974).

76. A. A. Anderson, "Marriage of Ruth," *JSS* 23 (1978):171–83; and E. Davies, "Ruth 4:5 and the Duties of the *gō'ēl*," *VT* 33 (1983):231–34.

77. See Lyn Bechtel, "Shame as a Sanction of Social Control in Biblical Israel: Judicial, Political and Social Shaming," *JSOT* 49 (1991):47–76.

78. The cases of Naomi and the poor widow may indicate that widows served as "trustees" for young sons until they became adults.

79. See Collins in chapter 3, pp. 130–35.

80. The accidental causing of a miscarriage is fined (Ex. 21:22–23).

81. There is little in the Hebrew Bible and early Jewish literature to suggest that adoption was commonly practiced. Because of his childlessness, Abraham thought to adopt his servant Eliezer (Gen. 15:1–6). Mordecai took Esther "to himself for a daughter" (Esth. 2:7, 15; author's translation). See S. Feigin, "Some Cases of Adoption in Israel," *JBL* 50 (1931):186–200; Marvin Pope, *Job* (AB: Garden City, N.Y.: Doubleday & Co., 1973), 233.

82. See I. Mendelsohn, "On the Preferential Status of the Eldest Son," *BASOR* 156 (1959):38–40. A common biblical theme is the displacement of the eldest or elder son by a younger one (e.g., Jacob, Joseph, David, and Solomon).

83. See Gottwald, *Tribes of Yahweh*, 263–67; cf. Ruth and Leviticus 25.

84. Gottwald, *Tribes of Yahweh*, 263. For blood vengeance, see Num. 35: 16–34; 2 Sam. 2:22–23; 14:4–11.

85. Otto Baab, "Fatherless," *IDB* 2 (1964):245–46.

86. One thesis is that the fatherless were the children of cultic prostitutes (Baab, "Fatherless," 246).

87. De Vaux, *Ancient Israel* 1:40; F. C. Fensham, "Widow, Orphan and Poor in Ancient Near Eastern Legal and Wisdom Literature," *JNES* 21(1962): 129–39; and Paula Hiebert, "'Whence Shall Help Come to Me?': The Biblical Widow," in Day, ed., *Gender and Difference*, 125–41.

88. See N. P. Lemche, "Manumission of Slaves," *VT* 26 (1976):38–59; and I. Mendelsohn, *Slavery in the Ancient Near East* (New York: Oxford University Press, 1949).

89. De Vaux, *Ancient Israel* 1:85.

90. A debt servant or slave freed for whatever reason is called a *ḥofši* (Lev. 21:2, 5; Deut. 15:12, 13, 18; Jer. 34:9–16).

91. See Christiana van Houten, *The Alien in Israelite Law* (JSOTSup 107; Sheffield: JSOT Press, 1991); and Frank A. Spina, "Israelites as *gērîm*, Sojourners in Social and Historical Context," in *The Word of the Lord Shall Go Forth*, ed. C. L. Meyers and M. P. O'Connor (Winona Lake, Ind.: Eisenbrauns, 1983), 321–35.

92. The complex history of the Levites cannot be discussed here. See Merlin D. Rehm, "Levites and Priests," *ABD* 4 (1992):297–310.

93. For an overview of this topic in the Old Testament, see A. Kuschke, "Arm und Reich im Alten Testament," *ZAW* 57 (1939):31–57.
94. Donald E. Gowan, "Wealth and Poverty in the Old Testament: The Case of the Widow, the Orphan, and the Sojourner," *Interpretation* 41 (1987): 341–53.
95. De Vaux, *Ancient Israel* 1:72–74.
96. The topic of rich and poor is a common one in Proverbs, especially in the collection of chaps. 10—22 (10:15; 11:28; 13:7, 18, 23; 14:20, 21, 31; 17:5; 18:23; 19:4, 7, 17, 22; 21:13; 22:2, 7, 16; cf. 3:27–28; 23:4, 7, 9, 16, 22–23, 26–27; 28:6, 11; 30:7–9). On the book of Proverbs, see Norman Habel, "Wisdom, Wealth and Poverty Paradigms in the Book of Proverbs," *Bible Bhashyam* 14 (1988):26–49; Raymond van Leeuwen, "Wealth and Poverty: System and Contradiction in Proverbs," *Hebrew Studies* 33 (1992):25–36; Harold C. Washington, *Wealth and Poverty in the Instruction of Amenemope and the Hebrew Proverbs* (SBLDS 142; Atlanta: Scholars Press, 1994); and R. N. Whybray, *Wealth and Poverty in the Book of Proverbs* (JSOTSup 99; Sheffield: JSOT Press, 1990). J. David Pleins argues that the perspectives on poverty in wisdom texts tend to reflect the ethos of a ruling elite in which wisdom was cultivated ("Poverty in the Social World of the Wise," *JSOT* 37 [1987]:61–78).
97. Van Leeuwen, "Wealth and Poverty," 33. According to wisdom literature, the creator established an order of justice and blessing that becomes embodied in wise teachings and communal law. Charity to the poor conforms to, strengthens, and actualizes this divine order of creation. As a result of good and wise actions, the community, including the poor, experiences well-being. Wickedness, including the neglect of the poor, contravenes this divine order and is harmful to the community, resulting ultimately in misfortune for the wicked. See Jacques Ellul, *The Theological Foundation of Law* (Garden City, N.J.: Doubleday & Co., 1960).
98. Rainer Albertz, *Persönliche Frömmigkeit und offiziele Religion* (Stuttgart: Calwer Verlag, 1978); and J. B. Segal, "Popular Religion in Ancient Israel," *JJS* 27 (1976):1–22.
99. A jar inscription from Kuntillet 'Ajrud and an inscription from a grave in Khirbet el-Qom, both dating from circa 800 B.C.E., appear to mention Yahweh and "his Asherah." See Klaas A. D. Smelik, *Writings from Ancient Israel* (Edinburgh: T. & T. Clark, 1991), 152–60; E. S. Gerstenberger, *Jahwe—Ein patriarchaler Gott? Traditionelles Gottesbild und feministische Theologie* (Stuttgart: W. Kohlhammer, 1988), 38–50; and P. K. McCarter, Jr., "Aspects of the Religion of the Israelite Monarchy: Biblical and Epigraphic Data," in *Ancient Israelite Religion,* ed. Patrick D. Miller, Jr., Paul D. Hanson, and S. Dean McBride (FS F. M. Cross; Philadelphia: Fortress Press, 1987), 137–55.
100. These figurines may have represented goddesses, or they may have been votive figurines of human women to secure fertility by magic.

101. See Tikva Frymer-Kensky, *In the Wake of the Goddesses: Women, Culture, and the Transformation of Pagan Myth* (New York: Free Press, 1992).

102. Westbrook, *Studies in Biblical and Cuneiform Law.*

103. See Blenkinsopp in chapter 2, pp. 78–81.

104. Hans-Joachim Kraus, *Worship in Ancient Israel* (Richmond: John Knox Press, 1966), 93.

105. Priests, who presided at formal worship services, had as their primary responsibility mediating between deity and people, a role that included especially the offering of sacrifice (Kraus, *Worship in Israel,* 100–101).

106. See especially Phyllis Bird, "The Place of Women in the Israelite Cultus," in Miller et al., eds., *Ancient Israelite Religion,* 297–320; idem, "Israelite Religion and the Faith of Israel's Daughters: Reflections on Gender and Religious Definition," in Jobling et al., eds., *The Bible and the Politics of Exegesis,* 97–108, 311–25; and Carol Meyers, "Of Drums and Damsels: Women's Performance in Ancient Israel," *BA* 54 (1991):16–26.

107. Conrad L'Heureux, "The Ugaritic and Biblical Rephaim," *HTR* 67 (1974): 265–74.

108. H. Brichto, "Kin, Cult, Land and Afterlife—A Biblical Complex," *HUCA* 44 (1973):1–54; Theodore J. Lewis, *Cults of the Dead in Ancient Israel and Ugarit* (Atlanta: Scholars Press, 1989); and Blenkinsopp in chapter 2, pp. 81–82.

109. See Blenkinsopp in chapter 2, p. 81.

110. See Carol L. Meyers, "Kinship and Kingship: The Early Monarchy," in *The Oxford History of the Biblical World,* ed. Michael D. Coogan (New York: Oxford University Press, forthcoming). Also see Gösta Ahlström, "Administration of the State in Canaan and Ancient Israel," *Civilizations of the Ancient Near East* 1 (1995):587–603; idem, *Royal Administration and National Religion in Ancient Palestine* (Studies in the History of the Ancient Near East 1; Leiden: E. J. Brill, 1982); Baruch Halpern, *The Constitution of the Monarchy in Israel* (HSM 25; Chico, Calif.: Scholars Press, 1981); and T. N. D. Mettinger, *King and Messiah: The Civil and Sacral Legitimation of the Israelite Kings* (ConBOT 8; Lund: C. W. K. Gleerup, 1976).

111. See above, pp. 173–74.

112. See Frank Frick, "Religion and Sociopolitical Structure in Early Israel: An Ethno-Archaeological Approach," *SBLSP* (1979):233–53; idem, *The Formation of the State in Ancient Israel* (Sheffield: Almond Press, 1985); E. W. Heaton, *Solomon's New Men: The Emergence of Ancient Israel as a National State* (London: Thames & Hudson, 1974); and T. N. D. Mettinger, *Solomonic State Officials: A Study of the Civil Government Officials of the Israelite Monarchy* (ConBOT 5; Lund: C. W. K. Gleerup, 1971).

113. See Blenkinsopp in chapter 2, pp. 85–92.

114. See John Bright, "The Organization and Administration of the Israelite Empire," in *Magnalia Dei: The Mighty Acts of God,* ed. F. M. Cross, Werner

E. Lemke, and Patrick D. Miller (FS G. E. Wright; Garden City, N.Y.: Doubleday & Co., 1976), 193–208; and Norman K. Gottwald, *The Hebrew Bible: A Socio-Literary Introduction* (Philadelphia: Fortress Press, 1985), 323–25.

115. Avalos, "Legal and Social Institutions," 621–23; and G. C. Malcholz, "Die Stellung des Königs in der israelitischen Gerichtsverfassung," *ZAW* 84 (1972):157–82.

116. See Gerhard von Rad, "The Royal Ritual in Judah," in *The Problem of the Hexateuch and Other Essays* (New York: McGraw-Hill Book Co., 1966); and Karel van der Toorn, "Theology, Priests, and Worship in Canaan and Ancient Israel," *Civilizations of the Ancient Near East* 3 (1995):2047–53.

117. For the king and royal religion, see J. H. Eaton, *Kingship and the Psalms* (SBT, 2d series, 32; Naperville, Ill.: Alec R. Allenson, 1976); Aubrey Johnson, *Sacral Kingship in Ancient Israel* (Cardiff: University of Wales Press, 1955); Keith Whitelam, "King and Kingship," *ABD* 4 (1992):49; and G. Widengren, *Sakrales Königtum im Alten Testament und im Judentum* (Stuttgart: W. Kohlhammer, 1955).

118. Walter Brueggemann, "The Social Significance of Solomon as a Patron of Wisdom," in Gammie and Perdue, eds., *The Sage in Israel,* 117–32.

119. Van der Toorn, "Theology, Priests, and Worship," 2050–52. For a comprehensive discussion of the temple, see Menahem Haran, *Temples and Temple-Service in Ancient Israel* (Oxford: Clarendon Press, 1978). Also see Carol L. Meyers, "Temple, Jerusalem," *ABD* 6 (1992):350–69.

120. Brueggemann, "Social Significance of Solomon."

121. Keith Whitelam, *The Just King: Monarchical Judicial Authority in Ancient Israel* (Sheffield: JSOT Press, 1979).

122. E. Neufeld, "The Emergence of a Royal-Urban Society in Ancient Israel," *HUCA* 31 (1960):31–53.

123. See Andrew Dearman, *Property Rights in the Eighth Century Prophets* (SBLDS 106; Atlanta: Scholars Press, 1988).

124. See above, pp. 85–92.

125. See Blenkinsopp in chapter 2, p. 89.

126. Ibid.

5

The Household,
Old Testament Theology, and
Contemporary Hermeneutics

LEO G. PERDUE

This examination of the development of the family in ancient Israel and early Judaism, including its religious and ethical practices, has to this point largely been an exercise in social history. To move from the discourse of social history to the word of Old Testament theology represents a significant challenge. Now we ask, "What does the understanding of the family in ancient Israel and early Judaism contribute to the larger discourse of Old Testament theology?" More specifically, "How does the family contribute to and reflect the Old Testament's understanding of God, creation, history, anthropology, and the chosen people?"

From Social History to
Old Testament Theology

Several assumptions underlie my move from social description to Old Testament theology. One assumption is that Old Testament theology should be systematic and constructive.[1] The systematic formulation of Israelite understandings of such theological categories as "God" and "chosen people" involves, to some extent, a modern imposition of a structure on varied literary materials arising from different periods, addressing diverse audiences, and offering disparate voices. Nevertheless, theology, whether contemporary or biblical, must by its necessity be constructive for contemporary understanding. The interpreter constructs, out of diverse materials, biblical understandings in a systematic form that makes sense to modern thought. This is not to say that such constructive, systematic work would have produced anything that would have made much sense to ancient Israelites, but it does to us.

The second assumption is the existence of a fundamental, unifying center to the theology of the Old Testament, not one that is contrived but rather one that emerges from the biblical text itself. This leads to the recognition that there are texts and understandings in the Old Testament that connect to this center, while others do not. Those not directly related to this center necessarily take on a secondary role in the formulation of Old Testament theology. However, the proposals as to the identification of this center vary significantly, ranging from God, election, and redemptive history to creation and salvation history and covenant, to name some of the most frequently mentioned possibilities.[2] As will be seen, the theological significance of the family in the Hebrew Bible offers us important insight in addressing this matter of a center.

The third assumption is that while Old Testament theology may wish to set forth a description of the teachings present in scripture, evaluation of the authenticity of this material is also necessary. The appropriate place for this evaluation, however, is debated: Should it occur in the initial formulation of biblical theology or in a critical review by contemporary theology? However, even an Old Testament theology that seeks to be only descriptive makes implicit evaluations.

The fourth assumption is that the historical particularities and disparate voices of the biblical witness are not to be ignored but rather to be elicited and articulated. These particularities and differences are to be integrated within the larger whole of a systematic Old Testament theology. Thus there are unity and continuity in the articulation but also diversity and discontinuity.

Israel's theological understanding of the family is discovered in its narratives about "houses of the fathers" (and occasionally, "mothers"); renderings of God in metaphors of social roles, drawn from society in general and the household in particular; laws and instructions that shape and direct human behavior within the family; and theological reflection, evidenced by references to God, explicit or implicit, in law codes, parenetic (moral) instructions, and prophetic pronouncements. These materials point to the emergence of several themes that contribute rather significantly to the construction of Old Testament theology: the household, the land, covenant, and solidarity and community.

The Family and
Old Testament Theology

The Purposes of the Household
and the Familial Roles of God

The household in the Bible occupies a central place in Old Testament theology and ethics. Much of what the Old Testament says about the character and especially the activity of God is shaped by discourse concerning the family. And much of what the Old Testament says about human morality concerns behavior within the context of the household. Indeed, the household of ancient Israel was one of two major social institutions that shaped theological reflection and discourse in the Old Testament and the subsequent formation of its theological traditions. The other social institution was the monarchy, followed later by the theocracy of the priesthood and the temple. In the second temple period, after the demise of the ruling house of David, the priesthood of the temple gradually shaped a theocracy that came to have significant religious and civil power amid the hegemony of the succeeding Persian, Greek, and Roman empires, which ruled over Judah as a colonial nation. This sacral theocracy of priesthood and temple provided significant theological language and understanding for the second temple period.

Throughout its history, ancient Israel's major understandings of God, creation, the nation, the nations, and morality were forged in large part by the social character and experience of the family household. Many of the key metaphors for imaging God, Israel, the land, and the nations originated in the household. The household's possession of and care for the land informed the theological understanding of God as the creator and provider of fertility, as well as the giver of the land to Israel's families. Major metaphors for Israel's self-presentation were drawn from household roles, especially those of the wife (the bride/wife of Yahweh), the son and the daughter, the impoverished kin (redeemed by Yahweh), and marginal members (debt servant, slave, resident alien, and sojourner). These are the principal theological metaphors that demonstrate how very important the social reality of the household became for theological reflection and articulation in the Old Testament. Indeed, the household not only grounded Old Testament theology in Israel's social reality but also became the primary lens through which to view the character and activity of God, the identity and self-understanding of Israel in its relationship to God, the value and meaning of the land as the *naḥalāh*

God gives to Israel, and Israel's relationship to the nations. The other social lens, in tension and often in conflict with the first, was the royal tradition. In the latter, God was the king, dwelling in Jerusalem, who chose his royal son to reign over the kingdom of Israel.

Yahweh's Role in Economics

In the Genesis creation narratives (1—2), God establishes the collective destiny of human beings and the purpose of human life at the beginning of the cosmos. The importance of labor as an activity necessary for existence and for helping to sustain the created order (Gen. 1:26–31; 2:5, 15, 18) is significant, though as a result of disobedience agricultural work becomes harsh and difficult (Gen. 3:17–19). The difficulty and even vanity of labor (see Eccl. 3:9–15; Ps. 127:1) are, according to the Yahwist, the result of divine curse of the soil, responding to human transgression (Gen. 3:17–19). While not valued in a positive way in the Old Testament, demanding agricultural labor was a necessity to survive (Gen. 1:29; 2:15; Ps. 128:2; Prov. 14:23; 16:26).

The Sabbath brought relief from toil for the household, including even its slaves and animals. The Sabbath was viewed as both a divine gift (see Gen. 2:1–3) and a commandment (Ex. 20:8–11; Deut. 5:12–15). Remembering the Sabbath, according to the Priestly source (Ex. 20:8–11), renews the order and life-giving power of creation that is the basis for household life, while its observance by the family in Deuteronomy 5:12–15 serves to remind the household that Yahweh liberated its ancestors from harsh slavery in Egypt.

Divine Blessing and Reproduction

Theologically construed, the reproduction of the household (including animals) resulted from divine blessing, which derived from faithful obedience to God.[3] God's commandment to the man and the woman in the garden, "Be fruitful and multiply, and fill the earth, and subdue it; and have dominion" (Gen. 1:28; 9:1 P), is grounded in the divine ordering of creation. The establishment of a new household by a man's leaving his parents to marry a woman was seen by the Yahwist to be the fundamental purpose of human creation (Gen. 2:21–24). The narratives of the ancestors in Genesis, centering on divine promise and fulfillment, incorporate this fundamental understanding of the family's reproductive commission (Gen. 12:1–4; 13:14–17; 15:1–6). Deuteronomy codifies this purpose and its enhancement by divine blessing within the law and the covenant (Deut. 28:4). The greatest curse was sterility and the cutting off of progeny, leading to the demise of the household (Deut. 28:18).

In the Old Testament, God is seen as the father who engenders life (Ps. 139:13–16; Prov. 8:22), receives the newborn on his knees to signal his paternity, and teaches Israel to walk (Hos. 11:1–3). God is also the mother, who conceives life within the womb, nourishes the fetus through its stages of gestation, and gives birth to the newborn (e.g., Deut. 32:18). As creator and sustainer, God forms the destiny of the child even before conception and provides, like a parent, sustenance and care throughout life (Jer. 1:5).

Divine Nurture

Divine authority and legitimation are given to laws and instructions that compel the household to nurture and care responsibly for its own members and for those outside the immediate family. The primary theological groundings of Israel's law codes and moral instructions are the traditions of God as creator and Yahweh as the liberator of the slaves from Egypt.

In Psalm 146, Yahweh is the God of Jacob, the creator of heaven and earth, and the righteous judge whose justice sustains his people and creation by supporting the poor and the oppressed, liberating prisoners, giving sight to the blind, lifting up those who are bowed down, loving the righteous, protecting the resident aliens, and upholding the widow and the fatherless.

In this portrayal of God as the righteous judge, the poor enjoy divine protection, especially from the ravages of wicked oppressors (Ps. 9:10–11 [ET 9:9–10]), and may call on their creator for deliverance (Ps. 34:6). In the wisdom literature, charity to the poor honors their creator and acknowledges the common origins of all humans, regardless of social status (Prov. 14:31; 17:5; 22:2).[4]

Elsewhere, God is the redeemer who freed the slaves from Egyptian bondage. This theology of liberation becomes the theological grounding for the legal requirement and moral imperative that Israel is to support the resident alien (gēr) and even, at times, incorporate resident aliens into the household. The children of Israel are to do so because they once were strangers (gērîm) in Egypt (Ex. 22:21; cf. 23:9). In the same context, the stranger, widow, and orphan are not to be afflicted,

for Yahweh will hear their cry (cf. Ex. 3:7) and bring punishment with
the sword and will make widows of Israelite wives and orphans of their
children (Ex. 22:22–24).

Deuteronomy often draws on exodus theology in setting forth its legal and parenetic teachings. Israelites are to love resident aliens, giving
them food and clothing, because the children of Israel themselves once
"were resident aliens in the land of Egypt" (Deut. 10:18–19, author's
translation). Justice to the resident alien, the widow, and the orphan is
not to be perverted, for the Israelite shall "remember that you were a
slave in Egypt and the LORD your God redeemed you from there; therefore I command you to do this" (Deut. 24:17–18). Elsewhere, Israel is
portrayed as a household of slaves whom Yahweh redeemed from Egypt
(Ex. 13:3, 14; 20:2; Deut. 5:6, 15; 6:12; 7:8; 8:14; 13:5, 10; 15:15;
16:12; Josh. 24:17–18; Judg. 6:8–9; Jer. 34:13).

God as Teacher

As the fathers and mothers of the households instructed their children, Yahweh taught (*môreh* = teacher; see Job 36:22) the children of
Israel. In the parable at Isaiah 28:23–29, God is the one who teaches
(*yārâ*) the farmer the knowledge and skill of agriculture. Yahweh also is
the one who instructs individuals and the people in the law and in ethical behavior (1 Kings 8:36; Job 34:32; Ps. 25:12; 27:11; 86:11; 119:33,
102; Isa. 2:3 = Micah 4:2; and Isa. 28:9–13) and who provides the
prophets and sages both the skill of rhetoric and the content of their
teachings (Ex. 4:12, 15; Judg. 13:8; Isa. 50:4–9).

The Divine Warrior

In early Israel (Exodus 15; Judges 5), Yahweh is the divine warrior
who issues the call for holy war against the enemy; assembles and then
leads the militia of families, clans, and tribes into battle; fights as a storm
god; secures victory; and distributes the spoils.[5] Even with the establishment of standing armies during the monarchy, the portrait of Yahweh as warrior continued throughout the first temple period (Deut.
7:16–26; Psalms 2, 24, 89, 97; Habakkuk 3) and into eschatological
thinking in the second temple period (Daniel 7, 12; Zech. 9:13–15;
14:3–4). During the monarchy, Yahweh was viewed by royalists as the
one who elected the ruler. According to the Deuteronomic History and
other royal traditions, Yahweh elected the dynasty of David to rule Israel (2 Samuel 7; Psalm 89), a role that included the conducting of war.

Yahweh became the lord protector and defender of the realm and its monarchy (Psalms 46, 48, 76).

God as Lawgiver and Judge

In ancient Israel and early Judaism, Yahweh was conceived as both the lawgiver and the judge (Ex. 20:2–17; Ps. 82:8). In addition, God was the one who either carried out indictments for violations or saw to it that the legal justice system did so. Israelite and Jewish law codes were religiously legitimated by the placement of their origins at Sinai, where Yahweh gave Israel the law (Exodus 19—Num. 10:10).

God as Head of the Household

Metaphors for both the representation of Yahweh and the portrayal of Israel's relationship to Yahweh are often drawn from the household. Yahweh frequently assumes the roles of the household, including father, husband, redeemer (go'ēl), and mother, while Israel (Judah, Zion/Jerusalem) is cast in the roles of wife, son and daughter, and marginal household members, including debt servants, slaves, resident aliens, sojourners, widows, and orphans.

Not surprising, in biblical theological reflection Yahweh is frequently viewed as the head of the household of Israel (Jer. 3:4) and as the father who was Israel's procreator (Deut. 32:6; Mal. 2:10) and who nurtured, supported, and loved his son Israel (Ex. 4:22; Isa. 63:16; Jer. 3:19; 31:9; Hosea 11) and his daughter (Lam. 2:13) or foundling (Ezekiel 16) Jerusalem/Zion. Yahweh is the father who teaches his child moral and religious instruction (see the "voice" of Wisdom in Proverbs 8—9).

God as Mother

Yahweh is occasionally presented as a mother who conceives, carries to term, and gives birth to Israel (Num. 11:12; Deut. 32:18). Divine "compassion" (rahǎmîm) is the plural of the word for "womb" (rehem), perhaps suggesting that the intensity of God's mercy and tender feelings for Israel is akin to that of the mother for the child who develops within her womb.[6] In Proverbs, divine Wisdom is personified not only as teacher but also as daughter, wife, and child (Proverbs 1, 8—9; cf. Sirach 24).

Yahweh as Go'ēl

Yahweh is often depicted in the role of the go'ēl who redeemed Israel from slavery (Ex. 15:13; Ps. 74:2; 77:15; 78:35). Yahweh is the go'ēl of

God's people and of righteous individuals (Job 19:25; Ps. 19:14; 78:35; Isa. 41:14; 43:14; Jer. 50:34), and Yahweh is the redeemer of widows and orphans (Ps. 146:9). This same redeemer is the special protector of the poor, acting to alleviate their suffering and oppression (Jer. 50:34). Indeed, in this role of protector, God required Israelites to extend to the poor the charity necessary for their sustenance and punished those who ignored this responsibility. It was Israel's encounter with the God of the poor in its historical experiences, especially the exodus, that provided the theological grounding for social legislation and action to address poverty.

God as Husband

The Yahwist's creation narrative points to the establishment of the household and the union of the man and woman, the becoming of one flesh, as the apex of creation (Gen. 2:21–24). Woman is, in Adam's words, "bone of my bone and flesh of my flesh" (Gen. 2:23; cf. 29:14; author's translation). In this creation story, Yahweh creates the wife as a partner or coworker within the household.

Marriage becomes a theological lens for understanding God and Israel. Yahweh is portrayed as the husband who takes Israel (or Jerusalem and Samaria) for his wife (Jer. 2:2; Ezekiel 16; Hosea 2). Monogamy, representing the covenant faithfulness of Yahweh and Israel to each other, is the favored way of representing divine election and community in terms of marriage, though Ezekiel points to Samaria and Jerusalem, two sisters, as married to Yahweh (Ezekiel 23). However, the unfaithfulness of Israel as wife in her devotion and obedience to Yahweh (Jer. 3:20) may lead to his divorce, humiliation, rejection, and abandonment of her (Jer. 3:1; Hosea 1—3), leaving her to be the victim of invaders unless he forgives and takes her back (Isa. 50:1; 54:6–7; 62:4–5; Jer. 2:2, 23–37; Hosea 2).

The Household and Israel's Theological Identity

Israel's identity and self-understanding as the people of God frequently are expressed in the titles of members of the household, including members related by kinship and marriage and marginal members as well. The makeup of the household provides the primary matrix and language system for the Old Testament writers' theological reflection and articulation.

The Households of Israel

Israel often understood itself as a community of clans and households. For example, the prophet Jeremiah, who came from the small farming village of Anathoth in the land of Benjamin, speaks of "all of the clans [mišpāḥōt] of the house of Israel" when introducing his oracle of judgment in 2:4–8. In this oracle the prophet draws on the faith traditions of the household—exodus, wilderness wandering, and entrance into the land—to contrast with Israel's history of apostasy after settling in Canaan. In the "Book of Consolation" (Jer. 30:1–31:40), Jeremiah addresses the Northern Kingdom, previously destroyed by Assyrian conquest, including both the survivors who live in exile and those who remain in Israel's former territory. In the oracle of salvation beginning at 31:1, he says on behalf of Yahweh, "I will be the God of all the clans [mišpāḥōt] of Israel, and they shall be my people." This is the covenant formula, which frequently expresses the relationship between Yahweh and Israel (cf. Jer. 7:23; 11:4; 30:22; 31:33; 32:38). Here the prophet bases Israel's future redemption from exile and the return of its captives to their homes on the everlasting love of God for his "clans, or residential kinship groups of families."

The specific term for "household" (bayit) is often used to speak of the nation as the "household of Israel" (bêt yiśrā'ēl), Ex. 16:31; 40:38; Lev. 10:6; Num. 20:29; Isa. 5:7; Jer. 2:4, 26; Hos. 1:4, 6; 5:1; 6:10; Amos 5:1). This term reflects the self-understanding of Israel as the nation formed from the ancestral household of Jacob (Israel). Thus the head of the household, a farmer, is to offer his confession during the harvest pilgrimage festival: Jacob/Israel is "my father," who descended into Egypt and there became "a great nation, mighty and populous" (Deut. 26:5–9).

Israel as Son

In addition to the frequent occurrence of the title "sons of Israel" as the name for the nation (Gen. 42:5, 21; Ex. 1:1, 7; etc.), Israel is metaphorically portrayed in the role of Yahweh's son. The northern prophet Hosea calls Israel the son of Yahweh, whom he loved and summoned from Egypt (Hosea 11). In this same judgment oracle, Hosea goes on to contrast Yahweh's continuing faithfulness to and compassion for his son with Israel's apostasy in following other gods, in particular, Baal. Yahweh was Ephraim's (Israel's) father, who taught him to walk. And while Yahweh as the divine judge exiles his own son, the compassionate father cannot give him up. Yahweh will have mercy and bring his son home from exile.

Jeremiah, especially in his early preaching (Jeremiah 2—6), often draws on the images and themes of Hosea. In the sermon on repentance in 3:1–4:4, Jeremiah uses the image of Israel as the son or sons of Yahweh. In spite of the fact that Israel was elected and placed among the sons of God, given a beautiful inheritance and patrimony among the nations, and came to call God "father," these privileged sons committed apostasy and became faithless (3:19, 22).

Jerusalem/Zion and Israel as Daughter

Another familial role often used in Old Testament theology is that of daughter. Daughter Zion is the personification of Jerusalem as the daughter of Yahweh. In Isaiah's lawsuit against Israel, he speaks of the Assyrian devastation, either the one that occurred with Sennacherib's invasion in 701 B.C.E. or an earlier one during the reign of Tiglath-pileser III in 734–733 B.C.E. This devastation left daughter Zion (Jerusalem) "like a booth in a vineyard" (Isa. 1:8; cf. 10:32; 16:1; 62:11; Micah 1:13; 4:8, 10, 13). In an oracle concerning the "foe from the north," Jeremiah compares the cries of daughter Zion (Jerusalem), uttered in response to the assault of the enemy, to those of a pregnant woman, shrieking in pain, when giving birth to her first child (Jer. 4:31; cf. 6:2, 23; Zeph. 3:14; Zech. 2:14; 9:9).

The Old Testament also portrays Yahweh as calling Judah the "daughter of my people" (bat-'ammî). This expression occurs especially in prophetic oracles of judgment when an enemy comes to invade Judah (Isa. 22:4; Jer. 4:11; 6:14, 26; 8:11, 19, 21, 22–23). In Jeremiah 6:16–30, a judgment oracle that speaks of the invading foe from the north, Judah is the "daughter of my people" who engages in rites of lamentation like a mother who mourns the death of an only child.

Israel as Wife

Israel is depicted by the prophet Hosea in chapter 2 as the faithless wife whom Yahweh divorces ("she is not my wife, and I am not her husband") for adultery (meaning, apostasy to other gods). When he casts her out, he also has no compassion on her children. Yet this oracle of judgment turns to salvation in Hosea 2:14–15: Yahweh will take Israel, his faithless wife, back to the wilderness and court her tenderly once more, and there she will respond as she did when first coming out of Egypt during the exodus (cf. Ezekiel 16, 23).

Jerusalem as Foundling

Israel is not only portrayed in the images and titles of household members related by marriage and birth. Titles, positions, and functions of marginals are also used to describe the nation's self-understanding and relationship to Yahweh. In Ezekiel 16, Yahweh comes upon an abandoned baby girl, exposed and left to die immediately after her birth. Even though she was the unwanted newborn of mixed parentage (her parents were an Amorite father and a Hittite mother), Yahweh sees her and admonishes her to "live." When she grows up and becomes a beautiful daughter, Yahweh marries her, though she afterward becomes faithless.

Israel as Slave

In describing Israel's origins in Egypt prior to the formation of the nation in Canaan, the Old Testament often refers to Israel as a slave ('ebed) in Egypt, whom Yahweh set free in the exodus (Deut. 5:15; 15:15; 16:12; 24:18, 22). Indeed, Deuteronomy in particular uses the theme of exodus liberation to provide the theological basis for its religious and social understanding. According to Deuteronomy, Israelites are to remember this tradition of their own slavery and liberation when commanded to support the poor and to include them within the community and protection of their own households. Thus, in Deuteronomy's reshaping of the law on Hebrew debt servitude and slavery, the released debt servant is to be liberally provided with goods, remembering that "you were a slave in the land of Egypt, and the LORD your God redeemed you." In addition, Israel is described as a "household of slaves," especially during its captivity in Egypt (Ex. 13:3, 14; 20:2; Deut. 5:6; 6:12; 7:8; 8:14; 13:5, 10; Josh. 24:17; Judg. 6:8; Jer. 34:13; Micah 6:4).

Israel as Resident Alien

The Old Testament draws on another marginal title to describe Israel's dwelling in Egypt, that of the resident alien (gēr). In Genesis 15:13, father Abraham is told in a theophany that his descendants will be resident aliens in a land not their own and will become slaves there (cf. Deut. 26:5–9). This collective memory is drawn upon when extending support to the poor and, in particular, to the resident aliens who dwell in Israel (Ex. 22:21; 23:9; Deut. 23:7). The high point of Israelite social ethics comes in the commandment to love the resident alien (Deut. 10:19) as oneself (Lev. 19:34), for in so doing, one actualizes God's own love and care for the stranger, that is, the other, who lives outside the immediate protection and support of his or her own family household.

The Family in Old Testament Theology:
The Land

Land tenure provided the economic base for the Israelite and Jewish household. Subsequently, a legal tradition developed that was designed to keep patrimonial land within the household or at least the larger clan. Land was not privately owned by the individual but rather was possessed by the household. When a household was forced to sell its land because of debts, the *go'ēl* of the family was to purchase it so that the extended household or clan could retain possession. Even then, the original household could later repurchase its land or at least could await its return at the time of jubilee. The levirate marriage was also designed to provide a deceased, childless husband offspring who would inherit his estate.

Israel's theological reflection on household land, and indeed, on the land of Israel and Judah in general, was grounded in the belief that the land was Yahweh's gift to the people and thus was not to be sold by households in perpetuity (Lev. 25:23–24). This meant that households, not kings or temples, possessed the land, because Yahweh, its owner, gave it not just to Israel in general but, more specifically, to its families.[7]

Yahweh's historical gift of the land is one of the central traditions of Old Testament theology.[8] Yahweh "gives" (*nātan*) the land to Israel to "inherit" (*yāraš*) as the *nahălâh,* "inheritance" (see Psalm 37). Yahweh's gift of the land is a fundamental feature of the larger understanding of the sovereignty of God. On the one hand, Israel possessed the land as a divine gift. On the other hand, the land continued to be Yahweh's, and he could take it back if the people were faithless. In the latter understanding, Israel was a tenant of the land (Jer. 2:7; 16:18; Ezek. 38:16; Hos. 9:3). Yahweh's gift of the land is thus like all other divine gifts, in that it was received by Israel and used for the benefit of its people. However, unfaithfulness would result in the loss of this gift as punishment. Indeed, the greatest punishment was the loss of the land and exile.

Israel's acknowledgment of Yahweh's continuing ownership of the land was indicated by offering the firstfruits to the sanctuary (Ex. 23:19). During the Festival of Weeks, the head of each household offered the first of the harvest to God and recited the ancient creed of God's salvific deeds (Deut. 26:1–11). Divine ownership of the land was also indicated by the affirmation that Yahweh, and no other deity, was the provider of fertility (Gen. 27:28; 49:25–26; Deut. 28:3–5; Hos. 2:10–11 [ET 2:12–13]). Indeed, the land is often called the "land of Yahweh" (Jer. 2:7; 16:18; Ezek. 38:16; Hos. 9:3).

The importance of the theological tradition of the gift of the land is indicated by its strategic locations in the literature of the Old Testament canon. The land is the culminating goal of Israel's redemptive history, as rehearsed in the Deuteronomic confession of faith in Deuteronomy 26:5–9. The divine grace demonstrated in Israel's liberation from Egyptian slavery is followed by God's obligations imposed on Israel in the law and the commandments (Exodus 20—Deuteronomy 34). Indeed, the gift and the continuing possession of the land that follow (Joshua—Judges) are predicated on faithfulness to this legal tradition, which acknowledges divine sovereignty over all of life. The gift of the land, in this case through conquest, stands at the beginning of Joshua and the Deuteronomic History (Josh. 1:1–9), and this tradition is celebrated in several of Israel's hymns and psalms of thanksgiving (Ps. 78:52–55; 105:7–11, 44; 136:21–22). Foreign conquest and exile from the land of Israel are construed by the prophets as divine judgment against a faithless people (Jer. 4:23–26; 9:10–11; 12:7–13; Hos. 2.16–23; 4:1–3; Amos 3:11; 7:11, 17), while the return of the exiles to the land is at the heart of prophetic oracles of salvation shortly before and during the exile (Isa. 11:10–16; 14:1–2; Jeremiah 30—31; Ezekiel 36—37; and Isaiah 40—55).[9]

In its understanding of the land as divine gift, Israel recognized that prior to its occupation of Canaan, other peoples inhabited this land. Thus Israel's theological comprehension of the land did not reside in some mythical understanding of the land as paradise or as the place of divine habitation or as the native soil of an indigenous people. In contrast to other nations of the ancient Near East, Israelites understood that the land was not theirs from the time of creation. Instead, the land of Canaan was Yahweh's promised gift to their ancestors, a promise realized in the settlement of the tribes.

This gift was expressed in two separate formulations that were eventually brought together: the promise to the ancestral fathers and the promise of liberation to the slaves in Egypt.[10] Peaceful settlement and conquest were the two different realizations of these two promises.

The promise of the land to the ancestors and their descendants is integral to the patriarchal narratives (Abraham, Gen. 12:7; 13:14–17; 15:7, 18–21; 24:7; Isaac, Gen. 26:2–5; and Jacob, Gen. 28:13–14; 35:9–15; 48:3–4). Even here, the promises came to be shaped by the understanding of household patrimony, for they were made to an ancestral founder of a household and his family that would extend into many future generations.

The second formulation of the promise is exodus and conquest. The exodus from Egypt had as its goal the possession of the land of Canaan, which God had promised to Israel as a gift or inheritance (Ex. 3:7–10; Deut. 4:21; 15:4; 19:10; 20:16; 24:4; 25:19; 26:1). This land is described as an inhabitable land, a "land flowing with milk and honey" (Ex. 3:8, 17; 13:5; 33:2–3; Num. 13:27), an expression that, while perhaps depicting the land in ideal fertility terms as viewed by seminomads, refers to the nourishment of farmers.[11] Yet, after Yahweh's liberation of the Israelites from Egyptian slavery, those who were rebellious were denied entrance to the land (Num. 13:22–33; 14:26–35; 20:12, 24; 26:64–65; 32:11). Joshua 2—11 rehearses the conquest of Canaan by "all Israel" and follows with the distribution of the land by lot as an inheritance (*nahᵃlāh*) to the various tribes and their clans and families (Joshua 13—19; see, e.g., 13:23, 28, 31; 15:12; etc.). Households were the recipients of this divine gift, which in this case was actualized by conquest.

Deuteronomy brings together the assurance to the ancestors and the promise to the slaves in Egypt and forges a broader theological tradition of the land (Deut. 1:8, 35; 4:21; 6:10–11, 18, 23; 7:8, 12–16; 8:1, 18; etc.). At the same time, Deuteronomy and the Deuteronomic History (Joshua—2 Kings) make the possession of the land contingent on the faithfulness of the people to the covenant (Josh. 23:12–16; 1 Kings 14:15). Thus the entwining of the theology of the gift of the land and responsibility to the covenant is central to Deuteronomy. In resting on the Sabbath, Israelites were to remember they were slaves in Egypt. Thus all members of the household, including slaves, are relieved of labor on the Sabbath. Charity, in the form of the produce left for the poor from the divinely given fields and orchards, is based on the corporate memory of enslavement and exodus liberation (Deut. 24:19–22).

Israel's claim to the land, then, meant that it would continue to be the "people of Yahweh" living in covenant with its God. The claim to the land had no other theological understanding. However, due to the impress of the royal tradition in Israel, this faithfulness to covenant responsibilities began, especially in Deuteronomy, to undercut some of the household tradition that integrated and sustained Israelite families (e.g., through the proscription of ancestor veneration and the celebration of the Passover not as a family ritual but as a pilgrimage festival).

The prophets warned and even promised that unfaithfulness to Yahweh would lead to exile and the loss of the land (Jer. 7:1–15; Amos 3:11; 7:11). Yet even this loss of the land in exile did not mean an end to the relationship with Yahweh. And the prophets held out the possibility of the return to the land as a theological hope grounded in the promise of God and the response of a faithful people (e.g., Isa. 11:10–16; 14:1–2; 60:21–22; Jer. 12:15; Hos. 2:16–23; Amos. 9:11–15; Micah 2:12–13).[12]

It is important to note that, theologically understood, the land is given not to Israel's and Judah's kings or even to their temples and priests but rather to the children of Israel in general, and in particular to their households from the very beginning of the nation. David did take Jerusalem, thus making it his own city, but he and his house did not own the land of Israel and Judah. Priestly Levites were even denied ownership of the land, thus having no *naḥălāh* (inheritance). Some remedy of their lack of land was provided in the postexilic period in the establishment of Levitical cities that at least included surrounding pastures.

The Family in Old Testament Theology: Solidarity and Community

The modern concept of individualism was not known in ancient Israel and early Judaism, though a basic understanding of individual responsibility within the larger corporate whole began to develop during the exilic period (see Ezekiel 18).[13] On the whole, however, the strong sense of corporate solidarity and community dominated Israel's and early Judaism's social and religious world.[14] The social and economic interdependence of members of the household produced the understanding of corporate identity and community that shaped people's relationships and lives. In the household, individual will and needs merged into the collective will and needs of the larger whole. The behavior of the individual affected the whole, and this was especially true of the head of the household, who embodied within himself the whole of the household (Ex. 20:5–6; Josh. 7:16–26). This collective good transcended the good of any individual member.

The marginal economic viability of many households produced an even greater sense of solidarity among their members.[15] However, when a household was no longer solvent, its surviving members dispersed and sought to take up residence in related households in the clan. In situations of economic duress, day labor, slavery, charity, and prostitution became the only options for survival.

Israel understood that its moral requirements as set forth by Yahweh were largely carried out in relationship to the members of the household. Marginal members, while "outsiders," were still connected to the family through their labor, producing of offspring, and occasionally even marriage and perhaps adoption. This moral responsibility also extended beyond the immediate household to the larger society, that is, the clans and tribes, and even to non-Israelites. The purpose of ethical action is not individual good fortune but rather the welfare of the community, beginning with the household and extending outward.

Theologically conceived, the divine election of Israel as a people and the formulation of a covenant with God placed on the nation's households the obligation to actualize economic justice. Deuteronomy expresses this corporate responsibility in social terms—"there will be no poor in your midst"—but provides for this responsibility a theological rationale: in so doing, "the LORD will bless you in the land which the LORD your God gives you for an inheritance to possess" (Deut. 15:4). Good was defined in terms of actions that would promote the well-being of the community, enhancing the lives of many thousands. Evil had to do with conduct that disrupted the solidarity and well-being of the community and that threatened both the viability of the household and the lives of marginals in the midst of Israel (Ex. 20:5–6 = Deut. 5:9–10; Ex. 34:7). Wrongs were thought to affect adversely the third and fourth generation, an understanding that reflects the multigenerational nature of Israelite households (Ex. 20:5–6). In the Deuteronomic History, the sins of the unjust (especially rulers) could affect negatively later generations (1 Kings 15:3; 2 Kings 21:19–22). At the same time, offenses of children could adversely affect the father (1 Sam. 2:12–4:18). The great commandment to love the neighbor as the self (and this was extended to include even the resident alien) was actualized in deeds that supported the integrity of the existence not only of the household but also of the marginal poor who lived outside the family's immediate protection (Lev. 19:18, 34). Extended outward to its largest boundaries of responsibility, the love of neighbor embraced the marginalized poor, who included the sojourner, the day laborer, the resident alien, the widow, the fatherless, and the Levite.

Exodus liberation became the fundamental faith of the community and led Israel to remember its experience as oppressed sojourners, resident aliens, and slaves in Egypt (Ex. 22:21; 23:9; Deut. 10:19; 23:7). This defining feature of the theological understanding of what it meant to be Israel obligated households to support, not to oppress or neglect, debt servants, slaves, sojourners, resident aliens, widows, the fatherless, and the Levites. In this understanding, ultimately it is Yahweh, the God of exodus liberation, who frees the slaves, listens to the cries of the oppressed, and is their defender (Ex. 22:26). Exodus faith became the theological grounding of the covenant obligations of the law and the administration of justice. For example, all members of the household, including even its slaves, were to observe the Sabbath, to experience its celebration, and to rest from their labor, because Israel was to remember—that is, to actualize in everyday life—its history of liberation as a house of slaves (Deut. 5:12–15).

This ideal of solidarity and corporate responsibility was not always realized, as the prophets indicate (Isa. 1:17; Jer. 7:6; 22:3; Amos). During the first temple period, royal policy dictated that loyalty and responsibility to monarchy, kingdom, and temple were to take precedence over loyalty and responsibility to the family household, the clan, and the tribe. The frequent failure of corporate responsibility for the poor was not always due to negligence, greed, or transferred loyalty. For example, the large number of refugees from northern Israel who migrated to Judah and particularly to Jerusalem after the Assyrian conquest of the Northern Kingdom undoubtedly placed enormous social strains on both the monarchy's and the household's capacity to provide care.

With the enormous disruption of family households caused by the Assyrian and Babylonian conquests and exiles, the strong solidarity that characterized the corporate life of Israelite society weakened considerably. An understanding of individual identity and responsibility began to develop in the exilic and postexilic periods (Deut. 24:16; 2 Kings 14:6; Jer. 31:29–30; Ezek. 14:12–20; 18:1–32). Even so, the strong sense of household solidarity and community reemerged in Jewish society in the second temple period, chastened by the recognition that individuals had a responsibility to the corporate wholes even as collective groups had for their members.

The Family in Old Testament Theology:
Covenant and Obligation

This understanding of solidarity and community became formally and morally expressed in Jewish society's theology of covenant and obligation, which defined the relationships between Israelites and God on the one hand and among fellow Israelites on the other.[16] Much of the covenant scholarship since the 1950s has focused on political treaties, in particular suzerainty treaties of the Late Bronze Age (1550–1200 B.C.E.) and loyalty oaths of vassals during the period of the later monarchy (eighth and seventh centuries B.C.E.), as the form and social location of the covenant (*bĕrît*) in Israel.[17] However, these analogies have rightly undergone significant criticism. The comparison of covenant in Israel with suzerainty treaties in the ancient Near East appear forced in certain key areas. For example, several of the important features of suzerainty treaties are not found in the key text of Exodus 20, where the so-called identification of the covenant parties, the historical prologue, and the stipulations are present. Absent in this chapter are the provision for deposit and public reading of the treaty (or covenant), the list of witnesses, and blessings and curses. These missing features have to be located in other biblical texts that are not at all related to Exodus 20.[18] In addition, the comparison of the Israelite covenant with loyalty oaths is too general to offer concrete evidence for influence or even specific similarities. If treaties and loyalty oaths did contribute in some fashion to the developing tradition of the covenants of Israel, especially the Sinai covenant in its Deuteronomic formulation, it is likely this influence would have taken place through the international dealings of the monarchy. I suggest that another, and perhaps even more formative, location for shaping the formal character and conceptual understanding of the covenant and its binding obligations is the household in ancient Israel and early Judaism.

Bĕrît probably derives from Hebrew *bārâ*, which includes the meaning "to choose, agree upon."[19] This suggests that the term issues from Israel's theology of election: God has chosen the ancestors, then Israel and its households, as God's community, and they in turn have chosen Yahweh to be their God. God has come to Israel in bondage to take up residence in this household, or God is the patron deity of the ancestral head of the household, whose descendants become the house of Israel. At its essence, covenant is viewed as a divine gift that Yahweh graciously bestows on Israel.[20] Yahweh's act of liberating the Israelites from Egyptian slavery precedes covenant and obligation, as the introduction to the Decalogue demonstrates (Ex. 20:2 = Deut. 5:6). Grace and election are prior to covenant and obligation, though incomplete without them.

In general, the Hebrew Bible speaks of five important covenantal relationships with God: those of the ancestors, Israel and its households, the house of David, the priesthood of Aaron, and creation. God's covenant with the households of Israel is presented often in the narrative discourse of the traditions of the ancestors and their families. This covenant is between the household deity, who came to be understood as Yahweh, and the ancestors Abraham, Isaac, and Jacob. In Genesis 15, Yahweh enters into a divine covenant (v. 18) with Abram (Abraham), identifies himself as the ancestor's "shield" (v. 1), and promises him descendants, a nation (vv. 3–6), and land (vv. 7, 18–21). The covenant between Yahweh and Abram is sealed through a ritual sacrifice (Gen. 15:9–11, 17). Later, in Genesis 17, the covenant between Abram and Yahweh is renewed. This time the covenant is sealed through the ancestors' name changes (from Abram to Abraham, Gen. 17:5, from Sarai to Sarah, 17:15) and through the ritual of circumcision (17:10–14). The promise of an heir and many descendants is reiterated (17:7), along with the promise of land for a "perpetual holding" (17:8). The household of Abraham is circumcised, including slaves born in the house and those bought from a foreigner (Gen. 17:27).[21]

In the course of shaping their household traditions, storytellers and bearers of tradition in Israelite clans and tribes created these and other foundation legends of the ancestors to articulate an understanding of covenant shaped by the social reality of the family. These ancestral legends spoke of the origins of the clans; of the establishment of a covenant relationship with the clan deities, who became eventually understood as the one God, Yahweh; and of the divine promises to households that legitimated their claim to their patrimony. These household legends of the ancestors eventually entered into the national saga of the Israelite people.

In addition to the ancestral households and their eponymic founders, covenant language is extended to include the households of Israel, especially at Sinai. Already in the ancestral narratives, the covenant is to include the descendants of the ancestors (Gen. 15:13–16, 18–21; 17:7–14, 19–21). However, it is especially at Sinai that Yahweh, having liberated the Israelites from Egyptian slavery, enters into covenant with the house of Israel (Ex. 20:2). This covenant, which encompasses a tradition formulated over several centuries, entails the Israelites' responsibility to acknowledge Yahweh as their lord, who liberated them from slavery, and to give obedience to his commandments, formulated within a continually growing legal tradition that encompasses various elements of social life and religious practice. This covenant, too, is ritually sealed with sacrifice (Ex. 19:5; 24:7–8; 34:10, 27–28) and continues to be renewed by later generations (Deut. 29:19). Much of the civil tradition that was placed within the Sinai covenant in the form of the obligations imposed on Israel concerns the life of family households. Thus much of the law developed by the Israelite and early Jewish legal system and preserved in biblical and early Jewish writings arose from the social matrix of the household. What is surprising is how very little law in the preserved legal tradition originated within or has to do with the monarchy.

The relationship of the house of David with Yahweh is also frequently portrayed in the language of covenant. In 2 Samuel 7, Yahweh offers to David and his house, through the prophet Nathan, an eternal covenant, guaranteeing that the house of David will continue to rule forever (cf. Psalm 89). The reigning Davidic king will be Yahweh's son (2 Sam. 7:14; cf. Ps. 2:7), and he will be the intermediary between Yahweh and Israel (cf. 1 Kings 8). Outside of promises and the Deuteronomic reshaping of the Davidic covenant to require the dynasty to follow the covenant of Sinai, there is no royal legal tradition preserved in the Hebrew Bible. The monarchy did exert limited influence on the content of the covenantal law of the Sinai tradition—for example, through the centralization of worship in Jerusalem, legislated in Deuteronomy probably during the reign of Josiah in the seventh century B.C.E. However, the influence of the royal house seems to have been marginal at best. With the end of the Davidic monarchy after the Babylonian conquest, this covenant was transferred to the Aaronic priesthood of the second temple (Num. 25:12–13; Neh. 13:29).

Finally, all creation, through the covenant with Noah, comes within the framework of a covenantal relationship with God the Creator (Gen. 9:8–17; Isa. 54:10; Jer.33:20, 25). This covenant, shaped in the period of the second temple, frames a universal relationship between God and humanity, other creatures, and all creation.

Johannes Pedersen has emphasized the understanding of covenant as the establishment of a sphere of life in which a strong sense of corporate solidarity and mutual obligations to fellow human partners and to God predominates.[22] Yahweh's covenant was established with the tribes of Israel but also with its community of households. This covenant established a relationship in which Yahweh bound himself to Israel and offered its people life and well-being, while they, in return, offered him their exclusive worship and devotion. The Sinai covenant, at least, was conditional, for the continuation of this covenant depended on Israel's faithfulness to Yahweh and to his divine obligations imposed on the community. Not surprising, the Davidic covenant was said by its loyalists to be eternal, even unconditional.

This means, then, that the Sinai covenant, while freely given, included obligation—to Yahweh as the God of election, whom alone Israel was to worship, and to covenant partners, that is, the other households of the nation. Covenant and obligation are not separate conceptions that only later are brought together but rather are interconnected, one with the other, from their very initial formulation.[23] In regard to the Sinai covenant, obligation took its form in divine imperatives expressed in the law, a point that is clear in the association of law and covenant at Sinai (Ex. 19:1–Num. 10:10). Much of this legal tradition, which grew over the centuries, was directed to the household and its socioreligious life within larger Israel.

Deuteronomy creates the first clear formulation of covenant theology, though it would be specious reasoning to argue that the elements of this construction were created out of thin air.[24] What seems most likely is that laws, customs, values, and practices originating within the development of the household and its larger social constructs of clan and tribe were placed within a theology of covenant that the Deuteronomic teachers and scribes began to put together in the eighth century B.C.E. This later law code points to the weakening of clan loyalties in favor of state control.[25] The centrality of the family household, not the monarchy, in the law codes of Israel clearly supports this view of the social origins of the covenant.

The family household is at the center of the relationship between Yahweh, greater Israel, and the land.[26] This means that the economic, social, and religious realms of ancient Israel and early Judaism were interrelated. The collapse of the traditional family household and the larger protective associations of clans would have had serious social, economic, and religious repercussions. Subsequently, a good deal of prophetic protest focused on the threat the monarchy posed to the family household and thus to the relationship between God, Israel as a people, and the land. The prophets depicted Yahweh as closely associated with and supportive of the household. If the household was undermined, then the relationship with Yahweh was threatened (cf. Isa. 5:8–10; Micah 2:1–3, 8–9; 7:5–7). And should the household have disappeared, Israel and early Judaism would have had to look elsewhere for a social reality to give shape to their theological articulation.

From Old Testament Theology to
Contemporary Theology and Ethics

The Limits of Social History

Many Jews and Christians take the Hebrew Bible seriously, for it is understood as scripture that is, in some way, authoritative and instructive for contemporary life. Yet to examine what the Hebrew Bible has to say about the family to contemporary, believing communities does not mean that an exegesis of biblical passages dealing with the household can lead directly to the formulation of absolutist, propositional, moralistic truths from scripture that, taken together, provide a handbook of "dos and don'ts" for the modern family in North America. To take this simplistic but wrongheaded approach involves several major difficulties.

First, the portrayal of the family in ancient Israel and early Judaism is incomplete. As the previous chapters have demonstrated, one has only a partial glimpse into the nature and character of the ancient Israelite and early Jewish family, since the limited textual and archaeological data are themselves not sufficient to flesh out all the details of this social institution. This incomplete picture also applies to the larger social world of ancient Israel and early Judaism in which the family was situated. Much about the family in the Hebrew Bible must remain the object of supposition and intelligent guesswork, hardly producing the stuff of divine fiat and authoritative prescription and proscription.

Second, as noted earlier, the family in Israelite and Jewish culture was dynamic, not static. This means that the nature and practice of the family even during a particular period, along with its theological and ethical valuations, are complex and diverse. And this diversity becomes even more apparent when considering the changes that occurred in both the institution and its different valuations during its cultural evolution. In other words, there are synchronic differences in the nature and assessments of the family, just as there are diachronic changes throughout ancient Israel's and early Judaism's social evolution.

Third, it would be foolish to attempt to single out the social institution of the family, along with its theological and ethical understandings, by removing it from the social and cultural moorings of a time gone by and then to transfer it to a radically different sociocultural reality in contemporary North America that is itself rather diverse. In other words, is it not inconsistent to think that the Bible's teachings about the family are immediately instructive and even authoritative for the family today but not to think that scriptural understandings of monarchy, slavery, economics, taxes, gender roles, and so on are just as pertinent for modern understandings of social and theological ethics in the contemporary world? To transfer biblical understandings of the family, without critical engagement, to the contemporary culture, even if one were to assume, for argument's sake, that these were monolithic and static, would necessitate the transfer of all the social, economic, and religious realities of ancient Israel and formative Judaism to the present. Who today could or would even wish to reestablish an ancient Israelite village society in Dallas–Fort Worth or in Chicago? Yet this is exactly what would have to happen, were one to argue that the portraits of the family in this volume, along with an appropriate theological and ethical formulation, provide authoritative social and moral paradigms for modern family life.

Nevertheless, this is not to say that the present characterizations of the family in ancient Israel and early Judaism are simply an antiquarian exercise, with nothing to contribute to contemporary theology and moral teaching in modern Christianity and Judaism. The question is how and what does the Hebrew Bible contribute to the formal and moral character of the modern family. In taking up this hermeneutical quest, the modern appropriation of biblical teachings about the family must follow the same winding pathways to contemporary theological and moral discourse that engage any other subject.

The Household and the Theological Question of Patriarchy

According to Priestly theology, woman and man were created in God's image, blessed, and commanded to populate the earth (Gen. 1:26–28) and to exert dominion over creation.[27] Even so, this sharing of the divine image did not lead to an egalitarian world for men and women in the Priestly document's legal code. The Yahwist pointed to the disobedience of the man and woman in the garden as the reason for the woman's multiple pregnancies, for the man's ruling (*māšal*) over her sexuality in order to produce needed offspring, and for the wearisome toil imposed on both sexes, which was necessary for households to sustain a subsistent life.[28]

Androcentrism is obvious throughout much of the Hebrew Bible. For example, genealogies are preponderantly male; legal codes are addressed to men, not women; masculine forms for generic speech are often used; most characters in biblical literature are male; men dominate in public life (rulers, judges, law, payment of women's vows, etc.); and only males can be priests.[29] This male-centeredness does, at times, cross the threshold and enters into male domination or patriarchy. These observations mean that, in speaking of the value of the biblical representation of the family for contemporary life, androcentrism and patriarchy impose significant challenges and impediments.

It is true that the household goes not only by the designation *bêt 'āb* but also by *bêt 'ēm* (Gen. 24:28; Ruth 1:8; S. of Sol. 3:4; 8:2; cf. Prov. 9:1–6; 14:1; 31:10–31). And there are numerous examples of the undermining of patriarchy that should be noted.[30] This undermining of the efforts to silence women's voices in scripture and of patriarchal domination indicates important ways that critical ethical reflection can negate the sometimes oppressive structure of biblical representations of family life and values and also can shape a more humane, faithful social expression of human community in contemporary life.

Toward a Criteriology for a Moral Paradigm

Let me propose, then, that the hermeneutic for engaging the Bible in contemporary theological and ethical discourse be shaped by a critical criteriology.[31] This criteriology should contain elements that together can be used to assess biblical themes and to evaluate their potential relevance for contemporary theological and ethical discourse.

First, is there a theological, ethical center or basic thematic core that is present in scripture and provides the unifying factor for biblical theology and ethics? Here I propose that covenant theology, which embraces both redemptive history and creation, provides the fundamental, thematic structure for the teachings of the Hebrew Bible and early Judaism.[32] This fundamental center, the polarity of salvation history and creation that is placed within the constructive and defining framework of covenant and obligation, is present in the various materials in the Hebrew Bible and in early Jewish texts that deal with the family. Indeed, this is also the structure for Israel's theological reflection about the household. Biblical teachings about the household are founded upon this theological base. But even more, I argue that the very origins of covenant theology took shape within the social reality of Israelite households and that this theology was later extended to include the households of Israel, the household of King David, the priesthood of Aaron, and, eventually, all creation. The ethos and practice of the household, in particular its strong sense of solidarity and community, provided an important social paradigm for theological reflection and discourse about God, Israel, and the world.

This center of covenant, consisting of fundamental assertions about the character and activity of God in history and creation, formed the basis and rationalization for laws, instructions, and proclamations about the family and about responsible moral life within the household. For example, all members of the household were to observe the Sabbath because Israel was to remember that it was once a house of slaves in Egypt (Deut. 5:12–15) or because it was on the seventh day that God rested from the labors of creation (Ex. 20:8–11). Texts, themes, and theological formulations that are remote from this center or that do not correlate with this center and its understandings are considered far less important. This means that not all of the corpus of the Hebrew Bible is equally appropriate for contemporary consideration in shaping the theological and moral discourse of modern culture.

Second, diversity is present in biblical texts that address any theological theme. This means that when theological diversity about the understanding of the family appears, the expression that best corresponds to the fundamental, thematic center of the Hebrew Bible is given highest priority for evaluating in relation to and then introducing into the contemporary conversation. In the diverse expressions of theological and ethical reflection on the family, some texts may contribute to modern discourse, and others may not.

Third, the Hebrew Bible speaks primarily not of the nature of God but of divine character construed through activity. This means that the Hebrew Bible describes the formation of human character and behavior as the appropriate response to divine imperatives and teachings that themselves issue from the character and activity of God. The Hebrew Bible does not represent an anthropology that speaks of ontology and a morality that points to intrinsic virtues within human nature. While such virtues are not necessarily to be ignored in moral formation, they do not represent the Hebrew Bible's primary area of interest in either theology—that is, the understanding of God—or theological anthropology—that is, the understanding of human character formed as a response to and then incorporation of the character and activity of God. This means that the revelation of divine character and activity, as well as human response to the same, becomes the avenue for understanding and expressing moral obligations that lead to appropriate human character formation and ethical actions. As those who stand within the traditions of Judaism and Christianity, contemporary believers are obligated to actualize in their behavior the character and activity of God.

Thus, from Israel's own theological reflection about the roles and functions of the household, including such matters as economics, nurture, education, reproduction, law, and protection, it becomes clear that these are grounded in and legitimated by the character and activity of God. The household was the theological lens, the ethical paradigm, and the human context for understanding the character and activity of God and for living out moral responsibilities to others. Thus God was the *go'ēl* who redeemed from slavery and death, the giver and sustainer of the household's land, the supporter and protector of the marginalized poor, and so on. This means, then, that humans, living in covenant with God, are to act accordingly.

Fourth, Israel's and early Judaism's understandings of divine character and activity changed somewhat through the course of history, but not radically. And Israel's moral responses to this dynamic understanding of God changed, but again, not dramatically. This suggests that the contemporary understanding of the family requires not only a consistent theological grounding but also one that is open to some variation. To engage in critical hermeneutics concerning the family means that diverse understandings of divine actions and the variety of human responses are often unavoidable.

This also means that to consider a response of ancient communities to divine character or activity an appropriate moral behavior for the present requires a careful and knowledgeable assessment of the historical and social situations in which these groups found themselves, the possible menus for responding, and the outcome of the responses. In other words, no ideal, absolutist theological or moral teaching exists that is equally valid for every Christian and Jewish community at all times and in every situation. Israel's own theological reflection was positioned within the concrete lives of households in changing and evolving social and historical circumstances.

Fifth, as we assay the biblical understandings of a topic or theme, we should question theological and moral teachings that appear to present themselves as absolutist instructions, transcending the limits of time and place. Teachings that appear to be proscriptive, authoritarian, and absolutist in character, whether the Ten Commandments or the instructions of sages in Proverbs, may not actually be so, since they are best understood as largely general commandments and instructions that those addressed must interpret and then apply to a particular time and place. In other words, in scripture a major responsibility is placed on the interpreter, standing within his or her community, to select, apply, and live out a particular teaching. Even in the ancient communities of Israel, "do not kill" was qualified by reference to particular situations. War and capital punishment, for example, were not proscribed by this commandment.

Sixth, in the interaction between teachings and the taught, equal weight, at the very least, must be given to the interpreter's critical appropriation or rejection. In other words, to appropriate a biblical teaching in the contemporary world requires that the interpreter be familiar not only with the world and discourse of the Bible but also with the reality and theological-ethical conversation of the contemporary community of faith. For example, the Jeremiah tradition presents the prophet as believing he has been instructed not to take a wife, for the times are hard and dangerous (Jer. 16:2–4). It would be foolish to take this admonition as teaching that marriage is not a valued social arrangement in the Old Testament or that celibacy takes the moral high ground over marriage. Rather, celibacy was appropriate for this prophet in this particular setting, and it might be appropriate for others found in comparably terrible and dangerous times, for similar reasons. Another example is the fact that demographic circumstances, economic requirements, and labor needs largely determine whether a society emphasizes the importance of overcoming infertility to produce many children. Large families are an economic necessity in households engaged in subsistence farming, but not in a well-fed, wealthy culture.

And seventh, a "hermeneutics of suspicion" must be added to the mix, especially in legitimating for the interpreter the role of critical engagement of biblical texts. This role takes note of the presence of biblical texts that at times subvert the patriarchy of some canonical literature and also recognizes the ideological caste of writings that seek to enforce submission to power and to enslave rather than, in the fashion of the God of the exodus, to liberate from oppressive structures of state and male power.

The Household, Old Testament Theology,
and Contemporary Hermeneutics:
Assumptions and Conclusions

Assumptions

Several fundamental assumptions have guided this overview of the
social history of the ancient Israelite and early Jewish family, its place
in Old Testament theology, and how it might contribute to contemporary theological and ethical discourse about the family.

1. To engage in theological reflection on the family in ancient Israel
and early Judaism as a biblical theologian or as a contemporary interpreter, one must begin with the reconstruction of the social history of the
family in this changing culture. The family in ancient Israel and early Judaism underwent some transformation during a period that extended for
twelve hundred years. In addition, scripture and early Jewish texts reflect
diverse understandings of the family that resulted not only from the evolution of Israelite and early Jewish social and political history but also
from evaluations by different social and religious groups, including the
court historians, sages, prophets, and priests who produced the Hebrew
Bible. To pick out, selectively and uncritically, passages from the Hebrew
Bible as authoritative prohibitions or imperatives for the contemporary
family is naive and misleading. Biblical texts that touch on the family first
need to be placed within critically reconstructed traditions that are situated within Israelite and early Jewish social and religious history.

2. These social understandings also should be placed within the
larger parameters of Old Testament theology and ethics. This allows
one to determine how Israelite and early Jewish theological and ethical
reflection interpreted the family within the operative framework of faith
and life and how the family contributed to Old Testament theological
and ethical discourse and understanding. This means, then, that Israelite and early Jewish understandings of the character and activity of
God, presented in the traditions of redemptive history and creation
within the fundamental structure of covenant and obligation, provided
the theological grounding and rationalization for laws, prophetic an-
nouncements, and parenetic (moral) teachings that addressed the family and its common life. In addition, the family household became the
basis of a shared human experience that provided a social lens through
which God, Israel, creation, the nations, and morality were seen.

In the Hebrew Bible, two major theological traditions converge: Yahweh's acts of salvation in history and God's creation and sustaining of the world and its creatures. Eventually overarching and relating these two traditions was the understanding of Israel's covenant with Yahweh and of the divine obligations imposed on those who existed within this relationship. Family life was carried out in a household that existed within Israel's covenant relationship with Yahweh, a covenant that was preceded by the liberation from Egypt and followed by the obligations at Sinai, which were imposed on those who chose to live in responsible relationship to God. These obligations issued from both the exodus event and God's offer to live in community with a particular people and, through this people, eventually with the larger world. Likewise, creation faith provided a theological grounding and rationalization for the moral character of social interaction within the family and with those outside the kinship structure. God's activity of originating and sustaining creation and, in particular, human creatures provided a theological paradigm for responsible human interaction among those within and outside the family. An important example is the gift of the land to Israel's households, which is grounded in the larger theological tradition of God as creator and God as the one who shapes human history.

3. The Hebrew Bible's social description of the household and its theological reflections on responsible existence within and outside the family must undergo a critical evaluation for their appropriateness for contemporary family life in North American culture. In other words, how do the various understandings of the family in ancient Israel and early Judaism speak authentically, if at all, as scripture to modern faith? Do these understandings of the characteristics of an ancient and radically different socioeconomic world point to authentic and legitimate efforts to incorporate basic elements of faith within family life?

4. Following on the preceding point, the fundamental assertions of ancient Israel and early Judaism about the character and activity of God in salvation history and in creation undergird the covenantal matrix for serious ethical reflection about actual human living within the social arrangement of the family. In addition, in Israel's theological reflection, reality was viewed as a household wherein God was father and mother, husband, and go'ēl (redeemer), while Israel was the son, daughter, wife, debt servant, slave, resident alien, and orphan. The household became the theological lens for viewing and understanding the identity of and relationship between God, Israel, creation, and even the nations. In this interpretation, in all questions of the moral life, including but not limited to the family, the church, and the synagogue, humans are to view reality

as a cosmic household in which God serves as parent and redeemer; to
see all people, including the poor, as family members who are to be nurtured, protected, and loved as the self; and to understand creation as the
gift, the *naḥālâh,* of God to all human beings. In addition, Jews and Christians, as members of this household, this symbolic world of life and
meaning, are to ask, "In what ways may our behavior actualize exodus
liberation in life, not just for the rich and powerful but also for the poor,
who have no access to power?" "In what ways may our behavior sustain
the beneficent order of creation, so that all may share in its bounty?" The
ways in which Israel and early Judaism attempted to implement these declarations of faith in social life in general and in family life in particular provide ethical paradigms for critical reflection and application, but not necessarily the form of imperatives or prohibitions and their specific content,
for contemporary family life that seeks to be morally responsible within
the context of modern Jewish and Christian faith.

The moral value of the specific economic, political, and ethical practices of this ancient culture is to be judged critically and primarily in
terms of whether these practices authentically and responsibly implement the basic affirmations of faith witnessing to the character and
activity of God that are represented in the traditions of creation and exodus liberation as placed within the theological structure of covenant
and obligations. Ultimately, the character and activity of the God of creation and salvation history, who chose to live in a responsible, covenantal relationship with Israel, provide the foundation and theological rationalization for moral discourse in the Hebrew Bible. God's character
and activity provide the authoritative structure—that is, the grounding,
legitimation, and rationalization—for laws and teachings about the
family. The specific implementations of this faith in Israelite and Jewish social and economic life provide for modern culture significant paradigms of the continuing effort of Israelites and early Jews to live faith-
fully and responsibly within the family, but they are not direct,
absolutist imperatives for contemporary existence that come to us unfiltered through critical theological evaluation.

The modern socioeconomic world is radically different from that of
ancient Israel and early Judaism. Thus it is primarily their representations of the character and activity of God and their theological reflections on family life, embedded in legal codes, prophetic announce-
ments, and parenetic teachings, that are appropriate for serious critical
evaluation in relation to modern discourse and behavior. We must ask,
then, how the theological statements embedded in the various genres

of the Hebrew Bible and in early Jewish literature appropriate the major traditions of salvation history and creation. What do these theological declarations say about the character and activity of God? How were these theological understandings used to shape family life in ancient Israel and early Judaism? And how are these biblical understandings of divine character and action to be appropriately actualized in contemporary family life?

Conclusions

I draw the following conclusions from this study:

1. The changes in Israelite and early Jewish society over the centuries inevitably impacted on the social unit of the family. But one may say, in general, that the ancestral household was the typical *form* of the Israelite and early Jewish family. However, what is "typical" should be distinguished from what is necessarily "normative," for ancient as well as for contemporary family life. For example, polygamy and even, although rarely, celibacy, along with concubinage and slavery, received social and even divine sanction. Few would argue that these are normative practices for contemporary family life.

2. Given that the form of the family represented in the Hebrew Bible and in the writings of early Judaism is the household, can one point to anything that is normative for modern households? To answer this question, one must ask if there is a fundamental theological understanding of the family in ancient Israel that, critically treated, may address contemporary life.

3. The most significant feature of the Israelite and early Jewish family that may serve as a social basis for contemporary ethical action is the corporate identity and solidarity of the ancestral household, which provided the primary locus for human existence, social interaction, social roles, moral value, and religious belief. Translated into theological terms, the family household provided the basis for shared experience and common reflection that led to the formation of Israel's understandings of redemptive history and creation within the framework of covenant and obligation. Covenant and obligation encompassed the theological theme of providence in creation and history. Covenant and obligation became the means by which Israel chose to define the relationships between God and the cosmos, God and Israel, God and the nations, and God and history. In other words, I suggest that the family household, in its diversity, is formed, shaped, and sustained by this core

of corporate identity and responsibility. In Israel's theological reflection and discourse, the household became the metaphorical or symbolic world for expressing the theological themes of covenant and obligation, redemptive history and creation.

The social reality of the family household, in addition to the monarchy, provides one of the two major paradigms for theologizing in the Old Testament. In many ways, the household became a microcosm of Israel's worldview. The competing tradition was that of kingship. These two traditions vied for allegiance, for they represented two very different ways of understanding God, Israel, history, creation, ethics, and the relationship of Israel to the nations.

4. To attempt to transplant gender roles, the roles of parents and children, polygamy, monogamy, celibacy, and a host of other specific features of the Israelite family into contemporary cultures would be naive. To do so would require the transplanting of Israel's entire society to the present. However, I propose that the household and its fundamental theological grounding in redemptive history and creation within the framework of covenant and obligation, if critically engaged, have meaning and import far beyond their historical and social embodiments in ancient Israel and early Judaism.

Ancient Israel learned to look at its social world and the world of creation as a household or as a village of households, in which members took up residence and dwelt, nurtured and protected one another, and provided care for the poor person, who was the "sibling" or the "neighbor" to be loved as the self. In the formation of our own ethical paradigm, informed by scripture, we, too, must learn to envision not only our own society but also all creation as a place for human dwelling and as a collection of family households, in which all peoples and creatures have a place to dwell and to live. In this global environment of village clans comprised of households, we indeed are responsible to and for one another, for the "good creation," and to the creator, savior, and sustainer who, as our just and faithful parent, redeemer, and spouse, not only continues to love and nurture us but also expects us to love and care for our neighbors as ourselves.

NOTES

1. Leo G. Perdue, *The Collapse of History* (OBT; Minneapolis: Fortress Press, 1994). See Horst Dietrich Preuss, *Old Testament Theology* (Louisville, Ky.: Westminster John Knox Press, 1995), 1:19–26.

2. Gerhard Hasel, *Old Testament Theology: Basic Issues in the Current Debate,* 4th rev. ed. (Grand Rapids: Wm. B. Eerdmans Publishing Co., 1991). Hasel points to the various options for this center, though his own assertion, that the center is "God," is too general to be helpful.

3. Claus Westermann, *Blessing in the Bible and the Life of the Church* (Philadelphia: Fortress Press, 1978).

4. See Leo G. Perdue, *Wisdom and Creation* (Nashville: Abingdon Press, 1994), 101–14.

5. See Theodore Hiebert, "Warrior, Divine," *ABD* 6 (1992):876–80.

6. Phyllis Trible, *God and the Rhetoric of Sexuality* (Philadelphia: Fortress Press, 1978).

7. Preuss, *Old Testament Theology,* 1:125.

8. See Walter Brueggemann, *The Land* (Philadelphia: Westminster Press, 1977); A. Ohler, *Israel, Volk und Land: Zur Geschichte der wechselseitigen Beziehungen zwischen Israel und seinem Land in alttestamentlicher Zeit* (Stuttgart: Katholisches Bibelwerk, 1979); A. G. Auld, *Joshua, Moses and the Land* (Edinburgh: T. & T. Clark, 1980); and Georg Strecker, ed., *Das Land Israel in biblischer Zeit* (Göttingen: Vandenhoeck & Ruprecht, 1983).

9. Second Isaiah prefers to speak of returning to Zion (Jerusalem), not to the land (40:9–11; 49:14–22; 51:3–11).

10. Walter Zimmerli, *Old Testament Theology in Outline* (Richmond: John Knox Press, 1978), 64–69.

11. Preuss, *Old Testament Theology,* 1:120–23.

12. Ezekiel speaks in 36:1–11 of a return from exile, when even the resident alien will inherit a portion of the land (Ezek. 47:21–23).

13. See Chapter 1 by Carol L. Meyers, "The Family in Early Israel"; George E. Mendenhall, "The Relation of the Individual to Political Society in Ancient Israel," in *Biblical Studies in Memory of H. C. Alleman,* ed. J. M. Myers et al. (Locust Valley, N.Y.: J. J. Augustin, 1960), 89–108. Baruch Halpern makes the intriguing argument that individual responsibility emerged in ancient Israel as a result of the monarchy's undermining of the solidarity of the traditional kinship groups of households, clans, and tribes ("Jerusalem and the Lineages in the Seventh Century BCE: Kinship and the Rise of Individual Moral Liability," in *Law and Ideology in Monarchic Israel,* ed. Baruch Halpern and D. W. Hobson [JSOTSup 124; Sheffield: JSOT Press, 1991]).

14. Walther Eichrodt, *Krisis der Gemeinschaft in Israel* (Basel: Helbig & Lichtenhahn, 1953); Johannes Pedersen, *Israel: Its Life and Culture, 1–2* (London: Oxford University Press, 1926), 263–310; J. R. Porter, "The Legal Aspects of the Concept of 'Corporate Personality' in the Old Testament," *VT* 15 (1965):361–80; Preuss, *Old Testament Theology,* 1:60–64; H. Wheeler Robinson, "The Hebrew Conception of Corporate Personality," in *Werden und Wesen des Alten Testaments,* ed. P. Volz et al (BZAW 66; Berlin: Alfred Töpelmann, 1936), 49–62; and Hans Walter Wolff, *Anthropology of the Old Testament* (Philadelphia: Fortress Press, 1974), 214–22. However, also see

J. W. Rogerson, "The Hebrew Concept of Corporate Personality: A Reexamination," *JTS* 21 (1970):1–16.

15. See Meyers in chapter 1. She refers to the paper by Ida Harper Simpson and John Wilson, "Proprietary Family Orientations of Black and White Farm Couples" (paper presented at the Conference of Rural/Farm Women in Agriculture, University of California at Davis, 1992).

16. See D. J. McCarthy, *Old Testament Covenant: A Survey of Current Opinions* (Richmond: John Knox Press, 1972); Lothar Perlitt, *Bundestheologie im Alten Testament* (WMANT 36; Neukirchen-Vluyn: Neukirchener Verlag, 1969); E. W. Nicholson, *God and His People* (Oxford: Clarendon Press, 1986); idem, "Covenant in a Century of Study since Wellhausen," *OTS* 24 (1986):54–69; R. Davidson, "Covenant Theology in Ancient Israel," in *The World of Ancient Israel*, ed. R. E. Clements (Cambridge: Cambridge University Press, 1989), 323–47; Zimmerli, *Old Testament Theology in Outline*, 48–58; Preuss, *Old Testament Theology*, 1:70–78; and Walther Eichrodt, *Theology of the Old Testament* (Philadelphia: Westminster Press, 1961), 1:36–45.

17. See George E. Mendenhall, "Law and Covenant in Israel and the Ancient Near East," *BA* 17 (1954):26–46, 49–76; George E. Mendenhall and Gary A. Herion, "Covenant," *ABD* 1 (1992):1179–1202; A. Grayson, "Akkadian Treaties of the Seventh Century B.C.," *JCS* 39 (1987):127–60; and S. Parpola, "Neo-Assyrian Treaties from the Royal Archives of Nineveh," *JCS* 39 (1987):161–89.

18. For a critical examination of covenant as suzerainty treaty, see D. J. McCarthy, *Treaty and Covenant* (AnBib 63; Rome: Pontifical Biblical Institute, 1963); idem, *Old Testament Covenant*; and E. W. Nicholson, *God and His People: Covenant Theology in the Old Testament* (Oxford: Oxford University Press, 1986).

19. Preuss, *Old Testament Theology,* 1:72.

20. J. Begrich, "Bĕrît," *ZAW* 60 (1944):1–11; Zimmerli, *Old Testament Theology in Outline*, 48.

21. See also Ex. 2:24; 6:4, 5; Lev. 26:42; 2 Kings 13:23; 1 Chron. 16:14–18 = Ps. 105:7–11; Neh. 9:7–8; Jer. 34:18.

22. Pedersen, *Israel*, 1–2, 263–310.

23. Zimmerli, *Old Testament Theology in Outline*, 53.

24. See Perlitt, *Bundestheologie im Alten Testament*.

25. See Naomi Steinberg, "The Deuteronomic Law Code and the Politics of State Centralization," in *The Bible and the Politics of Exegesis*, ed. David Jobling et al. (Cleveland: Pilgrim Press, 1991), 16–170, 336–38.

26. C. J. H. Wright, "Family," *ABD* 2 (1992):765.

27. See Carol L. Meyers, *Discovering Eve: Ancient Israelite Women in Context* (Oxford: Oxford University Press, 1988), 24–46.

28. Ibid., 95–109.

29. Phyllis Bird, "Women (OT)," *ABD* 6 (1992):953.

30. Trible, *God and the Rhetoric of Sexuality*; cf. the bibliography in Perdue, *Col-*

lapse of History, 197–227. In chapter 1 ("The Family in Early Israel"), Meyers notes that most biblical literature that speaks of the family is written from a male perspective. She suggests that patriarchy (or, in her view, "androcentrism") in ancient Israel would have developed after the period of Iron I when males and females originally were "farm partners."

31. Among the important studies on ethics in the Hebrew Bible, see J. Barton, "Understanding O.T. Ethics," *JSOT* 9 (1978):44–64; Bruce Birch and Larry Rasmussen, *Bible and Ethics in the Christian Life* (Minneapolis: Augsburg Publishing House, 1976); Bruce Birch, *Let Justice Roll Down* (Louisville, Ky.: Westminster John Knox Press, 1991); J. L. Crenshaw and J. T. Willis, eds., *Essays in O. T. Ethics* (J. P. Hyatt Memorial Volume; New York: KTAV Publishing House, 1974); M. Gilbert, J. L'Hour, and J. Scharbert, *Morale et Ancien Testament* (Louvain: Université Catholique de Louvain, 1976); Douglas Knight and Carol Meyers, eds., *Ethics and Politics in the Hebrew Bible, Semeia* 66 (1994); Horst Dietrich Preuss, *Old Testament Theology,* vol. 2 (OTL; Louisville, Ky.: Westminster John Knox Press, 1996); and R. R. Wilson, "Approaches to O. T. Ethics, *Canon,*" in *Theology and Old Testament Interpretation,* ed. Gene M. Tucker, David L. Petersen, and Robert R. Wilson (FS B. S. Childs; Philadelphia: Fortress Press, 1988), 62–74.

32. On the covenant, see Eichrodt, *Theology of the Old Testament,* 1:25–33. For the interactive traditions of salvation history and creation, see Claus Westermann, *Elements of Old Testament Theology* (Atlanta: John Knox Press, 1982).

Index of Hebrew Words

Index of Scripture and Other Ancient Writings

Index of Authors

Printed in the United States
102442LV00003B/103-114/A